D0291895

Reason and Democracy

Reason and Democracy

Thomas A. Spragens, Jr.

Duke University Press • *Durham and London 1990*

© 1990 Duke University Press
Printed in the United States of America
on acid-free paper ∞

Library of Congress Cataloging-in-Publication Data
appear on the last printed page of this book.

To

T. A. S. and C. S. S.

with thanks

———

Contents

———

Preface

The idea that rationality provides a standard for the good society has been widely discussed in recent Continental philosophy. Those conversant with that philosophical tradition will therefore not find great novelty in the contention that we should attend to the norms of rational practice as a useful and valid political guide.

For a number of reasons, however, this is a line of argument that has had very little discernible impact upon the recent enterprise of reconstructing liberal theory. For many Anglo-American liberals, rational practice is perceived as a neo-Hegelian idea in the service of neo-Marxist polemics. Hence they assume that it holds little relevance for their own concerns, seeing it as the offspring of a discredited metaphysic and as a hallmark of a dubious ideology.

Such an attitude is thoroughly understandable but nonetheless unfortunate. For the ideal of a society that conducts its affairs in consonance with the canons of rational procedure is fully compatible with the best historic ideals of liberal democracy. Indeed, I would argue that the norms of rational practice capture and express these ideals more accurately and more fully than any other single philosophical standard. Norms of rational practice become serviceable for neo-Marxism only when they are conjoined with the empirically contestable claim that liberal democracy systematically frustrates the prerequisites of rationally conducted politics—in ways that a socialist society would allegedly overcome. Moreover, an accurate account of the norms of rational practice requires no Hegelian derivation; and indeed such an account, I would argue, is impaired and distorted by Hegelian notions of absolute knowledge and dialectics.

What may be particularly useful and suggestive about this study, then, is that it remains largely within territory more familiar to and more habitable by those within the Anglo-American philosophical and political traditions. It takes its problematic from the "great tradition" of Western political theory; it finds its philosophical inspiration almost entirely from Anglo-American philosophy of science and of language; and it adduces lessons directly pertinent to issues raised by liberal and communitarian theories of democracy.

It may be relevant to note in this context, in fact, that the argument presented here grew out of two decades of reflection on the history and prospects of the liberal democratic tradition. It took its shape from the internal critique of liberal rationalism presented in two earlier books (*The Irony of Liberal Reason* and *The Politics of Motion: The World of Thomas Hobbes*) that antedated my own more recent and still partial acquaintance with Continental discussions of rationalism in politics. If that be a confession of intellectual parochialism—shared, I suspect, by most Anglo-American political theorists trained in the sixties—it also provides biographical confirmation of the claim that a political appropriation of norms of rational practice can be indigenous to Anglo-American liberalism and need not be a philosophical or ideological import.

I have written this book for a diverse audience. It does not purport to teach philosophers anything about philosophy. Rather, in a time-honored tradition, I seek to borrow ideas and insights from philosophy in order to apply them to issues of political theory. Several other types of reader will, I hope, find something of interest here: political theorists concerned about reason's role, if any, in a good society; political theorists interested in the philosophical foundations of liberalism and communitarianism; political scientists concerned with the ideals and logic of democracy; and graduate and advanced undergraduate students concerned with any of these issues.

Attempting to speak to a diverse audience in this way creates difficulties of expository strategy that I have not been completely able to surmount. I can only forewarn readers that all parts of the book will not be equally relevant to their own concerns and needs; and each segment of the intended audience should follow a reader's strategy adapted to its own purposes. Student readers may want to avoid getting bogged down in some of the philosophical issues that are not easily accessible to them, for example. On the other end of the spectrum, political theorists who are well acquainted with the history of modern political theory and who are familiar with *The Irony of Liberal Reason* and with Richard Bernstein's *Beyond Objectivism and Relativism* should probably skip fairly quickly over the first two chapters, because these cover ground that—although important for the overall argument—will be familiar to them.

Like all authors, I have accumulated indebtedness along the way. I especially am indebted to William Galston, Stephen Salkever, and two anonymous readers for their very helpful comments and suggestions. Their advice resulted in numerous revisions and improvements in the manuscript. I could not, however, act upon all their suggestions, and they bear no burden of responsibility for any flaws that remain in the book. Pat Tackney, Lillian Fennell, Mary Umstead, Mary Frances Davis, and Susan Emery all contributed to the task of manuscript preparation. Larry Malley and Reynolds Smith of the Duke University Press sustained and guided me through the publication process. And my family—Lynn, Jackie, Stephen, and Taylor—provided their support and toleration. My parents created the first rational society that I experienced, and in appreciation I have dedicated this book to them.

Reason and Democracy

Introduction

▬

This book is intended as a contribution to two distinct areas of concern among political theorists, one of them very longstanding and the other relatively recent. The traditional area of concern is the question of the role of reason in politics. The more recent area of concern is the interest in reconstructing liberal theory to accommodate contemporary philosophical insights and political realities. One of the implicit theses of this book, indeed, is that these two areas of inquiry should not be so distinct—that an appropriate understanding of the role of reason in politics is a crucial element in a satisfactory account of liberal political practices and ideals.

We might easily assume that little remains to be said about the role of reason in politics. So many of the epic political theorists have reflected on this issue that it is one of the principal thematic continuities of the entire tradition. For reasons that I hope to say something about, however—reasons relating to the dominance of the calculative ideal—the eventual outcome of the rationalist political tradition in the West has not been a happy one. When assimilated to positivistic conceptions of modern science, political rationalism has tended to lead us into Weber's "iron cage" of bureaucratic technocracy. Repelled by that specter, most liberal democratic political theorists have abandoned rationalist political norms altogether, looking for morally sound "habits of the heart" to suffice in the stead of apparently perverse reasons of the head. Some of the recent philosophical history of these developments were examined in *The Irony of Liberal Reason*,[1] to which this book is intended as a sequel.

Despite this impasse of political rationalism in the contemporary West, it is becoming apparent to some of the most astute philosophical commentators on politics that the resources of human reason cannot be so lightly abandoned. Whatever the frequent distortions of reason's powers and proper role in political life, healthy political practices cannot be arational or irrational. We should neither succumb to the iron cage nor join in the flight from reason but instead should seek to produce a philosophically defensible and politically humane understanding of what rational practice is all about. Such an understanding should recapture the essential insight embodied in Aristotle's conception of *phronesis*—the awareness that human beings are endowed with "a rational faculty exercised for the attainment of truth in things that are humanly good and bad." [2]

The assumptions that inform this inquiry have been ably stated by John Dunn in *Rethinking Modern Political Theory*. Neither the Kantian nor the utilitarian tradition in modern ethical theory, he writes, "has ever contrived to give a very coherent and philosophically satisfying account of the nature of the relations between human value, human agency, and the material universe. The more skeptical and pragmatist tinge of recent western philosophical conceptions of natural science and epistemology contrives to give less strained answers to these problems largely by dint of refusing to answer them at all—by pure evasion. At least in political philosophy, such evasive tactics, however elegantly deployed, will hardly suffice. Unless and until it can be remedied, the philosophical weakness of modern conceptions of practical reason will by itself preclude the construction of a political philosophy of any great power." [3]

Dunn concludes, then, that the most pressing task for political theorists today is to provide a more adequate account of "collective prudence" than has heretofore been offered. This book is intended as an initial contribution to precisely that task. By reflecting upon what recent philosophy of science and philosophy of language have taught us and by drawing the appropriate analogies, I argue, we can discern the outlines of a philosophically cogent and morally salutary conception of rational practice on the part of a political community.

Theories of liberal democracy, despite a great deal of recent attention to their reconstruction, have also exhibited considerable difficulty in escaping the philosophical confines mentioned by Dunn. Within the discipline of political science, the dominant account of liberal democracy has been the positivistic and pragmatic incrementalism of the pluralists. This account has its virtues, including moderation, sober realism, and the recognition of the importance of political culture and the role of elites. It also has its weaknesses, such as implicit conservatism, lack of vision, and complicity in the moral drift of philosophical emotivism. These weaknesses have become widely recognized.[4] But it would be hard to point to any constructive account of liberal democratic practice that has definitively replaced the pluralist depiction of that practice as the pursuit of equilibrium. The best attempts to provide such an alternative account have been those of Benjamin Barber, Theodore Lowi, and Jane Mansbridge.[5] Barber's vision of "strong democracy," Lowi's model of "juridical democracy," and Mansbridge's depiction of the need for elements of "unitary democracy" are each extremely valuable contributions toward moving our self-understanding beyond the pluralist balancing act. None of these students of democracy, however, goes very far toward refashioning the philosophical underpinnings of democracy. Lowi and Mansbridge are not specifically concerned to do so. And Barber's focus also lies elsewhere. When he does reflect on the constructive philosophical basis of his account, moreover, Barber remains largely within the ambit of skeptical pragmatism, citing as inspiration sources such as Dewey, Peirce, Oakeshott, and Montaigne. The argument for conceiving liberal democracy as a form of communal rational practice that I state in this book, then, is not really in tension with these accounts—with which I am highly sympathetic. Instead, my argument is intended to provide a framework within which their concerns can find what I would regard as more favorable philosophical grounding. The conception of rational practice articulated here could in this context, then, be said to have the same sort of role *vis à vis* these attempts to improve our understanding of democracy that Rawls intends his theory to have *vis à vis* our "familiar intuitions" about justice: it seeks to "organize these ideas and principles by means of a more fundamental idea within the complex structure of which the other ideas are then systematically connected."[6]

If recent advances in democratic theory on the part of political scientists either have been philosophically underdifferentiated or have remained essentially within positivist-pragmatist confines, the recent more philosophical excursions into liberal theory have only haltingly been able to advance beyond the utilitarian and Kantian perspectives that Dunn noted critically.[7] The flurry of current interest in rethinking liberal theory received its principal impetus from John Rawls's magisterial *A Theory of Justice*.[8] Rawls there mounted a strong critique of the widespread view that the democratic ethic was the utilitarian "greatest good for the greatest number." The utilitarian view, he argued, gave insufficient weight to the separateness of persons and thus insufficient protection to their integrity and autonomy. Instead, he argued, the philosophy of liberalism must be grounded in a philosophy of right analogous to Kant's "contract among rational beings." In philosophical principle—although not necessarily in political application—other recent liberal theorists such as Robert Nozick and Ronald Dworkin have agreed: liberalism is a philosophy of rights, not a calculus of welfare.

As Michael Sandel tells the story, I think correctly, this insurgency against utilitarianism on the part of those he calls "deontological liberals" has largely triumphed. The "new faith" has become, in fact, the "old orthodoxy"—one that has now begun to come under critical attack from those Sandel and others have called "communitarian critics of rights-based liberalism."[9] These communitarians include Sandel, Charles Taylor, Alasdair MacIntyre, and the coauthors of *Habits of the Heart*.[10] The burden of the communitarian position is that a healthy liberal society is not an aggregation of rights-protecting and interest-maximizing individuals but rather a community of public-spirited citizens oriented toward the common good. Some communitarians, as a consequence, identify with the tradition of civic republicanism, which they contrast with what they see as the rampant individualism of the liberal tradition.

If the contrast between rights-based individualism and common good-oriented communitarianism seems relatively clear in its outlines, at the philosophical level the issues that divide the disputants have become somewhat murky and confused. The philosophical essence of Sandel's critique of Rawls has been that "deontological liberalism" presupposes a metaphysic of "unencumbered" selfhood. That is, those selves who serve as the implicit bearers of Rawlsian rights are conceived and logically have to be conceived as "radically disembodied" subjects existing prior to and apart from their "contingent wants and aims." Such a conception, however, Sandel has argued, is not only inadequate in itself but is also an unsuitable basis for Rawls's own principles of justice—allegiance to which would seem to require selves who are tied to their fellows in more than an instrumental fashion.[11]

In contrast to this view of the "unencumbered self" he takes as intrinsic to rights-based liberalism, Sandel counterposes the writings of

Charles Taylor, Michael Walzer, and Michael Oakeshott. Each of these, he writes, "sees political discourse as proceeding within the common meanings and traditions of a political community, not appealing to a critical standpoint wholly external to those meanings."[12] He cites as exemplary of this "situated self" perspective Taylor's neo-Hegelian recourse to *Sittlichkeit*, Walzer's appeal to "shared understandings" or "an appeal to meanings internal to a political community not an appeal to abstract principles,"[13] and Oakeshott's depiction of healthy politics as a "pursuit of intimations."

In his most recent writings, however, Rawls for one seems to have deflected this line of criticism by changing his ground. The numerous Kantian references in *A Theory of Justice* Rawls now insists are to be understood merely as expository analogies and not as the presumptive metaphysical base of his principles of justice. Indeed, the principles of justice, he now argues, should not be construed as metaphysical at all. Instead, they should be seen as "political." Justice as fairness as a conception "starts from within a certain political tradition." It "draws solely upon basic intuitive ideas that are embedded in the political institutions of a constitutional democratic regime," and it "may at least be supported by what we may call an 'overlapping consensus,' that is, by a consensus that includes all the opposing philosophical and religious doctrines likely to persist and to gain adherents in a more or less just constitutional democratic society."[14]

If Rawls's lead is followed, then, there would seem to be no longer any gap remaining between the rights-based liberals and the communitarians concerning the philosophical basis of legitimate political norms. The distinction drawn by Sandel between deontological liberals who postulate transcendent grounds for individual rights based on a neo-Kantian metaphysic and their communitarian critics who look for situated selves' conceptions of the common good concretely grounded in historical traditions simply disappears. With respect to the alleged grounds or source of his liberal principles, Rawls is every bit as neo-Hegelian or historicist as Sandel depicts the communitarians as being. Sandel, for example, includes Walzer and Oakeshott as expositors of the communitarian "situated self" perspective. But now Rawls seems happily engaged, like Oakeshott, in the task of "pursuing the intimations" of a particular historical tradition whose moral intuitions he accepts as definitive. And Walzer likewise becomes his methodological kin rather than an adversary. Both he and Rawls, and presumably Sandel as well, now must interpret the "shared understandings" of their relevant communities.[15]

If the debate between the communitarians as understood by Sandel and the rights-based liberals as understood by Rawls is to continue, therefore, its locale seems likely to change. The issues of political principle and orientation may persist, but the contest is no longer over philosophical principles as much as it is over historical understandings. The disputants are not so much representatives of distinctive philosophical positions as they are rival hermeneuticists. Sandel's current project, as I understand it, is thus quite appropriately heavily historical in its focus, elucidating the communitarian strands of our traditional civic consciousness. It might likewise seem incumbent on Rawls to move beyond discussions of overlapping consensus in the abstract to demonstrate the actual presence in our tradition of those "familiar intuitive ideas" he cites as the ultimate source of his principles of justice. And Nozick too could easily get into the hermeneutic act: one criticism of his position denigrated it as a perfect expression of the views of the corner service-station owner; and, on the "shared understandings" criterion, that characterization would seem to serve as a warrant for approval rather than as a snide intellectual put-down.

The difficulty with this new hermeneutic mode of the debate is that historical investigation will inevitably find not only consensus but conflict of moral intuitions, not only understandings that are shared but other equally important understandings that are contested. Hence each disputant will be partially successful and partially unsuccessful in his or her attempt to find support for his or her own favored views in the ambiguous legacy of history and tradition. Our tradition includes Lincoln and Andrew Carnegie, Martin Luther King and Calvin Coolidge, the creators of Head Start and the defenders of substantive due process. Completion of their hermeneutic efforts by the contending parties will not resolve the issues that divide them but only give them a new dimension. Then what?

Rawls at least seems aware of the difficulties here, conceding that "the public political culture may be of two minds even at a very deep level."[16] But he must assume that this two-mindedness does not go all the way down, because in the same paragraph he anticipates the possibility of creating a synthesis of principles that "provides a reasonable way of shaping into one coherent view the deeper bases of agreement embedded in the public political culture of a constitutional regime."[17] Even assuming that sufficient consensus exists to permit the creation of such a synthesis, the presence of the "contending traditions" Rawls recognizes would seem to permit multiple contenders for this synthesis. How then are we to know which synthesis to embrace?

Rawls's argument at this juncture seems to acknowledge two possible answers, one leading into the political arena and the other at least part way back into the philosophical highlands that he wants to leave behind. First, he suggests, we may know the appropriate synthesis by its rhetorical appeal—by its capacity to elicit public acceptance. The right principles are not true principles in some metaphysical or epistemological sense. Instead, they are those principles that can prove themselves in the marketplace of ideas, as it were, by serving as the basis of an emergent "public understanding" of what our democratic society is all about.[18] Alternatively, or perhaps supplementally, these principles prove themselves by their capacity to "be seen as more appropriate than other familiar principles of justice to the nature of democratic citizens viewed as free and equal persons."[19]

Evidence to date would suggest that Rawls's principles will have mixed success in the political marketplace. And popular acceptance by itself is in any case an achievement but not an argument. At some point, then, we might suppose that Rawls and other rights-based liberals will need to foray somewhat deeper into the philosophical thicket to expand upon the rational bases of their doctrines. In Rawls's case, this need would seem to call for some elaboration of why his principles are to be seen as the most appropriate vehicle of association among "democratic citizens viewed as free and equal persons." And if, as he insists, that elaboration need not involve allegiance to some particular metaphysic of selfhood,[20] it would seem to require at least some underlying suppositions about human capacities and rational action.

The same burden would seem also to await the communitarians. Their own political values and concerns—their focus on community, civic virtue, and the common good—are at the moment as philosophically free-floating as those of the rights-based liberals. Most of the major communitarian treatises have essentially been critiques of views they find inadequate: critiques of liberal individualism (*Habits of the Heart*), of the "Enlightenment project" and its derivative emotivism (*After Virtue*), and of the deontological doctrines putatively endemic to rights-based liberalism (*Liberalism and the Limits of Justice*). When it comes to providing a constructive and affirmative philosophical foundation for the communitarian viewpoint, we find rather thin fare. Alasdair MacIntyre's creative reconstruction of Aristotle in his account of virtues, practices, and narrative quests is probably the most helpful contribution so far; but even MacIntyre would see his account in *After Virtue* as a somewhat partial and preliminary sketch. Other than that, the communitarians, concentrating on their critical analyses, have provided allusions more than arguments: neo-Hegelian allusions to *Sittlichkeit* and "constitutive" communities, allusions to "social ecology," and allusions to the traditions and norms of civic republicanism.

At this point, I would argue, the need for a more profound and explicit philosophical grounding for the norms of communitarian republicanism merges with Dunn's pleas for a more adequate theory of collective prudence. For, as William Sullivan observes in *Reconstructing Public Philosophy*, "the republican tradition has seen politics as essentially the application of prudence, an understanding that rests on a sense of practical reason missing from the liberal ideal of rationality."[21] In order to make their political values more than free-floating ideals or one possible understanding of our tradition among many equally plausible hermeneutic accounts, the communitarians would be well advised to take Sullivan's observations as the preamble for a constructive philosophical task: namely, to explain how their political vision embodies the norms of rational practice in pursuit of a common good.

Against this background of the traditional concern about the role of reason in politics and the more recent reawakening of interest in the philosophical basis of liberal democracy, this book can be seen as having several related purposes: to contribute to the project John Dunn adumbrates of fashioning a more adequate theory of "collective prudence"; to provide a plausible philosophical basis for the communitarian view of a healthy democracy as the rational pursuit of common purposes by free and equal citizens; and to provide a framework within which some of the perceptive efforts of recent theorists to improve democratic theory can be given a common home.

The book's principal theses can be sketched in the following preliminary fashion:

(1) The attribution of a significant political role to human rationality has been a persistent theme of Western political theories; and these accounts of political rationality have largely proceeded within the conceptual formats established very early by Plato and Aristotle (chapter 1).

(2) These accounts of political rationality have become increasingly narrow and inadequate, principally as a consequence of constraints and distortions produced by the dominance of the calculative ideal (chapter 1).

(3) Recent developments within the philosophy of science and the philosophy of language offer the resources for escaping these constraints and distortions and for reasserting in a profound way the practical dimension of all rationality (chapter 2).

(4) Reflection upon the necessary conditions of scientific inquiry and parallel reflection upon the conditions of successful linguistic achievement converge upon a specifiable pattern of constituent practices that can fairly be designated as "the constitution of rational enterprises" (chapter 3).

(5) By analogy, this pattern of rational practice can, to the extent that common purposes are present, be applied to political actions and institutions. Such an institutional embodiment of reason sustains a liberal form of *homonoia* and exerts an important centripetal counterforce against the fissiparous effects of individual passions and interests (chapter 4).

(6) Citizenship in a polity conducted in accord with the norms of rational practice logically entails certain specifiable rights and privileges. At the same time, certain obligations of citizenship are also logically specifiable (chapter 5).

(7) The ideal of politics as a rational enterprise provides an appropriate framework for rendering the best accounts of liberal democracy, both traditional and contemporary, philosophically perspicuous and coherent (chapter 6).

(8) The same ideal provides philosophical warrant for liberal democratic policies emphasizing a vital public sphere, robust public dialogue, enhanced citizen participation, protection of civic rights, the rule of law, a concern for equality, a democratic form of authority, and an insistence on the public responsibilities of democratic citizens (chapter 7).

In addition to the purposes noted earlier, this book can also be legitimately construed as an attempt to recall liberalism to its initial faith in the salutary power of reason in public life. The reconstruction of liberal theory should go hand in hand with the rehabilitation and refashioning of our understanding of practical reason. I say this despite MacIntyre's verdict on the inevitable failure of "the Enlightenment project" and Sullivan's comment suggesting that the liberal ideal of rationality was without a sense of practical reason. For the fact is that liberal rationalism was never sufficiently coherent in its origins to be as univocally deficient as these accounts would suggest. Many of the fundamental intuitions about the humanizing force of reason that informed early liberal critiques and aspirations were actually very astute. The problem was that they became associated with a philosophical attempt to perfect the powers of reason by rendering them wholly theoretical in the Aristotelian sense of that term. It was the pursuit of this systematically elusive theoretical certainty that had the ultimate effect of undermining the humane ideals of liberalism as it made the intuitions that sustained them increasingly unintelligible. Perhaps paradoxically, it is precisely the abandonment of the quest for certainty which liberal philosophy inspired that can make its ideals and intuitions once again accessible and persuasive.

One implication of my argument, therefore, is that the liberal and republican traditions are not so antithetical as much recent commentary would lead us to suppose. Certainly tensions exist between the two traditions, and they have different emphases and priorities. But the quarrels between them are better understood as internecine squabbling between fraternal camps than as a pitched battle between relentless adversaries. The gap between them has been depicted as greater than it is for two principal reasons. First, adherents of the civic republican viewpoint—perhaps because they have been unduly influenced by MacPherson's and Strauss's identification of liberalism with possessive individualism—have chosen to emphasize their differences with liberalism as they interpret it. And second, there has been a near-exclusive focus on the issue that does separate republicanism from the more individualistic strands of liberalism: the question of the relationship between private commerce and public good. When we look more broadly at the two traditions, however, and especially when we look at those aspects of Locke, Mill, and other liberals that do not fit into the narrow confines of Spencerian or Nozickean libertarianism, the gap narrows considerably. Locke, after all, spoke of community and common good; and Mill emphasized participation and the need for civic virtue. It is not, then, contradictory to conceive of the account offered here both as an attempt to reconstruct liberal theory and as an attempt to provide a philosophical framework for the concerns of contemporary communitarians. For the version of liberalism offered here is the complex and capacious common-good liberalism often characteristic of liberalism prior to 1850 rather than the simplistic and narrow individualist liberalism associated with laissez-faire and with post–industrial revolution commercialism. To put the point another way: I identify myself and the argument presented here as liberal, but I feel generally more at home with the civic republicans than with libertarians; and, if such conjecture be pardonable, I feel confident in supposing that Locke and Mill would have felt the same way.

Arriving at the views presented here has occasioned some mixed personal feelings; and I conclude by reflecting briefly upon these reactions.

Like many, I suppose, I was informed and impressed by Reinhold Niebuhr's critical analysis of what he called "the illusions and sentimentalities of the Age of Reason."[22] I have always since accepted as convincing his contention that the limitations of the human mind and the imperfections of the human heart preclude societies from ever transcending bias, conflict, and coercion. And I also accept his claim that some balance of power will always be a part of our best approximations of political justice. To speak, then, as I do here, of transforming and rehabilitating the faith of reason as an important part of liberal theory causes me both trepidation and chagrin.

I believe, however, that I can maintain my claims about the importance of reason in politics without forgetting counsels of realism. First, my argument is not utopian. I claim that norms resident in rational practices are valid in politics and that it is possible to adhere to these norms to a beneficial extent. How far imperfect human beings can institutionalize and adhere to these norms, however, remains an empirical question. On that question, realists are undoubtedly correct to insist on our limitations; but we should not therefore go to the opposite extreme of supposing reason to be impotent or useless in the social domain. Second, we should remember that even Niebuhr recognized that human rationality was an important resource in the quest for social justice. Reason, he wrote, could not alone restrain the will to power, but "reason ultimately makes for social as well as for internal order." He continued: "The force of reason makes for justice, not only by placing inner restraints upon the desires of the self in the interests of social harmony, but by judging the claims and assertions of the individuals from the perspective of the intelligence of the total community."[23] Finally, times change. If in Niebuhr's day an accurate social analysis was obscured by a philosophical sentimentalism that produced overly sanguine expectations about the future, today there is more danger from a philosophical cynicism that produces complacency or resignation about the present. Niebuhr worried that he might be perceived as a cynic; I worry that I may well be perceived as a sentimentalist. But there is not that much difference between us. It is more a case of which way the pendulum needs to be pushed in a given historical setting.[24]

Although my realist predispositions leave me somewhat uneasy about insisting upon the importance of rationality in politics, I find that the argument stated here alleviates a long-standing sense of political and intellectual discomfiture. I have always considered myself a political liberal in some fundamental intuitive way, but one who has found some of the prototypical versions of liberalism inadequate. Libertarian liberalism seems to me at best narrow and at worst morally disreputable. Liberal pluralism seems intellectually shallow and politically prone to complacency and a sense of drift. Utilitarian liberalism seems both protean and insufficiently alert to collectivist and elitist appropriation of its ideas. And the popular version of liberalism that transmutes it into straightforward egalitarianism seems somehow both odd and potentially perverse, seeming as it does to assume that the overriding goal of politics is social leveling rather than the complex achievement of justice, liberty, community, and social welfare.

Similarly, I always have been intuitively a rationalist—one who instinctively appreciates the value of reason and the demands of objectivity in all areas of human endeavor. But I have found the standard account of what rationality consists in seriously deficient and even repellent. It misconstrues objectivity as detachment and scientific learning as neo-Scholastic logic-chopping, and it either disqualifies reason from having any role in the realm of human values or it serves to legitimate scientific reductivism in that domain.

The recovery of the practical dimension of rationality and the understanding of liberal politics as an attempt to give political embodiment to the norms of rational practice helps me remedy these twin frustrations simultaneously. I can understand and give articulation to my most fundamental political and intellectual commitments, which previously were held more as intuitive sympathies. I can say that my rationalism embodies an allegiance to the complex norms of problem solving by human communities via the discipline of reason. And I can say that my liberalism represents a dedication to the form of social practice produced by the application of these norms to political problems—a complex and humane approach that encompasses liberty, equality, fraternity, participation, civic virtue, and legitimate authority.

At a minimum, therefore, writing this book has proved for me an important part of obeying the Socratic maxim "know thyself." And it has allowed me to fulfill a professional obligation of political theorists: to effectuate some coherence between philosophical perception and political action. More ambitiously, I hope that this book can help in the task of revitalizing the theory of liberal democracy by reconciling what is best in liberalism with what is most important in civic republicanism—doing so by grounding this synthesis in a conception of rational practice that conforms to what recent philosophy has taught us.

Chapter One Reason, Rational

Practice, and Political Theory:

The Making of a Problem

▬▬▬

"Reason" is not a name, but a philosophical symbol. It does not refer to a thing, something that can be kicked like a table or a rock. Instead, it stands for the power of organized feats of intelligence—the human capacity to make our experience intelligible. Because it is not transparently obvious what accounts for that capacity, giving content to the philosophical symbol requires interpretive judgment. And because the feats of reason stand as genuine achievements, these judgments ineluctably carry appraisive connotations.

The conceptual geography of the idea of reason approximates very closely the linguistic geography of the Greek *logos*. The word *logos* referred not only to the power of reason, but also to the capacity for speech. In addition, the stem of *logos* is incorporated into the Greek *logismos*, which refers to reckoning or calculation, and into our own logic and syllogism, which similarly refer to powers of deductive inference. And, finally, the stem of *logos* is also incorporated into the suffix "ology," meaning "the science of" something or other. When we put these various usages together and reflect upon the conceptual claims implicit in them, we can conclude that in Western parlance the power of organized intelligence is presumed to be paradigmatically displayed in three places: human speech or language, in calculative inference, and in scientific inquiry. To the extent that this is so, it also follows that philosophical reflection upon the nature and relationships of language, logic, and science is at the same time reflection about rationality itself.

Dominance of the Calculative Ideal

For a variety of reasons, *logismos* has dominated *logos* in the Western philosophical tradition. The three exemplars of reason—language, logic, and science—have not retained parity as bases for our understanding of rationality. Instead, it is the power of deductive inference—of logical calculation—that has seemed most exemplary of reason at work. It is not that language and science are actually deemed inferior, so much as it is that their rationality is seen as derivative of the force of reckoning. They are rational because and to the extent that they incorporate the resources of logical inference. Anything else found in speech is merely noise and anything else found in science a mere sociological curiosity.

The ascendance of the calculative ideal—the mathematicization of reason—is most evident and pronounced in modern philosophy, but the groundwork for this ascendance was clearly prepared in classical philosophy. The modern rationalists who sallied forth under the banner of "the geometric spirit" were not really abandoning their philosophical legacy. Whatever their rhetoric, they were revisionists rather than true revolutionaries. They were merely exaggerating one aspect of the classical conception of rationality at the expense of other aspects intermingled with it.

Plato's enchantment with the cognitive power of mathematics is especially obvious. Hobbes who, as his biographer Aubrey tells us, was "in love with geometry" saluted Plato as "the best philosopher of the Greeks" because he "forbade entrance into his school to all that were not in some measure Geometricians."[1] Our senses, in Plato's view, are at best very imperfect cognitive tools. Entrapped in the evanescent world of appearances, they can produce only beliefs (*doxa*) that do not amount to knowledge (*episteme*) in any profound or reliable sense of the term. Like Descartes, Plato concluded that the only way for our sense-imprisoned minds to surmount these limitations is through recourse to mathematical abstraction. Plato has Socrates ask Glaucon, "What form of study is there that would draw the soul from the world of change to reality?" After rejecting several attempted responses, Socrates gives as his answer "something that is universal in all crafts and in every form of knowledge and intellectual operation," namely "number and calculation." When the senses provide reports that are equivocal or paradoxical, "it is natural . . . for the mind to invoke the help of reason with its power of calculation [because] the properties of number appear to have the power of leading us towards reality."[2]

For all of his fascination with mathematical reason, however, Plato clearly interpreted its meaning within the context of his own essentialist cosmology and his cognitivist ethics. His Guardians, he admonishes, "are to practice calculation, not like merchants or shopkeepers for purposes of buying and selling, but with a view to war and to help in the conversion of the soul itself from the world of becoming to truth and reality."[3] However crucial the mathematical disciplines are to his educational program, and however paradigmatic they are for his conception of intelligence, they are only penultimate in status. They open the way for the rather mysterious process of dialectic—a process of reasoning that is alleged to produce a grasp of first principles, to obtain "an account of the essence of each thing," and to grasp "by pure intelligence the very nature of Goodness itself."[4] Rational knowledge for Plato, although clearly modeled upon number and calculation, always retains its axiological roots and its moral destination. Platonic rationality is mathematical in its form, but it is powered by *eros* and leads its possessors to the *Agathon*.

Despite his many differences from Plato, we can find in Aristotle a somewhat similar pattern of tempered fascination with mathematical reason. Given his biological orientation, his essentialism, and his moral cognitivism, Aristotle's conception of human reason cannot be unproblematically mathematical. He must allow for the noetic apprehension of form, and he insists that one who possesses "practical wisdom must at the same time be morally good."[5] Nevertheless, Aristotle also seems convinced that our knowledge is somehow imperfect unless it can be cast into deductivist form. The sciences should ideally be turned into Euclidean formal systems. As Jonathan Barnes writes in his introduction to the *Posterior Analytics*, "what Euclid later did, haltingly, for geometry, Aristotle wanted done for every branch of human knowledge. The sciences are to be axiomatized: that is to say, the body of truth that each defines is to be exhibited as a sequence of theorems inferred from a few basic postulates or axioms. And the axiomatization is to be formalized: that is to say, its sentences are to be formulated within a well-defined language, and its arguments are to proceed according to a precisely and explicitly specified set of logical rules."[6] His dedication to demonstration as the hallmark of real knowledge, moreover, even leads Aristotle to try to cast at least a part of the operations of practical wisdom into deductivist form through the not very illuminating notion of the practical syllogism.

In sum, in their different and distinctive ways, both Aristotle and Plato exhibited a profound attraction toward a mathematicized conception of rationality. For one, mathematics provided the pathway from *doxa* to *episteme*, from opinions about phenomena to knowledge of intelligible reality; and for the other, mathematics provided the ideal format for the presentation of scientific findings. In each case, however, the belief in the peculiar potency or perfection of *logismos* is constrained and tempered by equally powerful convictions that pull in a different direction—convictions, for example, that philosophy is inconceivable apart from the pull of divine *eros* and that science is impossible without the intuition into essential form supplied by *nous*.

Despite important exceptions, the prevailing tendency within modern rationalism has been to extend and consolidate the geometric ideal. The fascination with mathematical calculation as the paradigm for rationality in general has intensified, and the countervailing constraints have largely dissipated. Pascal may have coined the term *geometric spirit* in order to distinguish it from the more subtle form of reasoning he deemed essential to philosophic inquiry and to limit the influence of his adversary, Descartes. But it is Descartes who has triumphed. Indeed, by the eighteenth century, the *philosophes* had embraced Cartesian rationalism in a way that liberated it from the dualistic and fideistic restrictions he had scrupulously and self-defensively—but none too logically—placed upon it.[7]

If one recalls the nature and source of the constraints placed upon the mathematicization of reason in classical Greek philosophy and then reflects upon some of the central transformations that mark seventeenth-century cosmology, the consolidation of the geometric ideal should become readily intelligible. For it was their essentialist metaphysics and their associated teleological doctrine of motion that made it impossible for Plato and Aristotle to conceive reason as exhaustively mathematical. And it was precisely these notions that the seventeenth-century philosophical revolutionaries so happily jettisoned.

So long as the universe was believed to comprise a panoply of substantial forms, and so long as this universe was to be deemed intelligible, it was necessary to assume the existence of some valid cognitive powers not easily assimilable to mathematics. These cognitive powers had to be depicted as quasi-intuitive gestalt-discerning capabilities rather than as purely calculative operations. Hence the necessity of *noesis* as a complement to demonstration in Greek science. It required similar extramathematical intellectual operations to interpret the dynamics of end-oriented motions in order to comprehend the actualization of potential in specific cases. Once the universe was conceived in nonessentialist terms, however, these cognitive powers seemed super-fluous. If there were no forms out there to discern, it was not necessary to suppose any form-discerning intellect.

Once substances were replaced by matter and Aristotelian motion was replaced by mere change of place, in fact, mathematics might easily be seen as omnicompetent, uniquely suited for the apprehension of our world. "Primary qualities" are composed of measurable properties; and motion-in-space can be adequately and fruitfully represented in arithmetic notations. Thus, in his *Meditations*, Descartes could refer to "that corporeal nature which is the object of pure mathematics."[8] And Hobbes could take his bearings from the investigations of Galileo, who revealed what motion was all about by conceiving it mathematically. At a later time problems might arise with this metaphysical conception of a homogeneous mechanistic universe; but for the moment it was no strain to presume complete isomorphy between numbers and reality.

The other aspect of classical rationality that seemed to preclude any purely mathematical conception of reality was its axiological grounding. This aspect of the classical conception answered two questions about rational cognition: one relating to its location, the other to its motivation. The latter of these functions of the axiological hypothesis could be handled rather easily by a small change in anthropological analytics. All "motivations" including philosophic *eros* were assigned to the realm of the passions, a realm that could energize but was not included within the domain of the cognitive faculties. The love of the soul for the true, the good, and the beautiful that Plato and Aristotle conceived as internal to cognitive activity was simply interpreted as an impulse (now watered down into "curiosity") that could set reason in motion from the outside, as it were. This shift in the soul's geography was an important aspect, in fact, of the celebrated reversal in the soul's politics: the idea that reason was the slave rather than the ruler of the passions.

The second question under this heading, the one relating to the location of reason, has proved more intractable. Indeed, it is almost surely insoluble under the premises of seventeenth-century cosmology, a cosmology that paradoxically displaced human beings from the world altogether.[9] A variety of expedients were employed to handle this problem, none of them entirely satisfactory. One tack was to conceive thought as itself simply another form of matter-in-motion, an account championed by Hobbes. The Cartesian approach was to turn the differences between thought and matter into an ontological gulf between different substances and consequently to extrude reason from nature altogether. And a final tactic was to hope that the personal grounding of reason, being tacit in its deployment, could thereby simply be ignored or treated as nonexistent.

Despite this potentially worrisome difficulty, then, the clearly dominant judgment of the founders of modern philosophy—whether "empiricist" or "rationalist"—is that reason is fundamentally a process of mathematical analysis and calculation. The axiology of reason can either be shunted aside by conceptual rearranging or else ignored; and the complicating aspects of noetic intuition are no longer necessary to confront. "Intuitions" of a sort are still necessary, of course, to provide the first principles from which demonstrations can proceed. But these intuitions are themselves mathematical in both form and character—in character because they resemble the "clear and distinct" apprehension of the truth of mathematical axioms and in form because the "simples" thus intuited are mensurable.

The dominant tendency within modern Western rationalism has thus been to identify the powers of reason with the capabilities of mathematical calculation and deductive inference. The pattern is evident from the outset of modern philosophy in Hobbes, for example, who tells us: "in what matter soever there is place for addition and subtraction, there is also place for reason; and where these have no place, there reason has nothing to do . . . for reason is nothing but reckoning."[10] And the same assumptions remain controlling into twentieth-century accounts, such as Russell's propositional calculus, Carnap's "logische aufbau," and Wittgenstein's *Tractatus.*

With the ascendance of the geometric ideal, the three exemplars of reason—language, calculation, and science—are not accorded normative parity. Mathematical logic becomes the paramount exemplar of rationality, with language and science being subordinated to that standard. The power of reason is identified with the axiomatic clarity and the deductive rigor best embodied in the mathematical disciplines. Science and language are still regarded as important instances of rational endeavor, but only because and to the extent that they adhere to the standards of formal rigor established by mathematics.

This interpretation has produced as corollaries a characteristic diagnosis of failures in linguistic and scientific endeavors and a program for perfecting them. When language fails to produce clear understanding or when science fails to provide illumination, it is presumed that the failure is likely occasioned by a lack of adherence to the methodological norms of universal mathematics. Prophylaxis against such breakdowns in language and science could be guaranteed, then, if only we could construct a perfect language and if scientific propositions could be expressed in the terms of such a language. In short, the quest has been to purify language and science by turning them into internally rigorous and externally firmly anchored logical calculi. And whatever in language or science cannot be subsumed into a deductive system of this sort must be either cast aside as a distorting influence or at best disregarded as a nonrational irrelevancy.

The paradigmatic status accorded to the mathematical disciplines for our understanding of human rationality has produced real benefits but equally real costs. The geometric ideal has been a goad to precision in both language and science, and it has prompted the deployment of mathematical tools in enormously productive ways. On the negative side, however, the assiduous cultivation of this idealized account of reason has led us to misconstrue or to ignore important aspects of linguistic and scientific practice. And it has consigned large sectors of human experience to subrational status.

In particular, the appeal of the geometric ideal has made it exceptionally difficult to understand how reason might play a role in politics—just as it has made it difficult to understand reason's role in aesthetics and morality. If the essence of rationality is to be conceived as mathematical intuition and/or mathematical calculation, then rational practices must in some way embody these intuitive or calculative features. The attempt to model rational behavior in this fashion, however, generates some profound problems. Such a project in effect proceeds on the assumption that all genuine rationality—or at least rationality in its highest and best form—is theoretical. Rationality, that is, is depicted as precise, "eternal," contemplative or "observational," and certain in its conclusions. Practical reason must at least approximate these standards or else relinquish its claim to legitimacy. Since practical reason can never really "shape up" in this sense, however, the pressure created by allegiance to the geometric ideal leads to conceptions of rational practice that are distorted, incoherent, or excessively narrow. Those who fully appreciate these difficulties—but who cannot relinquish the mathematicized conception of rationality—may as a consequence abandon the notion of practical reason or rational behavior altogether, at least in their philosophical doctrines if not entirely in the tacit norms that govern their own lives.

As one should expect, given the foregoing analysis, these tensions are already visible in classical conceptions of rational practice, because Plato and Aristotle were inclined to accord normative priority to calculation and deductive inference. The problems with attempts to conceptualize practical reason and the role of reason in politics then become increasingly intractable in the modern era. Modern political theorists who consider political rationality tend to operate within the formal parameters set by Plato and Aristotle. But they then proceed to attenuate both the content and the ground of practical reason because of the pressure of the calculative ideal. The formulas remain, but the substance becomes both thinner and increasingly problematic with time.

Classical Praxis

Despite Aristotle's strictures against expecting more certainty than a given subject matter permits, and despite his distinction between theoretical and practical reason, the conception of rational practice in both his philosophy and that of his mentor, Plato, is shaped in important ways by their attraction to the mathematical ideal. In both instances, however, the potential difficulties intrinsic in the subjection of practical reason to mathematical norms are mitigated by the surrounding metaphysic. That metaphysic supplies contextual features that lend moral substance to what otherwise might be an abstractly formal rationality.

In Plato, rational practice can be defined by what philosophers do when they are creating the good society. Life "in most existing states" is a "mere dream," Plato asserts, "where men live fighting one another about shadows."[11] The philosopher's warrant to rule stems from his capacity to deliver his fellows from this unhappy dream world. And this capacity is, in turn, a function of the philosopher's rationality—his ability to perceive ensnaring illusions for what they are and to ascertain what is truly real.

"Happiness," Plato tells us, "can only come to a state when its lineaments are traced by an artist working after the divine pattern." The praxis of the philosopher-king, who is referred to in this context as "this artist," is a form of *mimesis*. The philosopher's first mimetic project is to fashion his own soul in the pattern of the divine order of the world. He contemplates the eternal order of the Forms, and "like one who imitates an admired companion" embodies that order in himself. If he is permitted to govern, his function will be to do the same for his fellows—"to mold other characters besides his own and to shape the pattern of public and private life into conformity with his vision of the ideal."[12]

The state, then, is a work of art. It is for this reason that Plato is so determined to regulate the tragic poets in his polis: they are the direct competitors of his governing philosophers, because both are mimetic artists. The crucial difference between the good *mimesis* of the philosopher—"the imitation of the best and noblest life"—and the suspect *mimesis* of the typical poet arises from their different capabilities to discern the truth. Poets are accomplished in the techniques of their craft, but only in the techniques. Their representational skills alone give them no access to the truth, no means of knowing whether what they represent is real or illusory. And if they beautify illusion, which their skills may permit them to do, their art can be a dangerously seductive threat to the spiritual health of their audience. The philosopher, in contrast, will artistically re-create only the images of the good, the true, and the genuinely beautiful.

These crucial powers of noetic intuition that enable the philosopher to know the truth are closely linked with and dependent upon mathematical intuition, in Plato's account. That is why the arduous training of the philosopher-king is so heavily devoted to the mathematical disciplines. In the first place, it is the capacity for mathematical abstraction that allows the philosopher to cast off unreliable sensory images in his quest for truth and goodness. Appearances can be deceiving, especially in the moral realm where the beauty that gives goodness its erotic power may be cosmetically falsified and grafted onto unworthy objects of desire. His mathematical training, Plato believes, will equip the philosopher to see through these ruses.

If mathematical powers provide the philosopher with a methodological prophylaxis against error, they sustain his moral noetic insight in another, ontologically grounded way as well. For Plato linked the forms of Goodness and Beauty very closely; he thought that the essence of beauty lay in balance, proportion, and harmony; and he was captivated by the Pythagorean discovery that musically harmonious relationships were expressible as mathematical ratios. Mathematical reasoning was, therefore, in his view neither purely analytic nor morally empty. Instead, it provided access to the moral order expressed in the music of the spheres.

The Aristotelian account of practical reason is not always easy to decipher. Considered as a body, Aristotle's characterizations of the rational faculty of *phronesis* are incomplete, seemingly inconsistent in important respects, and hopelessly muddy in others. Notwithstanding these difficulties, they provide a point of reference for much later speculation about rational practice; and like Plato's account, although in different ways, they incorporate mathematical imagery at crucial junctures.

Aristotle defines *phronesis* as "a rational faculty exercised for the attainment of truth in things that are humanly good and bad."[13] It is concerned with doing rather than with making, so it is not a craft. And it is concerned with things that do not exist by unalterable necessity, so it is not a science.

The prudent individual, by common acceptance, says Aristotle, is one who "calculates well for the attainment of a particular end of a fine sort."[14] The surrounding context of Aristotle's theory of the virtues and of politics, in addition, makes it clear that the ultimate "end of a fine sort" is to be understood as *eudaemonia*—a term sometimes translated as "happiness" but which is perhaps rendered more adequately as "human flourishing" in a larger sense.[15] Moreover, it is also clear that the ultimate end must be pursued within the setting of the *polis*, because human beings are by nature political animals. The end sought by *phronesis*, in short, is neither simple pleasure nor purely selfish. It is human fulfillment within a community.

Mathematical, or perhaps we should say quasi-mathematical, reasoning enters the picture in two places. First, Aristotle analogizes the perception of the ultimate end of *phronesis* to mathematical intuition in a very obscure and underdeveloped concluding paragraph to chapter 8 of book 6 of the *Nicomachean Ethics*. He tells us there that "prudence involves knowledge of the ultimate particular thing, which cannot be attained by science but only by perception. By this I mean not perception by any one of the special senses," Aristotle continues, "but the power of perceiving such a truth as that the irreducible figure in mathematics is the triangle, beyond which we cannot carry our analysis." And then Aristotle leaves his readers unedified and confused by concluding that "this mathematical perception deserves the name better than does prudence, which perceives a certain kind of truth by a process of a different order," without bothering to specify what "certain kind" or what "different order."[16]

Possibly this whole passage should be passed over altogether, since it is not only hopelessly muddy, but it also seems in tension with Aristotle's account in the *Posterior Analytics* of how first principles are intuited, with his own dialectical mode of argumentation on behalf of according *eudaemonia* the status of ultimate end, and with his insistence that accurate perception of the good for humanity requires both experience and virtue.[17] However, it is a notable passage despite its difficulties, for it exemplifies both Aristotle's desire to conceive the apprehension of the ends of practical reason as somehow akin to mathematical intuition and also the serious problems he had in handling the fundamental issue.

The other intrusion of mathematical reasoning into the Aristotelian characterization of *phronesis*, of course, is the depiction of the deliberative process involved as one of calculation. Once again, Aristotle does not spell out as fully as he might exactly what "calculation" means in this context. Obviously, it cannot be simply a matter of adding sums. It is a calculative process, however, in the sense that it involves the choice of the most effective pathway to the desired end—and therefore it embodies the kind of quantitative weighing that occurs in cost-benefit analyses.

By conceiving prudential judgment as calculation and by assimilating it to his notion of "deliberation," Aristotle comes perilously close to collapsing prudence into purely technical and instrumental rationality. His distinction between doing and making, together with his designation of virtuous activity (and prudence is a virtue) as intrinsically rather than merely contingently good indicates that this outcome runs contrary to his overall intent. Moreover, the Greek expression *pros ta tele*, translated as "means," does not necessarily connote a purely external relationship to the ends at stake, as the English rendition does.[18] Nevertheless, Aristotle clearly depicts prudential reasoning as a kind of deliberative calculation; he notes that "we do not deliberate about ends but always about means";[19] and at least some of his examples of this reasoning process are straightforward instances of lining up desired ends—for example, health and starting a business—with necessary or contributory causes—for example, eating light meat and having sufficient capital.

"Rationality in politics" is incarnated, then, on Aristotle's view, in the actions of wise, virtuous, and experienced people—the *spoudaioi*. Given positions of responsibility, these enlightened individuals display the practical genius of leaders like Pericles, since they "have the power of seeing what is good for themselves and for humanity,"[20] together with the capacity to discern effective ways to achieve these goals. They are not philosopher-kings, but they are the best real-world approximations of that utopian ideal type. It is their intellectual virtuosity in the moral and practical realm that makes it meaningful to speak of and desirable to foster rational praxis in political life.

Considering Plato and Aristotle together, then, it is clear that the philosophical legacy they bequeathed us assigned reason an important political role. Rationality provided light and sustained *dike*. Without its guidance, politics would resemble Matthew Arnold's bleak image of a "darkling plain where ignorant armies clash by night." Differing on some of the strategic particulars and on philosophical detail, Plato and his pupil nonetheless concurred that civilized praxis depends upon *sophia*.

It is also clear that their attempts to delineate the nature of practical reason were influenced by their attraction to the intellectual force and clarity of *logismos*. For Plato, mathematical reasoning seemed to have the power to release the mind from subservience to unreliable sensory images, to foster the abstract intellectual capacity needed to intuit the Forms, and to resonate with the harmonies of the ordered cosmos. For Aristotle, both the perception of the ends of *phronesis* and the weighing of its means were believed to be akin to mathematical intuition and calculation.

These conceptions of practical rationality as quasi-mathematical were intrinsically problematic, for reasons already adumbrated. Although wholly illogical minds may be difficult to imbue with practical reason, it is nonetheless not at all obvious how mathematical virtuosity can generate the capacity to appreciate the beauty of the Socratic soul or how logical acuity contributes to the discernment of the human good. What sustained these intrinsically problematic conceptions of practical rationality and what gave them moral content were the metaphysical assumptions that surrounded and permeated them. The influence of these metaphysical assumptions can be felt in the multiplicity of meanings and the richness of content found in the focal symbol of the *logos* itself. Pythagorean mathematical mysticism and an essentialist and teleological conception of *physis* converged upon the inference that human fulfillment is akin to harmonious development, is tended to by nature, and is perceptible by the *noesis* of able-minded and virtuous souls.

Against this background, it is already possible to anticipate some of the profound difficulties the whole ideal of reason in politics encounters in modernity. Because the mathematical format Plato and Aristotle tried to force upon practical reason was inherently problematic, and because the moral content with which they invested practical reason was a function of their metaphysics, the difficulties they confronted in this area of their philosophy could only intensify with the onset of modern philosophy. For two of the most characteristic features of modern philosophy have been the rejection of classical metaphysics and the tendency to identify rationality with mathematical reasoning. Modern philosophers of politics who have tried to adapt the idea of practical reason to the new philosophical setting, therefore, have seen problems in the received account turn into dilemmas and tensions turn into incoherencies. The neo-Platonists among them have found it ever more difficult to hear the music of the spheres; and the exponents of a de-Aristotelianized *phronesis* have seen that virtue lose most of its loveliness.

Modern Prudence: Transmuted Aristotelianism

The prudent individual, in Aristotle's influential formulation, was one who "calculates well for the attainment of a particular end of a fine sort."[21] To fill in this abstract definition, Aristotelian anthropology and essentialist cosmology identified the "particular end of a fine sort" as *eudaemonia* and saw it as attainable only within the communal life of the *polis*. As we saw, moreover, "calculating" was not conceived as merely technical computation of efficient means to an end, although Aristotle's account did not make the distinction entirely clear.

Many modern theorists who have sought to understand the role of reason in politics have taken Aristotle's abstract definition of prudence—just cited—as their starting point. With the dissolution of classical cosmology, however, the process of giving concrete content to the abstract formula has presented new opportunities and considerable difficulties. Informed by the new premises of modern philosophical naturalism, Aristotle's depiction of the virtue of prudence undergoes a twofold process of transmutation. On the one hand, it becomes increasingly technicized: the distinction between *phronesis* and *techne* is discarded and the feat of "calculating well" tends to become ends-means calculation in the narrow sense. On the other hand, the "particular end" whose attainment is at issue loses its grounding in a natural teleology.

As a consequence, its philosophical grounding becomes problematic; and under the pressure of modern positivistic and hedonistic philosophy the end seems no longer to be necessarily "of a fine sort."

Thus weakened, transformed, and usually watered down, the ghost of Aristotelian *phronesis* appears in the accounts of rational practice offered by some of the most eminent modern political theorists. Hobbes and Machiavelli, in somewhat different ways, inaugurate the modern era by attempting to offer us a "realistic" revision of classical prudence. Hegel gives Machiavelli's realistic prudence a superhuman incarnation. Mill refines Hobbes's account in the context of utilitarianism. And the problematics of the whole project—best exemplified in the groundlessness of what Mill termed "Art"—open the way to the Weberian complex of subjectivism and bureaucratic rationality so characteristic of our contemporary world.

The two intellectual revolutionaries who ushered in the modern era in political philosophy—Machiavelli and Hobbes—both provide a "new science" of politics that they deem a crucial resource in the fight against social chaos. In each case, the new science represents one possible way of adapting Aristotle's account of practical reason to the demands and limitations of the modern universe. Hobbes's "civil science" and Machiavelli's "new route which has not yet been followed by any one"[22] each represent in a different way a "realistic" reformulation of Aristotelian *phronesis*. "Realism" in each case has a dual meaning: first, it correctly suggests a kind of tough-minded antimoralism; and second, it indicates a rejection of what is seen as the metaphysical delusion of an idealist ontology of forms and final ends.

Machiavelli views the virtue of prudence as the ruler's principal resource—along with courage—as he grapples with fortune's fury. A successful ruler must be brave like the lion, but also shrewd and cunning like the fox. Machiavelli cannot give the prince courage. For that, he is on his own. But Machiavelli can, he believes, provide the knowledge essential for sagacious action. He can do this because prudence is grounded in experience, and he can offer two sources of the relevant experience. He can offer the lessons derived from his own career; and even more significantly, he can draw lessons from the historical record—once its significance is properly understood.

Most of those who look at history, Machiavelli complains, do so only to "take pleasure in the variety of events."[23] They are mere tourists in time, gawkers who fail to realize that they are getting only diversion from what could give them wisdom. Once it is recognized, however, that "heaven, the sun, the elements, and men [do not change] the order of their motions and power"[24] from one era to the next, historical learning acquires new potency. It serves as a laboratory of case studies, from which generalizations can be gleaned about the causes of success and failure in political undertakings. Plato would have his ideal ruler study philosophy so that he could intuit and then imitate the forms. Machiavelli disdains such study of "imagined republics and principalities which have never been seen or known to exist";[25] and he instead would have his ideal ruler "read history and study the actions of eminent men, see how they acted in warfare, examine the causes of their victories and defeats in order to imitate the former and avoid the latter."[26]

If in one sense Machiavelli's doctrine of good rulership turns Plato's doctrine of *mimesis* on its head—counseling the imitation of (real) historical events rather than the imitation of (imaginary) Ideas—in another sense his account of prudence replicates but eviscerates Aristotelian *phronesis*. The fruit of Machiavellian historical science comes in the form of prudential maxims: counsel to emulate so-and-so (eminent political figures of the past) who did such-and-such (followed certain strategies) and succeeded because of this-or-that (general causal patterns arising from human nature or from political dynamics). Like *phronesis*, Machiavellian prudence, to recall Aristotle's formulations, is "a rational faculty exercised for the attainment of truth in things that are humanly good and bad"; and the prudent individual is one who "calculates well for the attainment of a particular end of a fine sort." But the content infused into these formulas by classical anthropology and ethics is leached out in Machiavelli's hands. The "truth" in question is exhaustively existential, historical, and "realistic." The "humanly good" becomes *virtu* rather than classical virtue. And the "particular end" is only questionably of a "fine sort": despite some places where one can still construe it as the common good, in other places it is, at best, *raison d'etat* and, at worst, the unadulterated interest of the prince.

Machiavelli was, of course, a republican. And as such he was capable of attributing some capacities for prudence and deliberation to the people. He can even say, as he does in the *Discourses*, that "the people are more prudent and stable and have better judgment than a prince."[27] But in general he looks to the people to have good habits rather than to exercise good judgment. Perhaps because of his own background in statecraft, his account of prudence tends to focus upon the strategy of leaders; and it is to rulers rather than to the people that his prudential maxims are almost invariably directed. And, in that context at least, prudential "calculating well" emerges as purely "calculating" behavior in the colloquial sense of the term. It is merely competent scheming. Cesare Borgia can replace Pericles as an exemplar and prudence can be symbolized by the fox because prudence is essentially reduced to historically informed animal cunning. Machiavelli was not the simple diabolical figure depicted in Elizabethan drama and his motivations were both republican and patriotic. Nevertheless, purged of its traditional reference points in classical philosophy, his interpretation of the virtue of prudence tends to turn rationality into the *techne* of the powerful.

The political rationalism of the other contender for the "first major modern political theorist" title, Thomas Hobbes, resembles Machiavelli's in some important respects but also embodies some interesting new departures. Like Aristotle, Hobbes envisions the role of reason in politics to be that of "calculating well" in the pursuit of a compellingly important end. Like Aristotle, moreover, Hobbes conceives this end as a form of happiness whose pursuit is dictated by natural tendencies. Like Machiavelli, however, Hobbes fills this abstract formula with philosophically and ethically reductivist content that would have scandalized Aristotle (and did scandalize most of his own contemporaries). Finally, in a novel and bold step, Hobbes elevates rational practice into a theoretical science that is "practical" in its potential utility but not in its epistemological structure.

One cannot really understand Hobbes's account of the role of reason in politics by focusing on his concept of prudence. "Prudence," in Hobbes's vocabulary, no longer stands for a genuinely rational faculty. It is "re-conning" and not reckoning. It is an expectation of the future based only upon past remembrance and not upon knowledge of causes. As a consequence, prudence by itself is quite an unreliable guide. "Signs of prudence," Hobbes writes, "are all uncertain; because to observe by experience, and remember all circumstances that may alter the success, is impossible."[28] This criticism is obviously directly pertinent to the assessment of Machiavelli's version of the new science, one that Hobbes not surprisingly rejects as inadequate. Hobbes goes still farther. Because it is merely an accretion of brute experience, he argues, prudence is not a distinctively human faculty. "It is not prudence that distinguisheth man from beast. There be beasts, that at a year old observe more, and pursue that which is for their good, more prudently, than a child can do at ten."[29]

So much for noble *phronesis*. Hobbes means the demotion of the faculty of prudence not as a counsel of despair, however. Instead, it is merely a preliminary clarification that opens the way toward reconstituting the role of reason in politics in a new and potentially very powerful way. Reason, as Hobbes depicts it, indeed must play a crucial role in the extrication of human beings from the "ill condition" of "mere nature." The knowledge base for sound political action cannot be purely experiential, however. "The skill of making and maintaining commonwealths, consisteth in certain rules, as doth arithmetic and geometry; not (as tennis-play) on practice only."[30]

We know these rules, Hobbes tells us, because we can attain certain knowledge of the causes of political events. Science, generally, is a reckoning of consequences. It can demonstrate the necessary "conclusions" that must "follow" from given causes. When we obtain such demonstrative knowledge of cause and consequence in the area of human affairs, therefore, we have "moral and civil science," which affords us in a reliable fashion the foresight that experience-based prudence could give only in a very unreliable way. Moral and civil science can, in Hobbes's words, provide "those prospective glasses to see a far off the miseries that hang over [us], and cannot without such payments (i.e., being subject to the sovereign) be avoided."[31]

"Moral and civil science," then, is formally quite similar to Aristotelian practical reason, whatever the semantic fate of the term *prudence*. It is "calculating well" in "the service of a fine end of a particular sort." What is new is that, on the basis of the inclusion of human affairs within a mechanistic nature, it is now elevated to the status of a theoretical science. At the same time, and for similar reasons, it acquires the specifically technical interpretation that Aristotle resisted but imperfectly. "Calculating well," in short, becomes the certain deduction of particular complex consequences from the knowledge of their simple and universal causes—these being embodied in accurate definitions inductively obtained by a process of "resolution."

Hobbes's moral and civil science is what he would construe as an epistemologically perfected practical reason, Aristotle's *phronesis* pruned of its distinctions from technical reason and elevated to the status of theory. Its calculations are useful "because when we see how anything comes about, upon what causes, and by what manner; when the like causes come into our power, we see how to make it produce the like effects."[32] And what are the "effects" that are likely to be sought here? What is to be the "fine end" of the Aristotelian formula? Here, once again, Hobbes provides a deft reinterpretation to accord with his vision of nature and human passions. Like Aristotle, Hobbes assumes that this end is dictated by nature and best conceived as a kind of happiness. Hobbes's happiness, however, is not *eudaemonia*, but "felicity." Human beings are restless sorts by nature, Hobbes avers. Thus their happiness "consisteth not in the repose of a mind satisfied." Instead, felicity is "a continual progress of the desire from one object to another."[33] There is no *summum bonum* that, once attained, produces contentment. Rather, "there can be no contentment but in proceeding."[34] The ultimate end, therefore, is a negative one to be avoided rather than a positive one to pursue: it is the absence of proceeding that violent death brings. This is the *summum malum*, as Leo Strauss puts it, that in Hobbes's account takes over the functional role of the highest good. It is the negative ultimate end. The dead have no pleasures: their proceeding—and hence their felicity—has terminated.

By transforming the idea of practical reason to conform it to the specifications of the new cosmology—a causal law-governed universe devoid of hierarchic ends—Hobbes gives it its definitive modern shape, definitive for the empiricist tradition, at any rate. Later writers may revise some aspects of the model, and they do not necessarily acquiesce in the definitive end—avoidance of violent death—Hobbes claims to be established by nature or in the psychology that informs this claim. Nevertheless, practical reason within the modern empiricist tradition remains to this day essentially what, in outline at least, it was for Hobbes: namely, a theoretical science of cause and effect that can become technically efficacious when conjoined with stipulated purposes.

These twin "realistic" transmutations of *phronesis* have proved definitive for modern appropriations of Aristotelian practical reason. The persistence of the Machiavellian archetype of reason in politics is seen in Hegel's account of reason in history, for example. And Hobbes's moral and civil science reappears with only marginal modifications—as far as the basic pattern is concerned—in Bentham's felicific calculus and Mill's account of the logic of the moral sciences.

Without for a moment denying the many original elements in Hegel's philosophy, it nonetheless requires no procrustean distortion to depict

Hegel's doctrine of rational activity as a reconstruction of Aristotelian *praxis*—mediated by Machiavelli's account of prudence. Hegel begins his general introductory lectures on the philosophy of history with a reference to Anaxagoras and his testimony that "Reason rules the world"; and he next recalls Aristotle's judgment that this recognition marked Anaxagoras as being like a sober man among the drunken. Hegel's *Geist* is, then, that very Reason that indeed rules the world by determining the course of history. *Geist* is Aristotle's *nous* that operates not merely through nature and space—as Greek cosmology allows— but also through history and time. Reason must create itself—actualize its potentiality—by objectifying itself in the world and then attaining self-awareness through reflection. *Geist* has its own ends, its own purposes, which it realizes "with infinite power."

In Hegel's *Weltanschauung*, reason is no longer a human faculty. Instead, it is an autonomous, self-creating, suprahuman ego whose autobiography is world history. Human beings, conversely, are not the subjects of rationality but its objects. They are the vessels within which Reason incarnates itself rather than being rational agents in their own right. World-historical individuals may embody rationality by conforming their passions to the Spirit's purposes; but the purposes themselves are not theirs, and "once their objective is attained, they fall off like empty hulls from the kernel." Accordingly, *phronesis* is in parallel no longer conceived as a human capacity. *Phronesis* consists, recalling Aristotle's definition once again, in "calculating well for the attainment of a particular end of a fine sort." And this is what the historical activity of the Spirit consists in. The Spirit "calculates well" on behalf of its purposes. This is the "cunning of reason: it sets the passions to work for itself, while that through which it develops itself pays the penalty and suffers the loss."[35]

The content of this "transcendental" prudence is Machiavellian craftiness, in effect. Spirit "uses" its objects like Borgia used Remirro de Orco, whom he unleashed to pacify the Romagna and whom he then cut in half and left in the public square at Cesena. And, like Machiavelli, Hegel finds here nothing to blame. He counsels his listeners to understand and accept the ways of the Spirit, which are not our ways, and to emulate the believer who is content that "it is not I but the spirit that dwells within me." Where Hegel departs from Machiavelli is in his fusion of the two forces whose struggle Machiavelli saw as the very stuff of history: fortuna and prudence. In this context, Hegel performed his dialectical feat of reconciling opposites into a higher unity rather neatly. On his account, fortuna is no longer chance and prudence no longer a merely human capacity. Instead, fortuna has become rational and prudence has attained transcendental status. Their union is consummated in the cunning of Reason.

And what is the "particular end of a fine sort" to whose attainment the cunning of Reason is devoted? The end is the self-realization of Spirit, the actualization of its potentiality. And in what does this fulfill-ment consist? It consists in the *eudaemonia* of self-contemplative activity that Aristotle had identified as the hallmark of divinity. Where Hegel departs from Aristotle is in his insistence that this fulfillment of the divine Idea can only be achieved through historical embodiment. Only at the end of time will the Idea attain the happiness of its unique *theoria*. And its mode of activity within the temporal struggle is the true *praxis*. As creator of the world, God must possess practical as well as theoret-ical reason.

Human beings are thus dispossessed of practical reason, which they now confront as a divine being beyond them. If prudence be thus hypostatized, what then is it "prudent" for mere mortals to do? Either, it seems, human beings are simply to accept the power and dictates of Reason, "being still and knowing it is God" as it were. Or, for those of an activist disposition, they might claim to be "conscious master build-ers of their own freedom" (the phrase is that of the Polish Hegelian, August von Cieszkowski), taking it upon themselves to actualize Rea-son's ends that have been vouchsafed to them.

In neither the former "right-wing Hegelian" nor the latter "left-wing Hegelian" response do human beings behave like the *spoudaioi* of Aris-totle. In neither case do they themselves embody practical wisdom, striving amid the uncertainties of life to achieve an imperfectly know-able human good. Instead, they become passive acolytes of whatever History brings them, obedient to what they see as the realization of the Rational. Or else they claim to be practitioners of a posttheoretical *praxis*—technicians of the truth. But both outcomes, by liberal and republican standards, offer defective accounts of reason's role in poli-tics. Instead of promoting a civic life in which people reason together in pursuit of a common good, the Hegelian hypostatization of Reason tends to force a choice between fatalism and technocracy. Machiavellian prudence, elevated to divine status in the guise of a cunning *Geist*, tends to undermine democratic procedure—even though putatively in the service of "freedom."

The other modern transmutation of Aristotelian "calculating well in the service of an end of a fine sort"—the Hobbesian nomological policy science—reappears with only minor modifications in nineteenth-century utilitarianism. From the vantage point of "reason in politics," Jeremy Bentham is a romantic version of Hobbes. When Bentham tells us that "Nature has placed mankind under the governance of two sovereign masters, pain and pleasure,"[36] he simply reiterates Hobbes's psychology of appetite and aversion. The principles of legislation endorsed by Bentham are simply a form of the "reckonings" in Hobbes's moral science, in which the consequences of various legislative acts for the balance of pains and pleasures are calculated. And when Bentham pursues his dream of being the warden of multiple Panopticons scattered across the face of England, he is placing himself into the role of Hobbes's Sovereign. The only real difference is that Bentham is optimistic where Hobbes is modest with respect to the Sovereign's ultimate ends. Hobbes, with his bleak calculus of natural human dissociation, was content to hope that the Sovereign could keep the peace and thereby forestall the ultimate pain of civil war. Bentham, more enthralled by the potential powers of social *techne*, hoped to make his subjects happy.

The technical calculus of the Benthamite legislator can be effective, moreover, only because his subjects are also in their own way prudent people. Governed by pain and pleasure, they calculate with acuity how to avoid the one and gain the other. "When matters of such importance as pain and pleasure are at stake, . . . who is there that does not calculate?"[37] Thus the utilitarian Sovereign can be a prudent technician who maximizes the general happiness because the objects of his legislative stratagems themselves calculate adeptly on behalf of their individual pleasure.

The abstract formula of Aristotle's *phronesis* here remains intact: prudent people "calculate well" in the service of a "particular end"—although an end of a compelling but not a "fine" sort. The reduction of the human good to simple and undifferentiated pleasure ("pushpin is as good as poetry") and the purely means-ends account of calculative deliberation turn the nobility of the practically wise into the pettiness of the shopkeeper (as Marx complained) on the one hand and into the oppressive legal *techne* of the legislator on the other hand. Neither lawgiver nor subject reason practically in any civil, humane, or complex fashion concerning the attainment of the human good. They simply tally pleasures and reckon consequences.

John Stuart Mill, himself the product of an experiment in Benthamite education, was acutely aware of the problems with Bentham's philosophical reduction. He tells us that "few great thinkers have ever been so deficient" as Bentham in intellectual subtlety. And he says that Bentham "saw in man little but what the vulgarest eye can see."[38] Mill was also opposed to Hobbes's authoritarian doctrines, as he was to Comte's. Moreover, he represents his logic of the moral sciences as a distinct advance over the logic of both Hobbes and Bentham, whom he criticizes as exponents of "the geometrical or abstract method" in social science. Nevertheless, a careful examination of Mill's explicit account in *The Logic of the Moral Sciences* reveals that he departed only marginally from their accounts of the nature and relationship of social science and rational practice. He tries to introduce a conception of utility more sensitive to qualitative differences than Bentham's crude calculus, using this norm in place of Hobbes's social peace. But he depicts the rational pursuit of ends as a technical application of cause-consequence laws; and his account of the discernment of the "fine ends" to be pursued is remarkable mostly for its almost complete absence. In the end, only Mill's uncritical acceptance of the norm of utility and his hopeful account of human *eros* separates him from Weberian decisionism.

Small differences aside, Mill's explicit account of the role of reasoning in politics found in the *Logic* is formally very similar to that of Hobbes. Both conceive rational practice as the conscious artificial production of desired effects by controlling what science tells us to be the relevant causes. Mill, like Hobbes, offers a doctrine of "foresight and control." The theoretical science of politics will contribute the necessary knowledge of cause and effect through its ascertainment of laws of nature. Art, or *praxis*, then rearranges these truths of science into the most convenient order for practice and acts upon them. "When the circumstances of an individual or a nation are in any considerable degree under our control, we may, by our knowledge of tendencies, be enabled to shape those circumstances in a manner more favorable to the ends we desire than the shape which they would of themselves assume." And Mill writes, in a language markedly similar to Comte's, of using "artificial means . . . to accelerate the natural progress insofar as it is beneficial."[39] In his own career, Mill was a model of deliberative rationality and the virtue of *phronesis*. But his explicit epistemology of rational action is an account of social *techne* in which human beings are, as Hobbes put it, both "matter" and "artificer."

Mill's conception of how the theoretical science of society will be practically deployed to bring about social progress is vague and problematic in two important respects. First, who is to be the "artificer" and on what authority? Second, what is the status and origin of what he terms the "ultimate principles of conduct"?

Mill is systematically vague on the "who governs" issue. Whenever he speaks of "foresight and control," he speaks in the passive voice ("artificial means may be used"), in impersonal terms ("the exigencies of practical life require"), or in universal terms. Mill's horrified reaction to Comte's later writings and his devotion to liberty and representative government make it clear that he had no technocratic rule of *savants* in mind. But what he did have in mind is never clearly articulated. In all likelihood, Mill felt the question was not all that crucial, because his beliefs about *how* the advance of speculative science would influence politics made the *who* question superfluous. Mill tells us that "social existence is only possible" because our powerful selfish inclinations can be "disciplined" by "subordinating them to a common set of opinions."[40] With the advance of knowledge, however, "the number of doctrines which are no longer disputed or doubted will be constantly on the increase."[41] Thus the progress of the moral sciences will produce "common opinions," and that consensus is what will govern.

Careful reflection as to what this "common system of opinions" would consist of, however, reveals that Mill has a serious difficulty here—a difficulty that Comte and Hobbes can handle in ways not available to him. If a common system of opinions is to be taken to refer to the truths (soon to become common because they can be experimentally demonstrated) of moral science, the question is: how can the reception of these truths counteract the disruptive influence of selfish interests? What gives these theoretical truths their practical efficacy? Hobbes has an answer in his psychology. People stumble into civil war only because they "know not the causes of war and peace." Once they understand the relevant cause-effect relations, their dominant passion for self-preservation will give effectuating force to this theoretical knowledge. Comte's answer is that the truths of theory are normative as well as descriptive. Theoretical sociology generates not merely flat descriptions of fact, but it distinguishes order from anarchy and identifies the "definitive state" of society. The common system of opinions that positive science will provide, on Comte's account, then, includes self-legitimating ideals whose moral force can combat anarchic individual interests. Mill, however, shares neither Hobbes's psychology nor— in this respect, at least—Comte's epistemology. He is very clear that science includes only indicative assertions and no imperatives.[42] Hence the truths of moral science have no moral force. And he attributes no overwhelming priority to fear in his psychology. Hence he cannot look to that as the civilizing passion.

For Mill, thus, it all comes down to the nature and the status of the doctrine of utility. Utility, he avers, is the universal standard, the ultimate practical end, whose acceptance and application are requisite to convert the speculative truths of the social sciences into practical precepts. In order for his vision of the progressive subordination of factious self-interest to the unity of common opinion to be persuasive, then, Mill must provide a compelling account of the appeal and power of the utility principle.

Why should the general happiness be a compelling end? Mill's capsule justification in *Utilitarianism* is a logical *non sequitur:* "each person's happiness is a good to that person, and the general happiness, therefore, a good to the aggregate of all persons." Behind this fallacy of the whole, however, lies Mill's stated conviction that "the influences are constantly on the increase which tend to generate in each individual a feeling of unity with all the rest." This increased social solidarity that accompanies "an improving state of the human mind" Mill attributes to two factors. The first of these is an increased cognitive appreciation of human interdependence that he believes the understanding of social forces to include. Second, and most important, Mill attributes to the human psyche a "powerful natural sentiment" that "will constitute the strength of the utilitarian morality," to wit: "the desire to be in unity with our fellow creatures, which is already a powerful principle in human nature, and happily one of those which tend to become stronger, even without express inculcation, from the influences of advancing civilization."[43]

Here, then, is Mill's substitute for Hobbes's fear as the civilizing passion. The general happiness principle acquires its force by appealing to Mill's version of Rousseau's "natural sympathy." Mill's optimistic prognosis as to the beneficent application of the knowledge acquired by the moral sciences rests upon a psychology of Eros without Thanatos. Like Freud, Mill seems to posit a libido "whose purpose is to combine single human individuals, and after that families, then races, peoples and nations, into one great unity, the unity of mankind."[44] Missing from Mill's hopeful vision, however, is the lurking aggressiveness that Freud believes can only be repressed or sublimated and never eliminated. Ultimately, then, Mill's account of the uplifting role of reason in politics is dependent upon the conviction that emergent social science will provide a convincing display of interdependence and that this display will enhance and augment the natural sympathy of one human being for another.

Because Aristotle also believed expressly in the natural sociability of mankind, and because Mill strove valiantly both in *Utilitarianism* and at the end of his *Logic* to reinvest "utility" with some of the qualitative features that Bentham had denied it (the "higher meaning" of happiness, says Mill, is "rendering life not what it now is almost universally, puerile and insignificant, but such as human beings with highly developed faculties can care to have"[45]) it could be said that Mill's version of political rationality constitutes a reasonably good adaptation of Aristotle's views to a modern setting. Such a characterization, I think, is probably fairly accurate; and the features of Mill's political theory it relies upon help to account for the richness and complexity of his view of democratic government. Apart from the inevitable substantive modifications, however, there are two formal differences between Mill's rational practice and Aristotle's *phronesis* that need mention. These may seem somewhat superficial, but what lies behind them has profound consequences.

The first formal difference with Aristotle is one Mill shares with Hobbes and other moderns: Aristotle's practical means/ends "calculations" become identified with the cause/effect propositions of nomological science. And because of this identification and the ontology implicit in it, these calculations become indistinguishable from those of a craft. In short, a distinction between *phronesis* and *techne* that Aristotle had some difficulty sustaining is abandoned outright. The second difference seems at first to be merely semantic, but it reflects some deeper shifts than merely verbal ones. Here I am referring to the reversal of roles of theoretical and practical reason in the context of rational action. For Aristotle, the calculations were practical, the ends (on some interpretations, at least) grounded in *theoria*. For Mill and the other exponents of nomological social science, the "calculations" upon which rational practice depends are theoretical in status; and the ends are practical.

Because these semantic crossed wires are the product of fundamental ontological shifts rather than purely arbitrary emendations, they open the way for an even more profound reversal that neither Mill or Aristotle would have liked: namely, the conversion of this form of political rationalism into political irrationalism by circumscribing the scope of reason. This transformation parallels the transition that occurs between the rationalism of Kant and the irrationalism of his self-styled philosophical heir, Schopenhauer. Its points of departure are clearly visible in Mill.

Near the conclusion of his *Logic*, Mill writes: "A scientific observer or reasoner, merely as such, is not an adviser for practice. His part is only to show that certain consequences follow from certain causes, and that to obtain certain ends, certain means are the most effectual. Whether the ends themselves are such as ought to be pursued, and if so, in what cases and to how great a length, it is no part of his business as a cultivator of science to decide, and science alone will never qualify him for the decision." Who then is entitled to render these practical evaluations? And on what basis? For Mill, it is the moral philosopher who can determine practical ends on the basis of his *philosophia prima* that deals with "first principles of conduct."[46] The persuasive ultimate standard thus established, of course, he believes to be the utility principle. Mill struggles, however, when it comes to specifying the basis for this standard.

Thwarted by his empiricist ontology from finding any objective grounds for utility, Mill finally is forced to concede that its "ultimate sanction," like that "of all morality," is "a subjective feeling in our own minds." Mill refers to this feeling as "the conscientious feelings of mankind," and he concludes that moral obligation has "its seat in human consciousness only" and its force is "exactly measured by" the "strength" of a person's "own subjective feeling."[47] One gathers that Mill believes these "conscientious feelings of mankind" to be natural, universal, and at least somewhat altruistic. That is why he can expect the advance of the social sciences to bring an increase of social unity in its train. In this respect, one could say, Mill stands with Kant and Rousseau in finding the locus of morality "within" the "invisible self" but at the same time believing the moral demands thus located to be common, binding, and eternal.

Suppose, however, that this inner noumenal world is not so common and universal as Mill, Rousseau, and Kant believed on the basis of their own introspection. Suppose instead that the contents of the "subjective feelings" are ascertained by an empirical investigation, and suppose further that this investigation discovers a wide variety of "subjective feelings" that conflict rather than cohere. Absent recourse to claims of "false consciousness," and apart from a successful effort to reconcile the conflicts in a larger synthesis of some sort, the scenario for the role of reason in politics changes rather dramatically. We can ascertain rationally only facts and relations of succession among them; but as for what the facts mean or for what we should do about them, reason has nothing whatever to say. The ends of *praxis* are now subjectively determined in a more radical sense: they are posited as an act of rationally unrestricted choice on the basis of "preference" or "taste" or "sentiment" or "will" or "metaphysical speculation." At that point, taking only a small step that Mill provides little evidence or logic to forestall, we enter the world of Max Weber.

In Weber's account, the causally related objective facts that social science's theoretical reason describes to us constitute a humanly meaningless domain of Kantian "phenomena"—a "vast chaotic stream of events which flows away through time."[48] Any value or meaning or purpose these events might have has to be imposed from the outside by the free choice of noumenal (human) beings. This is, in Mill's terms, "Art" providing the "end" for science to pursue; but the difference is that Weber does not suppose that "Art," the residue of practical reason, has anything cognitively based to offer or anything unanimous to report. Instead, the ends or values are radically subjective in origin, a freely chosen "demon" that orients the soul. "The fruit of the tree of knowledge," Weber writes, "consists in the insight that every single important activity and ultimately life as a whole, if it is not to be permitted to run on as an event in nature but is instead to be consciously guided, is a series of ultimate decisions through which the soul—as in Plato—chooses its own fate, i.e. the meaning of its activity and existence."[49] Because Weber's moral ego is ontologically homeless in a way that Plato's soul is not, moreover, its choice embodies the "dreadful freedom" of the existentialist hero. Weber's moral hero is more like Atlas, who must bear the world on his shoulders, than he is like Sartre's Orestes, who is dizzied by his freedom. But both are, in Sartre's words, "outside nature, against nature, without excuse, beyond remedy, except what remedy I find within myself."[50]

This Weberian cosmos stands at the end of the attempt to adapt Aristotelian *phronesis* to modern philosophy. In it, rational practice is simply technical efficiency. Rationality is a meaningful concept *vis à vis* politics only in the context of determining the means "adequate to the realization of an absolutely unambiguously given end."[51] Concerning the ends themselves, reason has nothing whatever to say. What remains of Aristotelian prudence is only the "calculating well" part, now conceived as a means-end calculus *simpliciter*. The "particularly fine ends" to which *phronesis* had been devoted have, in the Weberian and emotivist view of things, fallen altogether into the void.

To summarize, then, it is evident that the Aristotelian formulation of the role of reason in politics as a prudent calculation of appropriate measures directed toward some compelling end has an important place in modern political philosophy. It is also evident that, following upon the demise of classical cosmology with its essences and implicit moral hierarchies, the difficulties already nascent in Aristotle's own thought are encountered with renewed force. In particular, Aristotle's problematic efforts at distinguishing the calculations of *praxis* from the means-ends alignments of *techne* are often abandoned outright, and the "particular fine ends" become ever more particular and ever less fine. Hobbes and Machiavelli give priority to those ends deemed most "compelling" and in so doing replace Aristotle's higher goals with the most basic ones of power and self-preservation. Hegel elevates Machiavelli's cunningly prudent ruler into the creative Idea of the social universe. Bentham hopefully but crudely turns prudence into a calculus of pleasure. Mill seeks to improve upon Benthamite reductionism by reintroducing a qualitative dimension to utility but leaves this "fine end" grounded only in "subjective feeling." And Weber, like the emotivists, finding no objective basis or universality to these feelings, leaves the ends of rational practice contingent on our choice of demons.

By reference not only to Aristotle's intentions but also to the civilizing and humanizing potential of practical reason, none of these modern adaptations of prudence is adequate or compelling. But it is hard to see how the inadequate options they present can be surmounted unless we could reenter the classical cosmos or until we can escape the constraints placed by the geometric ideal upon our conception of rationality.

Modernizing Platonic Rationality: Natural Light and Social Harmony

Alongside the attempts to formulate a compelling and useful modern doctrine of Aristotelian prudence, efforts have also been made to give the Platonic conception of political rationalism modern philosophical grounding and modern political relevance. We shall here note only a few of the more notable manifestations of this enterprise, with the same intent as in the previous section: to demonstrate the persistence of this mode of understanding the role of reason in politics, to identify some of the principal transformations occasioned by evolving philosophical premises, and to note some of the major difficulties encountered by the exponents of this approach. The common strand that we followed in the previous section was the Aristotelian phrase "calculating well for the attainment of a particular end of a fine sort." In this section, the common theme will be the quasi-mathematical rational intuition of a harmonious order that possesses erotic appeal and invites *mimesis*.

The most explicit and systematic early modern attempt to give Platonic rationalism a convincing contemporaneous form was that of the small but notable group of English prelates and dons known as the Cambridge Platonists. This group—Benjamin Whichcote, Henry More, John Smith, Ralph Cudworth, and Nathanael Culverwel—received their inspiration from the neo-Platonic Christian humanism of Marsilio Ficino and tried to use what they learned there to clear a pathway through the acrimonious and divisive theological and political controversies of their day. Rejecting both the "thin, airy knowledge" of Scholasticism and the reductionist "seemings" of Hobbes, the Cambridge Platonists insisted upon the axiological character and the fundamental trustworthiness of human reason. Reason was for them noetic, fueled by *eros*, and attuned to the divine *logos* of the world.

The Platonists' insistence on the axiological grounding of human reason allowed them to maintain reason's moral competency. Reason was not merely theoretical, but had real practical force. It was "the candle of the Lord," to invoke Whichcote's apt phrase, a light to guide our way through a perilous world. It was Cicero's "right reason," capable of apprehending morally substantive natural laws. In Culverwel's words, "the vigor and triumph of Reason is principally to be seen in those first-born beams. . . ; I mean those first bubblings up of common Principles, that are owned and acknowledged by all."[52]

The doctrine of this group of thinkers, then, was Platonism in an early modern key. They took the neo-Platonist account of the soul and its rational *eros* and Christianized it, partly and reluctantly Cartesianized it, and democratized it. The Christian component is very clear, of course. The Platonic Good is God, Platonic *eros* the love of God, Platonic rationality the "candle of the Lord." The Cartesian element is reflected in the language of "inner" and "innate," although the Platonists resisted without great success the inclination of others to assimilate the inner faculty and innate capacity of which they spoke to the doctrine of *res cogitans*. The democratic aspect of their thinking stems mostly from their Christian universalism: all people, and not philosophers only, bear the divine likeness in their souls. If anyone fails to know the Good, it is owing to sinful will and not to the alloy of grosser metals in the soul.

The Cambridge Platonists fought a losing battle, however, at least at the level of explicit philosophical doctrine. Plato was both a heathen and an ancient; and the Cambridge school lived in a time dominated by a dedication to biblical Christianity and by a fascination with new philosophy. In England, it was Bacon and the bishops who triumphed. The Platonists' sole true philosophical heir was Shaftesbury, and he in turn had no lasting following in his own land. Where he did have an impact was in Germany, where Herder, Schiller, and Goethe found inspiration in his doctrines of nature and aesthetics. In this manner, the ideas of the seventeenth-century English Platonic rationalists metamorphosed into one component of another century's German romantic Idealism.

Despite their failure to win the philosophical battle on their home front, however, the ethical and political content of the Platonists' thought survived in other vessels. One of these was the political theory of Locke and another was a popular version of moral Newtonianism. And to the extent that their influence is felt in these places, the Platonists can be seen as contributors to liberal constitutionalism and to the more benign strand of Enlightenment rationalism.

Clearly, Locke was no Platonist in his ontology, in his epistemology, or even in his philosophical psychology. He accepted and expounded the increasingly dominant empiricist position in these fundamental areas. It is not surprising, then, that standard commentaries accord the Platonists little influence over Locke's ideas.[53] On moral, political, and religious issues, however, Locke's views were strikingly similar to the moderate and rationalist views of the Platonists. In these areas, Locke seems to have embraced and given voice to the temperament, attitudes, and moral orientation of his many Platonist associates, even if he could not accept their allegiance in matters of first philosophy. The occasions for such influence, certainly, were many—and willingly chosen by Locke. For besides reading Culverwel carefully, Locke joined the congregation of St. Lawrence Jewry in London when Whichcote became its vicar; he was a regular guest in the Lombard Street *salon* of one of London's most influential Latitudinarians, Thomas Firmin; and the person Locke's biographer describes as "closer to Locke than any other human being"[54] was Damaris Cudworth, daughter of the Cambridge Platonist.

The central themes of Locke's *Letter concerning Toleration, The Reasonableness of Christianity*, and parts of the *Second Treatise* could have taken the Platonists' treatises and sermons as texts. Whichcote writes that "truth lies in a little compass and narrow room";[55] and Locke in the *Essay concerning Human Understanding* seeks to establish where the boundaries of that narrow room lie—to "set the bounds between the enlightened and dark parts of things, between what is and what is not comprehensible by us."[56] Culverwel argues that "there's nothing in the mysteries of the Gospel contrary to the light of Reason";[57] and Locke sets out to demonstrate the reasonableness of Christianity. John Smith writes, "the Common Notions of God and Virtue imprest upon the Souls of men, are more clear and perspicuous than any else, and they . . . display themselves with less difficulty to our Reflexive Faculty than any Geometrical Demonstrations";[58] and Locke argues that "the measures of right and wrong might be made out . . . from self-evident propositions" and that these moral truths may be "as incontestable as those in mathematics."[59] Whichcote admonishes the overly zealous: "Our fallibility and the Shortness of our Knowledge should make us peaceable and gentle: because I may be mistaken, I must not be dogmatical and confident, preemptory and imperious";[60] and Locke uses a similar fallibilist argument in his *Letter concerning Toleration*. Despite his ostensive empiricism, then, one could fairly conclude that Locke carried over some of the most important contentions of the English Platonists into his own depiction of the role of reason in politics.

Equally clear and striking is the Platonist interpretation given to Newton's cosmological theories by some of his leading popularizers. That Newton had uncovered the fundamental principles of the natural order was a commonplace of the eighteenth century. But less clear were the moral lessons to be learned from Newton's discoveries. What was the human meaning—the implications for the conduct of life—of Newtonian philosophy? The answer given to this question by one of Newton's most able and widely read popular expositors construed Newton's vision of the cosmic order in a decidedly Platonic fashion. The Newtonian world is here depicted as a model of cosmic harmony that exerts a profoundly erotic pull upon the soul of anyone who contemplates it. The words of this Newtonian, the Scottish mathematician Colin Maclaurin, could almost have been written by Plotinus. In his disputation with the Gnostics, Plotinus writes of the beauty of the phenomenal world: "Heavy and senseless must be that mind which could contemplate all the visible beauties, this harmony, and this imposing arrangement, this grand panoramic view furnished by the stars in spite of their distance, without being stirred to enthusiasm, and admiration of their splendor and magnificence."[61] And Maclaurin interprets the moral lesson of the Newtonian cosmos in the following almost identical manner:

> Our views of Nature [reveal] that mighty power which prevails throughout, acting with a force and efficacy that appears to suffer no diminution from the greatest distances of space or intervals of time; and that wisdom which we see equally displayed in the exquisite structure and just motions of the greatest and subtilest parts. These, with perfect goodness, by which they are evidently directed, constitute the supreme object of the speculations of a philosopher; who, while he contemplates and admires so excellent a system, cannot but be himself excited and animated to correspond with the general harmony of Nature.[62]

The truths of Newtonian empiricism are in this way infused with Platonic moral substance. Nature now serves as Agathon. It embodies a perfect order and harmony that "excites and animates" the soul who contemplates it. Because the precise content of this moral order is ambiguous, moreover, it was possible for Enlightenment philosophers so inclined to give this Newtonian order a secular and democratic rendering. Condorcet, for example, could assert that "the rights of men are written in the book of nature."[63] And Jefferson could write of the "self-evident" truths of human rights and equality in the Declaration of Independence, an account that he saw as "the common sense of the subject."

Each of these attempts to reconcile the moral content of classical philosophy with modern empiricism was, despite the enthusiasm or assurance of the expositors, fundamentally unstable in philosophic terms. Locke's effort to maintain some of the truths of "right reason" and religion in the context of his epistemological and metaphysical empiricism enmeshed him in tensions and contradictions that have led critics in his own day and in ours to characterize him as a Hobbes in conventionalist disguise. Similarly, what Condorcet and other devotees of natural right saw written in the book of nature was largely a reflection of their inherited moral convictions. The underlying problem is best discernible, perhaps, in the comparison of Plotinus with his Newtonian counterpart, Colin Maclaurin. For although both of them focus upon the philosophical *eros* they believe to be excited by the heavenly order, there is a basic difference between them. Specifically, Plotinus sees the visible harmonies of the phenomenal world as mere reminders or representations of an intelligible suprasensible reality beyond them. They are analogies of transcendent Being, not Being itself. For the Newtonian philosopher, in contrast, if the colloquialism may be excused, "what you see is what you get": Newtonian nature is Reality itself. What this difference means is that the moral beauty "found" in the Newtonian order lies in fact in the eye of the beholder. And more literalistic eyes or more timorous ones might with equal justification read in the visage of nature a very different message than that of Maclaurin's neo-Plotinist hymn. Rather than being morally uplifted, one might easily be dispirited and disappointed by the mechanistic essence of this new cosmos—like the character in one Enlightenment dialogue who asked, "Tell me, Sir, did you not formerly have a more elevated view of the universe?" Or one might respond, like Pascal, with fear and trembling at the human emptiness and nonhuman dimensions of Newtonian space. Or those of more activist and secular disposition might see in the cause-effect relations of the Newtonian cosmos an invitation to manipulate social forces in the direction of their own desires.

It was David Hume, especially in his *Dialogues on Natural Religion*, who inflicted mortal wounds on the widespread conviction that Newtonian rationalism and Lockean empiricism could sustain the moral hopes of the Enlightenment. Locke's argument on behalf of natural law and moral Newtonianism both relied in crucial ways upon an argument from design. Locke, for example, writes in his *Essays on the Law of Nature* that our sense experience can reveal to us "the visible structure and argument of this world" and perceive it to be "in every respect . . . perfectly and ingeniously prepared."[64] As Hume's cool skepticism made evident, however, a corpuscular and mechanistic metaphysic left human rights and goods homeless and inaccessible to an epistemology founded on its premises.

Indeed, Hume himself almost surely did not appreciate how deeply his criticisms struck at any empiricist moral philosophy, for they ultimately undermined his own attempt to place morality on an experimental footing. Immanuel Kant, however, did appreciate the radical force of Hume's critique, which, he wrote, roused him from his "dogmatic slumber." As Kant recognized, Hume's analysis demonstrated the impossibility, at least within a Newtonian cosmos, of grounding any moral theory in the external world of phenomena. If morality was not to be ultimately a groundless chimera, it had to be given a different foundation altogether. Kant's attempt to provide this new foundation, I think, can appropriately be seen as the final retreat of Platonic practical reason in the world of modern philosophy.

The term *retreat* is chosen advisedly, for it is the essence of Kant's philosophical strategy. He simply concedes the whole exterior world to Cartesian *res extensa* ontologically and to Humean heteronomy behaviorally. The phenomenal world is conceded to be mere matter in motion, and human behavior insofar as it is a part of that world is conceded to be causally governed by self-interest. But this is only part of the story, Kant then insists, and it is the fundamental mistake of materialists such as Holbach or utilitarian moralists such as Hume that they unwittingly take the part for the whole. By looking only at the world of phenomena, in fact, they render themselves incapable from the very outset of grasping human nature. Kant's complaint against these philosophers is the same as Rousseau's complaint against those who similarly look outward in their attempts to "know mankind": "Instead of a being, acting constantly from fixed and invariable principles, instead of that celestial and majestic simplicity, impressed on it by its divine Author, we find it only the frightful contrast of passion mistaking itself for reason, and of understanding grown delirious."[65]

The way to escape this conceptual impasse—and the tendency toward a "lax and low" interpretation of morality that follows upon it—Kant also finds in Rousseau's anthropology. Human beings, says Rousseau, are animals with a difference. We are animals in that we are subject to the laws of physical nature. Unlike beasts, however, we are spiritually free to resist the bondage of that nature. "Nature lays her commands on every animal, and the brute obeys her voice. Man receives the same impulsion, but at the same time knows himself at liberty to acquiesce or resist: and it is particularly in his consciousness of this liberty that the spirituality of his soul is displayed. For physics may explain, in some measure, the mechanism of the senses and the formation of ideas; but in the power of willing or rather of choosing, and in the feeling of this power, nothing is found but acts which are purely spiritual and wholly inexplicable by the laws of mechanism."[66]

The duality captured in this passage, Kant believes, is not simply metaphorical. It instead reflects the ontological peculiarity of human beings who uniquely inhabit two distinct levels of being: the phenomenal and the noumenal worlds. Insofar as we inhabit the phenomenal world, we are, like beasts, automata driven by the compulsions of instinct and inclination. Insofar as we inhabit the noumenal world, we are radically free beings bound only by laws we set for ourselves. The moral tension to which human beings are uniquely subject arises from the tension between the two coexisting realms. "If I were only a member of the world of the intellect, all my actions would conform perfectly to the principle of the autonomy of pure will; if I were only a part of the world of sense they would be assumed to conform wholly to the natural law of desires and inclinations. . . . The moral 'ought' is then the necessary 'will' of a member of an intelligible world and he conceives it as an 'ought' only to the same extent that he considers himself a member of the world of sense."[67]

Reason is, in Kant's account, identified with the noumenal world. It is part of the world within rather than the world without. Indeed, it is the very essence of that world, providing the principles by which it is regulated; and it is only through their reason that human beings know anything whatever about the noumenal world. (Concerning that world, Kant writes, we "may know nothing other than that there pure reason alone makes the law."[68]) The moral role of reason in Kant's philosophy, therefore, is the same as it is in Plato's. Reason is the charioteer who must subject the appetites to its control if the soul is to be properly ordered. The concrete rendering of the participants in this moral struggle for control of the soul is, however, quite different in Kant from what it is in Plato. By conceding nature to phenomena and confining reason to the interior realm, Kant transforms *nous* into "pure reason." And the command of this abstract reason is a behavioral version of the logical categorical demand to avoid contradicting oneself: "Act only on a maxim by which you can will that it, at the same time, should become a general law."[69]

The reduction of the *logos* of reason to logic alone is thus complete. The exclusion of all "heteronomous" elements, which are conceived as merely mechanical and appetitive, produces this inevitable result. "Rational behavior," as a consequence, can no longer be conceived as the noetically mediated communion with the Good. It must instead be much more ascetically conceived as a rather Calvinistic dutiful conformity to the "good"—now defined as universal law. Kant insists that his abstract and interior constriction of *nous* into a categorical logical mandate is an advance, both morally and philosophically. Given all that he conceded to the dead hand of a mechanized "nature," it could be granted that he at least made the best of a bad bargain. His "pure" practical reason at least incorporates and operationalizes one crucial feature of moral behavior, namely the voluntary forfeiture of any pursuit of preferential treatment or status based on self-interest.

Kant purchases the a priori status of his practical reason and its prophylaxis against "heteronomous" passions at a very high price, however. Just as his pure reason is a thin and abstract substitute for the ontologically robust *nous*, so he can offer only a tepid and watery substitute for the motivating power of *eros* that fueled it. With all "inclinations" or "desires" banished as morally unworthy and potentially corrupting, the fidelity to duty that Kant enjoins is sustained by its logical appeal alone.[70] Kant was aware of the problem, noting the necessity "that reason . . . not impotently raise its wings in the empty space of transcendent concepts which we call the intelligible world without being able to move." (Recall here that *eros* was characteristically depicted by the Greeks as having wings.) And he conceded that he could not in fact explain how the wholly logical appeal of pure practical reason could motivate the will. "How the mere principle of the universal validity of its maxims as laws . . . can supply an impulse of itself without any object of the will in which one could antecedently take any original interest," he writes, "is beyond the power of human reason to explain." He insists, nonetheless, that the appeal of pure moral duty is strong, indeed being "so much more powerful than all other impulses."[71] His abstract logician's "Good," he contends, holds compelling charm for all minds that are "not wholly spoiled for abstraction."[72]

If pure practical reason must stand in constant danger of losing its motivating power, it also proves simultaneously precarious in its content. For just as Kant can only attribute to his principle an erotic power he cannot explain, so he gives his principle its full moral content by stipulation and sleight of hand. The crucial transition in this regard occurs between the original purely logical form of the categorical imperative—act only on a maxim you can will to become universal—and its final form as a version of the golden rule—"act so as to treat man, in your own person as well as in that of anyone else, always as end, never merely as a means." This translation is justified by Kant on the grounds that "rational beings are called persons" whose "very nature constitutes them as ends in themselves."[73] Kant skips very lightly over this crucial definition and attendant stipulation. But it is precisely at this point that he gives the game away, however inadvertently. For these claims are both crucial to giving pure reason its moral content, and at the same time they are admissible only on grounds that exceed the limitations that constitute reason's purity. When "rational beings" become "persons" a purely logical construct becomes human, but only because heteronomy comes stealing covertly in the back door. We know implicitly what "persons" are. They are, we also appreciate implicitly, more than bare "rational beings." And it is in fact only because of this "more" that we respect them and attribute to them the status of "ends in themselves." What begins as a logical mandate turns into a genuinely moral imperative, then, but only by means of a step—namely, definitionally reembodying reason into human persons—that violates the very standards of ontological asceticism that are allegedly being deployed.

The swift and ironic reversal of Kant's pristine moral absolutism into the profound relativism of much neo-Kantian philosophy, therefore, is neither entirely surprising nor inexplicable. One need only identify and reject the sleight of hand that permitted Kant to infuse his logical imperative with his Protestant conscience, and one is then left with the morally empty bare formalism of neo-Kantian jurisprudence. Once the Newtonian fixity Kant attributed to the "moral world within" dissipates, his "rational will" fragments into a cacophony of wills that arbitrarily confer a plurality (instead of necessarily conferring a uniformity) of meanings upon the phenomenal world. And when that happens, we are delivered into the philosophical world of Max Weber, where competing "values" are placed by radically free subjects upon an in-itself-meaningless objective reality.

At this point, in short, the career of Platonic practical reason in modern philosophy arrives at the very same terminus reached by its Aristotelian counterpart. Mill's account of the moral sciences (which gives a modern version of Aristotle's "calculating well in pursuit of an end of a fine sort") and Kant's account of moral imperatives (which gives a modern version of Plato's quasi-mathematical apprehension of right order) open by the same trapdoor into Weber's cosmos of bureaucratic instrumentalism and "demonic" ends. For in both cases, the ontologically attenuated remainder of practical reason ("Art" for Mill, "pure practical reason" for Kant) proves easily vulnerable to relativist critique. These conceptions embodied the philosophers' "can't helps," the notions of the human good they took as certain: utility for Mill, the golden rule for Kant. But in both cases, it was easy to argue that these ends were merely stipulations generated by their own "subjective" faiths: in Benthamism and Christian pietism respectively. Especially as they became informed by Darwinian assumptions about flux and relativity rather than by Newtonian assumptions about eternal regularity, philosophers found it hard to escape this skeptical conclusion. G. E. Moore might attempt to resurrect the objective good in the form of non-natural properties; but the manifest deficiencies of his intuitionism made it only a brief interlude on the road to emotivism.

Careful examination of the logical development—perhaps logical disintegration would be a more apt characterization—of the idea of practical reason in modern political philosophy would thus seem to lend credence to Alasdair MacIntyre's judgment that "the contemporary vision of the world . . . is predominantly, although perhaps not always in detail, Weberian."[74] At least at the rather rarified level of philosophical speculation about rational practice, that claim seems well warranted. The perennial Western predisposition to assimilate reason to logic pushes us toward a Weberian outcome, once the remnants of classical essentialism and axiology are brushed aside. Utilitarians and Kantians have tried to retard the slide into subjectivism and hedonism that Mill and Kant already saw to be well under way in Bentham and Hume. But, as we have seen, the objective groundlessness of their moral philosophies leaves them easy prey to the skeptical and tough-minded who would speed us toward a Weberian, or emotivist, or Nietzschean destination. Having lost its grounding in the modern objective world of causal mechanism, practical reason loses first its intelligibility and then its capacity to sustain a humane and civilizing political life.

Practical Reason and Theories of Liberal Democracy

Theories of liberal democracy have been profoundly shaped by these philosophical developments. Early theoretical accounts tended to exhibit the Enlightenment faith in the moral capabilities of unaided reason and presumed that minds liberated from oppression and superstition would accept the idea of natural rights. As late as the end of the eighteenth century, Condorcet could write with confidence that "the rights of man are written in the book of nature."[75] And since the new simplifying and precise methods of scientific analysis were presumed competent to decipher this book of nature, the bases of a free, equal, tolerant society seemed secured.

This faith was relatively short-lived, however, as indeed it deserved to be in strictly philosophical terms. As Carl Becker observed on the final page of his book *The Declaration of Independence*, "throughout the nineteenth century the trend of action and the trend of thought . . . gave an appearance of unreality to the favorite ideas of the age of enlightenment."[76] Hume's cooly skeptical arguments seemed to block reason from having any role in ascertaining moral truth, leaving it instead the slave of the passions. And he likewise undermined the whole idea of moral design in the book of nature. The idea of common humanity succumbed to the kind of doubt expressed by de Maistre: "The constitution of 1795 is made for Man. . . . I have seen, in my time, Frenchmen, Italians, Russians, etc.; but as for Man, I declare I have never met him in my life."[77] And Jeremy Bentham could heap ridicule on natural rights as "nonsense on stilts."

Until very recently, then, most twentieth-century theories of liberal democracy have either been utilitarian or skeptical. On the one hand, democracy is seen as the pursuit of the greatest good for the greatest number. On the other, it is depicted as a society where individuals are mutually tolerant because all values are relative.

Each account has its problems, however. Utilitarian norms are thoroughly democratic in the sense that all utils have equal weight—and hence the pleasures of each are accorded equal treatment. Wholly apart from the question of whether the greatest happiness principle proves ultimately determinate,[78] however, utilitarianism seems a deficient basis for liberal democratic practices. If it is egalitarian, utilitarianism need not be liberal. It does not in the first place, as Rawls observes, "take seriously the plurality and distinctiveness of persons."[79] Correlatively, it does not take sufficiently seriously the integrity and autonomy of persons. Liberty and justice thus both become at best contingent virtues—normative only to the extent that they please the fancy of the greatest number. One can build a utilitarian case for liberty, as Mill did; but it is left precariously resting upon debatable empirical propositions. Or it might be set aside altogether, as Bentham seemed on occasion willing to do, writing of the objects of his legislative plans: "call them soldiers, call them monks, call them machines, so they were but happy ones, I should not care."[80]

On the utilitarian account, then, the substantive egalitarian norms of democracy may be validated, but the whole procedural complex of civil rights, liberties, and protections of democratic procedure lose their footing and therewith their significance. Utilitarian democracy is government for the people, but not necessarily government of or by the people. And justice, as an end of government, loses its autonomy and priority. It is not only Rawls and the others that the utilitarian standard would set aside, but traditional accounts like that of Madison, who wrote; "Justice is the end of government. It is the end of civil society. It ever has and will be pursued until it be obtained or until liberty be lost in the pursuit."[81]

Skeptical liberalism offers itself as a moderate and civilized way of living in a Weberian cosmos of plural and purely subjective competing values. Hans Kelsen, with his depiction of democracy as the logical practical correlate of value relativism, and T. V. Smith, who celebrated compromise as the essence of democracy, were articulate spokesmen for this viewpoint. And the regnant liberal pluralism, with its close association with methodological positivism and ethical emotivism, would seem clearly heir to that tradition. In each of these theories, toleration is the paramount democratic norm, equilibrium among competing group interests is the end of liberal politics, and the political broker who bargains and compromises is the democratic hero.

But skepticism alone proves a narrow and precarious basis for liberal democratic practices. Toleration and stability are important, but other important aspects of a good society such as justice and community find little sustenance in the pluralist vision of things. And even toleration may be on shaky ground here: no claims of objective right or good are admissible to use as warrant for bending others to your will, to be sure; but for the same reason no claims of objective right or good stand as obstacles to simple expressions of the *libido dominandi*. When reading the works of the liberal skeptics, it is hard not to remember the words of Leslie Stephen: "I now believe in nothing, but . . . I mean to live and die like a gentleman if possible."[82] One does not worry, then, about the skeptical pluralists themselves, who are generally humane and morally sensitive people. But one does worry about those who, on equally good logic, might play nihilistic Smerdyakov to their doubting Ivan. And even at its best, the view of liberal democracy they offer seems a limited and tepid one.

The deontological liberals who achieved prominence in the seventies have in effect played Kant to the pluralists' Hume. Rawls, Gewirth, Dworkin, and Nozick have each clearly sensed the ultimate precariousness of skeptical liberalism, whether or not they see it as a "lax and low" habit of morality, to use Kant's phrase. And they likewise recognize the deficiencies of utility-maximizing democracy I have just mentioned. Like Kant, they want us to "take rights seriously," and also like Kant, they would base these rights not on a conception of teleological nature but on a conception of rational selfhood.

The theories of deontological liberalism, however, exhibit difficulties that—not surprisingly—tend to mimic the problems of Kant's own project: infusing the (morally relevant) heteronomous properties of persons into his allegedly purely logical rational beings—thereby making them morally robust enough to warrant the status of "ends in themselves," and reading his own "can't helps" into "pure practical reason" as well. Gewirth's project of deriving human rights simply by logical inference from the nature of human beings as "prospective purposive agents" replicates the first of these Kantian difficulties. Key steps in the reasoning, depicted as purely logical, in fact embody conceptual additions that might be warranted on moral grounds but that are illicit under the professed constraints of the argument.[83] Rawls, Nozick, and Dworkin, on the other hand, each seem to stipulate their own ultimate norms—"fairness," liberty, and "equal concern and respect," respectively—into their construction of the definitive moral situation (for example, Rawls's "original position") or their depiction of the dimensions of rational selfhood (for example, the contrast between Rawls's "unencumbered" selves and Nozick's fully vested selves whose "assets" are all intrinsic to their identity). In addition, perhaps because of the egalitarian content of his stipulated norm, Dworkin exhibits a tendency to backslide into using utilitarian criteria when he deploys his theory on concrete political cases.[84]

The communitarian critics of rights-based liberalism, in turn, have also seemed more adept at discerning the weaknesses of others than at articulating a philosophical basis for their own viewpoint. They concur with the deontological liberals' rejection of utilitarianism as too implicitly reductive and potentially collectivist a basis for justifying liberal democracy. But they doubt the adequacy of the rights-based liberalism offered as a substitute. In particular, the communitarians believe that a healthy liberal democracy must be a community oriented toward the common good; and it seems clear to them that rights-based liberal theories either disdain those aspects of a polity altogether (as in Nozick) or else provide an inadequate and distorted account of them (as in Rawls).

Because the constructive philosophical underpinnings of the communitarian viewpoint are so relatively underdeveloped, it is probably more accurate at this time to speak of a communitarian impulse than of a communitarian theory of liberal democracy. In the context of their critiques of liberal individualism and deontological theories, the communitarians have at times looked to Aristotle or to Hegel for inspiration. As they themselves recognize, however, neither Aristotle nor Hegel can simply be deployed *in toto* as a persuasive philosophical groundwork for a theory of liberal democracy.[85] Aristotle attracts the communitarians because of his account of prudence, because of his conception of the *polis* as a natural community, and because of his insistence that political life is oriented toward the human good. But his teleology was based upon an outmoded metaphysic, he was focused upon the small city-state, and the essential egalitarian and pluralistic features of liberal democracy find little support in his philosophy. Hegel attracts with his account of the state as a human project that has ineluctable moral dimensions and with his view of the self as constituted by its communal relationships and commitments. On the other hand, Hegel's historicist metaphysic, his philosophical certitude, and his emphasis upon positive freedom at the possible expense of "negative" civil liberties are less appealing to adherents of liberal democracy.

What seems needed is a theory of liberal democracy that is grounded in a viable philosophy and that incorporates the toleration of the skeptics, the rights of the deontologists, and the general welfare of the utilitarians into a normative conception of a political community. But a basis for such a conception within the usual channels of modern philosophy seems genuinely hard to find. For, as we have seen, the prevailing assumptions of modern philosophy have tended to generate a pattern of oscillation among emotivist, utilitarian, and neo-Kantian theories—none which is fully adequate to the task at hand.

At this point, the impasse in our understanding of practical reason and the philosophical dilemma of liberal democratic theory converge. The dominance of the calculative ideal of reason has made a theory of collective prudence difficult if not impossible. But one potentially attractive and plausible way of understanding and justifying liberal democratic practices is to construe them as an attempt to embody the norms of collective prudence—to see liberal democracy as a community of citizens who pursue their common good in accord with the canons of rational practice.

Although liberal democracy has always received—and will undoubtedly continue to receive—support from a variety of philosophical quarters, understanding liberal democracy as communal rational practice in politics has, *prima facie*, several attractive features. For one thing, it is a perspective that resonates with the intuition so powerfully present at the birth of liberalism—the intuition that the faith in reason and the ideals of liberal democracy are not merely historically associated but are logically related in some fundamental ways. Moreover, a philosophy of rational practice seems sufficiently complex and capacious to incorporate the whole range of norms and values found in liberalism—liberty, equality, participation, toleration, rights, and community—rather than singling out and elevating one of them at the expense of all the others.

This, then, is the possibility I wish to explore in the following pages: the possibility that a theory of liberal democracy can be based on a philosophically viable conception of rational practice, thereby reconciling the concerns of the communitarians with what is best in the skeptical, utilitarian, and deontological versions of liberalism. For, so I shall argue, recent philosophical developments—specifically in the philosophy of science and the philosophy of language—open this possibility to us in a way previously foreclosed. What these developments offer us is the prospect of breaking the hegemony of the calculative ideal over our understanding of the life of reason, of rediscovering the practical dimension of all feats of rationality. And that achievement offers the further prospect of relearning—and perhaps even learning better—something that classical philosophers, early liberals, and civic republicans all have known: that politics at its best is a communal embodiment of reason's work in the world.

Chapter Two Rationality in
Science and Language:
From Syntax to Pragmatics

The neo-Platonist disposition to logicize rationality has persisted force-fully into the twentieth century. It is manifest not only in the wide-spread use of the term *rational* as a synonym for *logical*, but also in the tendency to construe scientific inquiry as applied logic and to interpret languages as imperfect logical calculi. This overly constrained and idealized account of rationality has benefited us by stimulating the enormously productive and important mathematical components of science and by goading all disciplines toward greater rigor and clarity. It has, however, had several unfortunate consequences. It has afflicted us with polarized lenses in our perceptions of science and language, screening out the elements of scientific and linguistic rationality that do not fit its confines. And it has, by the application of its overly stringent criteria for inclusion within what has become an ever-shrinking circle of reason, pushed increasingly extensive areas of human cognition and practice into an amorphous slag heap of allegedly irrational (or at least nonrational) phenomena. Especially significant for our concerns here, these unfortunate consequences have distorted or discouraged any ade-quate understanding of the genuine and significant role of rationality in politics.

For this reason, it is quite important for contemporary political philosophy to recognize that the last three or four decades have wit-nessed significant alterations and improvements in areas of philosophy that have direct bearing upon our understanding of human reason. Against the background of the dominance of the calculative ideal, the past several decades have seen what can be characterized as a piecemeal rebellion against the hegemony of *logismos* over *logos* and "ology." Our best contemporary accounts of scientific inquiry and of linguistic practice add up to a persuasive case that neither science or language are properly conceived as, or properly judged by the standards appropriate to, formal calculations. Instead, both science and language are more complex and sophisticated forms of rational practice with a discernible structure of their own. Although neither as fully specifiable nor as precise as the formal structures of mathematics, moreover, these forms of rational practice are neither shapeless nor anomic. We can characterize their *modus operandi* and their constitutive norms with some assurance. And these characterizations, in turn, provide us with the basis for an understanding of human rationality that is both more adequate and more capacious than the account that has hitherto dominated modern philosophy.

In this chapter, then, I provide a brief sketch of what seem to me the most relevant accomplishments within the philosophy of science and the philosophy of language. I argue that these accomplishments are significantly complementary, converging upon the reintroduction of some of the traditional hallmarks of practical reason into our general conception of reason. And finally, I argue that resident within this enlarged conception of reason as one of its constitutive features are identifiable procedures, dynamics, and institutions—what might be called the "politics" in reason. These procedures, dynamics, and institutions in turn will provide the grounds and the reference point for the later contention that it is meaningful to speak of rationality in politics and salutary to subscribe to the norms of good practice derived from that conception.

Scientific Rationality: From Explication of Logic to Critique of Judgment

Whatever the controversies that still percolate within the very lively discipline of the philosophy of science, it is clear that the center of gravity has shifted very substantially in that field between 1950 and the present day. Even the most cursory exploration of the leading work in philosophy of science, then and now, readily reveals significant differences in the concerns, the assumptions, and the problems of those working in that area. Before 1950, the philosophy of science centered around the explication of logic. Today, logical issues still have their place, but the major issues in the field can be characterized as centering around a critique of scientific judgment. And implicit in this shift has been the gradual emergence of a conception of scientific rationality that is larger and more complex than the conception that equated reason in science with applied logic.

From the 1920s into the 1950s, the philosophy of science was dominated by the assumptions and research goals of logical empiricism. This approach carried the geometric ideal into the twentieth century and sought to bring it to new heights by appropriating the tools of contemporary mathematical logic. Like Plato and Aristotle, the adherents of logical empiricism conceived of science as *theoria:* contemplative, demonstrable, and vested with the precision and objectivity of logic. Like Enlightenment epistemologists, the logical empiricists aspired to positive knowledge, although they did not have the Enlightenment hopes that this knowledge would include moral illumination.

It was no mere accident that almost all of the founders and leading early practitioners of logical empiricism were physicists or mathematicians. Their paradigmatic "exemplars" of legitimate and successful scientific reasoning were taken from these fields that were most familiar to them. The impressive achievements of theoretical physics and the accomplishments of mathematical logicians, as for example that of Russell and Whitehead in *Principia Mathematica,* not only served them as the prototypical instances of scientific progress but also functioned as a model for emulation by all the sciences. This disciplinary focus—and the hope for a unified *methodos* of science based upon it—gave the logical empiricists another point of continuity with Enlightenment rationalism, since Enlightenment rationalism also took its prototypical cases from the mathematicizing sciences and also hoped to guarantee future scientific advances by universalizing the methods of these sciences.

In terms of scientific theory construction, the logical empiricist model was essentially identical with that stated forthrightly by Sir John Herschel, himself building upon the tradition of positivistic rationalism, in the nineteenth century: science should "stand or fall by the result of a direct appeal to the facts in the first instance, and of a direct logical deduction from them afterwards."[1] The epistemic bedrock of science was Herschel's "direct appeal to facts" encountered in experience. This was the base of science in "observations"—which were construed as unproblematic reports of unambiguous data. It seems evident that this account of observation was profoundly empiricist, philosophically speaking, but not very empirical. That is, it is a depiction of observation that owes little to the complex, skillful, and often problematic observations of real-world scientists and owes a great deal to the abstract accounts of observation and observables found in Hume and Mach. "Observations," in short, were conceived as discrete and atomic Humean "impressions" that could be naively, passively, and unproblematically imprinted upon the mind of an unbiased and biologically normal observer.

If the observables provided the hard and certain base of scientific theory, the process of theory construction itself was construed in terms of logical formalism. A scientific theory, then, was to be a logical calculus that was hooked into the world through the incorporation of the data into the formal system. The ideal scientific theories were law statements that could be combined with statements of relevant circumstances to deduce empirical consequences. These logically derived consequences could then be compared with the facts and the truth or falsity of the theoretical hypotheses ascertained by the congruency, or lack of congruency, between the logical deductions and the empirical realities.

The research program of logical empiricism was dictated by this conception of knowledge and of scientific theory. Some adherents of what has come to be termed the "received view"[2] of scientific practice were content to use it as simply an abstract ideal. For the logical empiricist account to be more decisively convincing and more concretely useful, however, it seemed to require some additional specification and clarification. Some of the necessary elaboration of the paradigm or disciplinary matrix, to borrow Thomas Kuhn's nomenclature, related to the nature and content of the empirical observables, and some of it concerned the theoretical structures. In addition, some clarification of the linkages between these two halves of scientific theory—the logical and the empirical—seemed necessary. And finally, it seemed both necessary and practically highly useful to clarify and to apply the criteria implicit in the received view for discriminating between genuine science and pseudo-science.

On the side of the observables, a central task of the logical empiricist research program was to specify more fully both the nature and the content of the hard, atomic facts that provided the alleged bedrock of scientific theory. This task led on the one hand to an attempt to designate the protocol sentences that met the criteria for direct reports of experience and composed an acceptable observation language. On the other hand, this task produced a debate over whether observation statements should be understood as phenomenalist reports of sense data or as physical descriptions of things possessing observable properties.

On the side of theory, the logical empiricist program led to efforts to rationally reconstruct scientific theories into tight logical systems. The most important aspect of this project was to reconstruct scientific explanations into hypothetico-deductive form. Successfully reformulating scientific theories in this manner would help to sustain and exemplify the logical empiricist contention that fully developed scientific theories were causal explanations susceptible to syllogistic expression, in which causal law statements were the major premises, statements of conditions the minor premises, and factual reports of empirical effects the conclusions. Such demonstrations would also help validate the corollary contention that scientific explanations were formally isomorphic with predictions of future effects from known causes.

Discussions of the linkage between the observation language and the theoretical algorithms focused on the appropriate "correspondence rules" for giving theoretical terms solid footing in unambiguous empirical data. These rules were to incorporate and give force to appropriate criteria for giving reliable definitions to theoretical terms: theoretical terms were to be "ostensibly" defined by pointing, as it were, to the observables to which they referred. One famous version of ostensive definition was the "operationism" popularized by P. W. Bridgman: the meaning of a term in this view was considered synonymous with the operations employed in using it.

Because the correspondence rules served to specify what counted as acceptable theoretical terminology, discussions about them were closely connected with the logical empiricist criterion for scientific admissibility. No theoretical terms were acceptable unless they could be grounded in direct experience, and no explanations were scientifically acceptable unless they were verifiable by direct experience. Thus no discipline that necessarily deployed theoretical terms or explanations not susceptible of such empirical validation could claim the status of a science. Because statements that did not meet the verificationist criterion were deemed not only scientifically inadmissable but cognitively empty, in fact, all nonscientific assertions became stigmatized as actually meaningless: they must either be purged as fraudulent or delusionary, or in some cases they might be reinterpreted as subjectivist expostulations. Magic and metaphysics generally were considered as falling under the fraud and delusion heading; and ethics and aesthetics were considered in need of reinterpretation as essentially emotive rather than cognitive, as expressions of feeling rather than as truth claims.

Historical case studies that examined the actual development of concrete areas of science were not included in the agenda of the logical empiricist research program. Such inquiries might be anecdotally interesting but they were not deemed relevant to the understanding of scientific knowledge. Especially once the hope that an inductive logic of discovery could be formalized had dissipated, the process of inquiry no longer seemed philosophically interesting. Because it could not be reduced to applied logic, the "context of discovery" was written off as nonrational. Scientific rationality was confined to the "context of justification," wherein the finished propositions generated by the scientific disciplines could be assessed by the norms of logic and empirical verification.

Each of these elements of the logical empiricist research program encountered difficulties. The attempts to refine and solidify its account of scientific rationality seemed instead to reveal that account's limitations and internal problems.

Specifying the nature and context of the observation language, for example, proved to be an extremely tricky undertaking. As for the nature of the observables, both the phenomenalist and the physicalist characterizations carried discomfiting implications. The phenomenalist interpretation endowed the observables with the incorrigibility that was desirable, but at the price of inviting solipsism and a pluralist Babel of individual sense-experiences. These flaws in the phenomenalist interpretation led to the general triumph of the physicalist interpretation; but the latter account did not survive closer examination unscathed either. The physicalist designation of the observables as things in the world and their directly observable properties saved the objective grounding of the observation language, but it surrendered the incorrigibility of observations and seemed logically to depend upon an intersubjective consensus for its warrants. And this dependency on an intersubjective consensus, however unproblematic it might seem to be in the exemplary cases of physics, opened the way epistemologically to conventionalism. It was as if the empiricists had asked Hume and Condillac to provide their philosophical supper, but Bishop Berkeley had catered their dessert uninvited.

As for the content of the observation language, specifying that also proved difficult to do in a fully satisfying way. If the eligible constituents of the observation language were determined by rigorous and parsimonious standards, a great many scientifically relevant observations seemed not to be included. It took a good deal of gerrymandering, at best, to construct real-world scientific observations out of data that took the form of "red, here, now." On the other hand, if the observation language were broadened to include the more complex and sophisticated observations that seem to constitute the data base of real world scientific inquiry, the observables seemed to lose their desired hardness and simplicity. In addition, the line between pure observation terms and theoretical terms became cloudy at best.

Specifying the criteria for acceptable theoretical terms and tying them down to their observation base also proved to be problematic. Some very useful theoretical concepts in science proved upon examination to be only partly or indirectly tied to observations. As a consequence, either some palpably important and useful component terms of scientific theories had to be embarrassingly construed as in some sense illicit, or else the whole interrelated program of correspondence rules, ostensive definition, and reduction sentences had to be revised and relaxed. The latter choice seemed to be the only acceptable alternative, so theoretical terms were deemed allowable even if subject only to "partial interpretation" by reference to an observation language. Once the correspondence rules and the derivative principle of operationism were so relaxed, however, the verification criterion of cognitive significance underwent a parallel relaxation. And at that point, the empiricist program lost the epistemological bite that made it interesting, radical, and distinctive.

The deductivist account of scientific explanation that came with the view of scientific theories as logical systems also came under criticism. Some important scientific explanations could indeed be usefully formulated as deductive inferences from theoretical covering laws. In other instances, however, the deductivist model seemed inapplicable; and in still other cases it could be rendered applicable, but not in any very useful or significant manner. In these latter instances, relevant explanations could be pounded into deductive form and covering laws invoked, but neither the deductive form nor the covering laws seemed to add any illumination to otherwise intelligible explanations.

Finally, although some philosophers of science seemed content to write off the process of scientific discovery as nonrational and consequently as beneath philosophic interest, many others found this abdication—and the very stringent and limited criteria for rationality that dictated it—disturbing. Writing off the context of discovery in this fashion left an important part, possibly the most important part, of science unexplained and unintelligible. Even granting the role of hunches, chance, and intuition in scientific inquiry, it seemed misleading to imply that nothing distinguished this process from random conjecture. In philosophical terms, moreover, the sharp distinction between the contexts of discovery and justification brushed aside the important question Plato posed in the *Meno:* how is it that anyone knows where to look for an answer he or she does not already have? In other words, a theory of knowledge that had no theory of learning seemed deficient.

The setbacks and complications encountered by the logical empiricist program inspired its more loyal adherents to work more diligently to "save the appearances"—to patch up the holes, overcome the paradoxes, and remedy the apparent incompetencies in the basic framework. At the same time, however, critics emerged from several quarters in the 1950s and 1960s to challenge the received view of scientific rationality at its core. There were essentially two major sources of this challenge: first, the carryover into the philosophy of science of the fundamental assault upon all sense-datum accounts of language and learning found in the later philosophy of Ludwig Wittgenstein; and second, reflection upon actual scientific practice by scientists or historians of science uncowed by the a priori proscriptions of the received view. The most important critics of logical empiricism who centered their critique around the insights of Wittgenstein were Stephen Toulmin and Norwood Hanson.[3] The most important critics of the received view who drew principally upon their experience or study of science-as-practiced were Michael Polanyi and Thomas Kuhn.[4] Important contributions to the antiempiricist critique were also made by two students of Karl Popper: Imre Lakatos and Paul Feyerabend. Feyerabend radicalized Popper's doubts about empiricism into what he did not flinch from styling as epistemological anarchism; and Lakatos found himself suspended somewhat uncomfortably between an appreciation of the insights of the new "moving picture" approach to scientific understanding and a deep commitment to Popper's objectivism and to his focus upon the rational reconstruction of theories.[5]

Just as the adherents of the received view had differed among themselves on important details, so also the critics of the received view were not of one mind in all respects. Nevertheless, their work contained many important common themes.

First, a common complaint was the inadequacy of any account of scientific theory that focused exclusively upon logical formalizations. Theories, the critics agreed, were not simply logical systems. Moreover, it was insisted that the logical syntax of scientific theories could not be fruitfully abstracted from the "semantics" of theory "interpretation." Instead, syntax and semantics were indissolubly connected in the complex task of theoretical conceptualization. Hanson's comments in his article "The Interpretation of Scientific Theories" might be fairly taken as representative here:

To take the interpretation out of geometrical optics is to take the optics out of optics. The *theory* of geometrical optics (in the positivists' sense) is simply geometry, not optics, at all. . . . To restrict one's philosophical attention, focusing now only on syntactical structure, and later on the host of semantic issues involving interpretation and meaning—this is to have failed to recognize that "physical theory" is an *indissolubly* complex concept to begin with. Complexity never constitutes a good argument for reluctance to undertake analysis. We can all grant that. But complexity is not confusion. When analysis results in destroying complexity in the name of clearing up confusions, to that extent it destroys the concept in question. It slices it out of existence. . . . To chop theories apart into *formalism* and *interpretation*—and then to identify only the formalism with the "theory"—is the simple mistake of misplaced discreteness.[6]

The critics also came down hard upon what they saw as the primitive, misleading, and unsustainable notion of observation as passive reception of sense impressions that informed the received view. In this respect, they echoed the earlier complaint of Kant against Hume: percepts without concepts are blind. Hanson, Kuhn, and Polanyi each appropriated and deployed some of the findings and contentions of the gestalt theory of perception in this context. Discrete and passive impressions, by and of themselves, the critics insisted, are quite meaningless apart from organizing patterns imposed upon them. To cite Hanson again, "the atypical signal registrations of inebriates, idiots, and infants may constitute *de facto* interpretation-free sense encounters with phenomena. But these certainly are not observations—not in any sense that the last five hundred years of scientific inquiry would recognize as an 'observation.'"[7] Instead of being the passive reception of atomic and indubitable sense data, then, all observation in any relevant epistemological sense must be construed as an active process of grasping and interpreting these data.

This revisionist understanding of both theory and observation has several important corollaries. Because semantic interpretation cannot be sliced out of theory construction and because meaningful observations require some hermeneutic construction by reference to *gestalten*, the clear division between allegedly pure and heterogeneous theory and observation language cannot be maintained.[8] Scientific perceptions are, to some extent at least, "theory-laden." It also followed that there could be no fully neutral nor incorrigibly reliable algorithm for theory choice. Deciding that one theoretical explanation was superior to another in science was rarely if ever a simple matter of "deciding on the basis of the evidence," as if the evidence spoke the verdict on its own.

This absence of a neutral algorithm of theory choice meant that the verificationist program and the criteria of meaning and demarcation that went with it had to be set aside. Any attempt to lay down "precise rules for making or testing assertions of fact," Polyani argued, "is condemned to futility from the start. For we can derive rules of observation and verification only from examples of factual statements that we have accepted as true before we know these rules."[9] And Kuhn expressed parallel doubts about the conventional claims for the verifiability and falsifiability of scientific theories:

> Verification is like natural selection: it picks out the most viable among the actual alternatives in a particular historical situation. Whether that choice is the best that could have been made if still other alternatives had been available or if the data had been of another sort is not a question that can usefully be asked. . . .
>
> Clearly, the role thus attributed to falsification (i.e., by Popper) is much like the one this essay assigns to anomalous experiences, i.e., to experiences that, by evoking crisis, prepare the way for a new theory. Nevertheless, anomalous experiences may not be identified with falsifying ones. Indeed, I doubt that the latter exist. . . . If any and every failure to fit were ground for theory rejection, all theories ought to be rejected at all times.[10]

A final corollary of the revisionist view of science is a blurring if not a breaking down of the distinction insisted upon by the received view between the context of discovery and the context of justification. If there are no crucial experiments in the full sense, then it follows that justification is a more complex and less univocally determinative process than the logical empiricists' depiction supposes. And if scientific justifications require some of the kinds of judgments mandatory for the pursuit of scientific discoveries, then it is arguable that the same "logic" employed in theory appraisal may characterize theory development. In Lakatos's terms, the warrants for accepting a given research program as justified are almost synonymous with the reasons for pursuing further discoveries within that program; and these latter reasons in their turn provide the clues, leads, and relevant categories for directing the pursuit of new insights.[11]

As the revisionist attack gathered force, depth, and adherents, it inspired counterattacks that focused principally upon what were taken to be the untenable and unsettling implications of its major contentions. Almost uniformly, the counterattacks manifested and invoked what Richard Bernstein has aptly termed the "Cartesian Anxiety." As Bernstein observes, Descartes gave archetypal expression to a persistent fear that has haunted Western rationalism: either we must find firm and unshakable foundations for our convictions, or else we shall fall into the abyss. "With a chilling clarity Descartes leads us with an apparent and ineluctable necessity to a grand and seductive Either/Or. Either there is some support for our being, a fixed foundation for our knowledge, or we cannot escape the forces of darkness that envelop us with madness, with intellectual and moral chaos."[12]

By virtue of their declaration that no fixed Archimedean point exists for our knowledge, the defenders of the received view insisted, the revisionists would push us over the precipice and into this intellectual and moral chaos. Without fixed reference points to impose standards and determine choices, science would sink into pure subjectivism and the drawbridge of civilization's defense against political barbarians would be let down. Writing in review of Polanyi's *Personal Knowledge*, for example, May Brodbeck characterized the author as one of those "obscurantists" who "deprecate reason in favor of faith or feeling" and participate in "the disavowal of objective truth." She concluded her review by saying that "it is time once again to stand up and be counted against the forces of irrationalism, wherever they appear, in no matter how benign a guise."[13] The Cartesian "grand and seductive Either/Or" cited by Bernstein was very much in evidence in these polemics. Either one must hold to an objectivist conception of knowledge or one is ipso facto a subjectivist. Either one holds to neutral and fully specifiable criteria for theory choice or one is a conventionalist and relativist. Either one conceives science as logical and impersonal or one is an irrationalist. And if this parade of imaginary horribles was mostly invoked by the holdouts for the fundamentals of the received view, the revisionists were not wholly exempt from responsibility for this dichotomized depiction of the alternatives. Seeking language to etch their disagreements with the objectivist tradition, its critics sometimes used terms that in unqualified or unelaborated formulation could foster a justifiable concern for those holding fast to the truth that scientific inquiry is neither undisciplined nor irrational. Kuhn, for example, wrote that a decision to accept a new paradigm at an early stage "can only be made on faith" and approvingly cited and denominated non-scandalous Max Planck's observation that "a new scientific truth does not triumph by convincing its opponents and making them see the light, but rather because its opponents eventually die."[14] Reading these words, Kuhn's detractors could be excused for worrying whether rational argumentation in scientific controversy, however conceptualized, was being swept aside.

Attempts to characterize a discipline such as the philosophy of science, to identify its center of gravity, and to assess the nature and significance of contemporary trends within it are always hazardous and contestable. Nonetheless, there seems good warrant for believing that the elusive "mainstream" of philosophy of science has moved beyond some of the constraints and polarized polemics of only a decade or two ago. Those sympathetic to the aspirations of the received view now seem willing to acknowledge the inevitability of some fairly profound alterations in the traditional empiricist epistemology. In this respect, they have followed in a rhetorically more subdued form the lead of Lakatos, who despite his intention to keep alive the ideal of rational reconstruction conceded the accuracy of many of the revisionists' critical strictures and sought to show how irrationalist conclusions need not follow. On the other hand, the revisionists, with the possible exception of Feyerabend, have generally tried to make it clear that their reservations about the received view did not entail a rejection of a belief in the disciplined, rational, and progressive character of scientific inquiry. In the postscript to the second edition of *The Structure of Scientific Revolutions*, for example, Kuhn took pains to disassociate himself from epistemological relativism. Even though he continued to maintain that no unambiguous neutral criteria for theory choice can be decisive, Kuhn nonetheless affirmed that "it should be easy to design a list of criteria that would enable an uncommitted observer to distinguish the earlier from the more recent theory time after time." And the later theory is properly seen as superior. "Later scientific theories are better than earlier ones for solving puzzles in the quite often different environments to which they are applied. That is not a relativist's position, and it displays the sense in which I am a convinced believer in scientific progress."[15]

Although sharp disagreements persist among philosophers of science in many respects, it is possible to discern the emergence of a rather broad general consensus in recent years—a consensus moving toward a new synthesis that escapes the forced either/or straight-jacket of the earlier polemics. The original thesis, stemming from Enlightenment neo-Platonism, held that science was "rational," meaning objective in the sense of logical, neutral, and precise; and science was progressive, meaning linearly cumulative on the basis of firm foundations. The antithesis, whether real or alleged, held that science was not simply logical or straightforwardly cumulative, and therefore science was neither rational nor progressive. The emerging view, in which these oppositions are *aufgehoben*, is that science is both rational and progressive, but its rationality cannot be confined to mere logic or specified by wholly neutral criteria, and its progressiveness is not characterized by continuous accretion of knowledge upon unalterable foundations.

Despite their differences, most contemporary philosophers of science would, I believe, share both the premises and the aspirations expressed by Dudley Shapere in his recent paper on "The Character of Scientific Change":

Scientific change seems to be pervasive and deep, extending far beyond mere alteration of factual belief. Yet on the other hand, the philosophically-minded historian (or the historically-minded philosopher), in his rightful reaction against Whiggish history and positivistic philosophy, seems often to have gone too far in the other direction, forgetting that one also cannot look closely at modern science without being impressed by the fact that its claims *are* better than those of its predecessors.

Can justice be done to both these claims without returning to the absolutes of the Platonic-Kantian-positivistic tradition or falling into the relativism of its latest critics?[16]

Science, as we are now coming to understand it, is not—essentially—a process of computation or applied logic. Logical inferences play a significant role in scientific thought, but they are simply one of the tools in the scientific arsenal and not the defining feature of scientific rationality: logic can be deployed in unscientific ways, and logic alone is inadequate to perform some of the most crucial cognitive tasks in scientific inquiry. The rationality that defines and informs scientific investigation and explanation is, instead, a disciplined but not fully objectively specifiable process of intelligent judgment—a process of judgment that, moreover, is almost inconceivable apart from the shaping and sustaining influence of a scientific community that is organized and governed in particular ways.

The crucial agent of scientific inquiry is the scientific discipline—with "discipline" here being construed in its concrete communal enterprise sense (e.g., as in the phrase, "members of the discipline") rather than in the sense of an abstract body of propositions. The scientific discipline is a community of inquirers constituted by a shared allegiance to certain central values and goals, by a shared acceptance of certain broad paradigms or theories, and by a common focus upon a given set of intellectual problems demanding resolution and intellectual tasks awaiting completion. The values and goals include the actuating normative premises of science, such as those expressed in the ideal of scientific "objectivity," broadly defined: a belief in the importance of making the world intelligible, fidelity to the truth, and a commitment to quarantining one's own biases. The paradigms and theories include those broad conceptual frameworks that define the entities populating the area under investigation and those explanatory models that seem—for the time being, at least—warranted by their performance. The problems and tasks are those of further clarification, refinement, and extension of the model and/or the exploration of potential or apparent counterinstances that strain the model. Each of these levels of constitutive norms, theories, and problems, moreover, overlaps and interacts with the others to some extent. A scientist can identify problems, for example, only against the background of the discipline's theoretical matrix; and the acceptance of these theories relies to some degree upon the same belief in the orderliness of nature that in turn sustains the discipline's dedication to the pursuit of truth.

The principal attentions of any scientific discipline at a given time will be focused upon the tasks of understanding and problem solving that follow from its body of theory. These efforts of extension, refinement, and clarification on the one hand and investigation of possible anomalies or counterinstances in applying the theory to the real world on the other hand make up the concrete substance of the discipline's "research program." In their different ways, both the puzzle-solving activities of normal science (to use Kuhn's term) and the attempts to understand and evaluate apparent counterinstances to expectations fostered by the discipline's accepted theories constitute scientific "testing." The testing process rarely if ever conforms to the idealized and simplistic conception of proceeding via crucial experiments, however. Instead, it is a more complicated and long-term process of assessing a theory's persuasiveness—or, more likely, of a whole cluster of theories' persuasiveness, since most scientific theories are implicated in multiple ways with neighboring theories and concepts.

Established paradigms, theories, and research programs are rarely abandoned—even in the face of fairly massive counterinstances and explanatory incapacities—unless some alternative theoretical framework and corresponding research program can be adumbrated. At that point, a competition is likely to ensue between the alternative programs, in which adherents of each try to demonstrate its superiority over the other. This task of adjudicating between competing research programs and deciding which to pursue is not an easy one. Rational argumentation and "demonstrations" in the general sense are possible, of course; but unequivocal and clearly decisive reasons or evidence are rarely adducible. It is likewise possible to specify, in general terms at least, the relevant criteria for rational theory choice. The most important of these criteria include the competing programs' relative explanatory capabilities, especially the capacity to provide satisfactory resolutions for problems that otherwise remain vexing and unmanageable. Also an important criterion is the heuristic power of the competing programs, their relative utility in anticipating previously undiscovered facts or in generating auxiliary hypotheses that turn out to be useful in their own right. The coherence of a program's theories with other theories and concepts deemed acceptable on independent grounds makes another good argument on its behalf. The scope of a program's theoretical framework is also a relevant consideration, as is its simplicity and elegance in accounting for the data.

Choice among competing research programs and the theories they contain is, then, by no means arbitrary. Relevant criteria exist, good reasons may be given, and evidence may be searched out and brought forward. But careful and difficult judgments are nonetheless called for, and where the balance lies may be impossible to ascertain with any confidence at a given time or with genuine certainty at any time. No serious research program is likely to fail by all standards, or it would never have been developed in the first place. Conversely, no contending research program is likely to be wholly successful by all standards, or it would not have inspired competitors. Different theories may do better on one criterion than on another: one theory may have great heuristic power but little coherence with other accredited theories and little structural elegance, for example, while its competitor can handle certain disciplinary anomalies with greater ease but possesses only limited heuristic capability. Moreover, the criteria themselves are not established by divine decree; neither are they unequivocal in meaning nor are they always unambiguous in application. What counts as theoretical simplicity, for instance, may not be altogether obvious. Likewise, no straightforward and neutral measure exists for determining what an important—as contrasted with a trivial—anomalous occurrence is. As a consequence, the most knowledgeable and objective scientist may not know which path to follow at some junctures of his research. For the same reasons, it may be rational to continue to pursue a previously productive research program suffering from increasing problems— what Lakatos calls a "degenerating problemshift"—in the hopes that it may yet prove able to overcome these problems, generate new discoveries, and exhibit explanatory potency. And it may also be rational to shelter an emergent research program that shows good potential even if it cannot currently compete effectively across the board with an established rival—rather like protecting an "infant industry" in an important area of the economy.

Against the backdrop of these understandings, contemporary philosophy of science has evolved from an explication of logic into what can best be characterized as a critique of judgment. Scientific inquiry can no longer be convincingly conceived, even in abstractedly idealized form, as a marriage of logically rigorous calculations and neutral empirical data. It instead embodies a sophisticated process of interpretative judgment, involving a complex dialectic between highly skilled perceptions and the evolving conceptual patterns that organize them into an intelligible whole. Understanding scientific rationality, therefore, requires understanding the nature and basis of these interpretative judgments.

It is for this reason that careful attention to concrete historical cases of scientific advances have assumed such an important role within the contemporary philosophy of science. Only a few decades ago, the study of such cases was left to historians. Since scientific reason was believed to be adequately encapsulated within a priori and abstract logical imperatives, case studies could be considered philosophically irrelevant. The abandonment of the geometric ideal, however, has mandated attention to historical cases for good philosophic reasons. The pragmatic turn in contemporary philosophy of science no longer allows abstract logic to dictate what scientists "must be" doing, but rather recognizes that we must look empirically at what scientific reason does to know what it is.[17] An explication of logic can proceed with cavalier disregard of the imperfect real world. But a critique of judgment must have something to critique.

Most contemporary philosophers of science take it for granted that science is rational in its procedures and progressive in its results. They recognize at the same time that the logical empiricism of the received view cannot adequately explain these admirable scientific qualities. They therefore are looking attentively at scientific practice in order to provide some new and more adequate answers to the questions: how and in what way is science progressive; and what are the warrants and procedures that make science rational? To answer these questions, the most important task is to understand what goes on in the multiple skilled judgments that go into successful scientific inquiry. Among these judgments that scientists make and that philosophers of science must understand are the judgments essential to interpreting observational data to make them into genuine scientific perceptions, seeing a problem, selecting heuristically important problems for exploration, identifying anomalies and distinguishing them from trivial counterinstances that can eventually be explained within the parameters of existing theory, assessing research programs, balancing the claims of the multiple warrants for accrediting theories, and assessing what is to count as legitimately scientific. This concern with good scientific judgment, moreover, cannot be set aside on the traditionally invoked grounds that such judgments may play a role in discovery but not in justification. Justifications have the advantage of hindsight, but they depend upon the same kinds of perceptual, conceptual, and strategic judgments that discovery requires.

By their recognition of the autonomy of scientific rationality, contemporary philosophers of science have rescued "ology"—the rational *methodos* of organized inquiry—from the hegemony of *logismos*. The rationality evident in the disciplined and immensely productive cognitive practices of science cannot be reduced to logical operations. The scientist as rational actor cannot adequately be depicted as combining the passive reception of impressions with a similarly passive acquiescence in the conclusions of logical deduction. Rather than working like a well-programmed computer, the scientist works more like a judge—weighing and assessing ambiguous and sometimes conflicting evidence, evolving standards and criteria to handle his or her problems, and deciding what constitutes the right thing to do in light of the goals and constraints of the enterprise.

Considered in the context of the long-standing philosophical debate about the relationship and relative merits of *theoria* and *praxis*, this reorientation in the philosophy of science carries with it some important and potentially radical implications. From Aristotle's depiction of the scientist as contemplative, through the seventeenth century's radicalization of the elevation of theory over practice, right up to the deductivism of the received view of science, the power of science has been attributed in part to its approximation to the contemplative ideal of *theoria*. The rationality of *praxis*, in alleged contrast to the presumed precision and passive "objectivity" of scientific theoretical rationality, was deemed at best second-rate and at worst wholly spurious.

In light of our revised understanding of scientific rationality, this long-standing systematic bias against the imperfection of practical reason seems wholly unwarranted. Indeed, the very coherence and relevance of the idealized image of the *bios theoretikos* seems questionable. Even our most precise and most successful cognitive enterprises incorporate and rely upon the problem-solving judgments traditionally definitive of practical reason. These features of rationality may be minimized or rendered tacit in the most abstract and mathematicized sciences, but they cannot even there be eliminated altogether.

This reorientation in our conception of scientific rationality provides both an impetus and a substantive basis for reevaluating our understanding of rational practice and the political implications that might be drawn from that understanding. Before confronting those issues directly, however, it will be useful to note some of the analogous developments in our understanding of the third of our exemplars of rationality—namely, the rationality of "the word" (*logos*).

Human Language: From Logical Syntax to Speech Acts

The direction of the philosophy of language in the past several decades has paralleled in significant respects that of the philosophy of science. The parallels are not adventitious. In fact, the developments in the two fields do not merely run in a similar direction along separate tracks; they have instead overlapped and fed upon each other at crucial junctures. The conception of scientific theory as a logical calculus was sustained by the same premises that informed the modern quest for a perfect language. And the pivotal figure in recent philosophy of language— Ludwig Wittgenstein—has also served as a major reference point for several of the leading revisionist philosophers of science.

As Hobbes noted in his chapter of Leviathan entitled "On Speech," "The Greeks have but one word, *logos*, for both speech and reason."[18] The question in the philosophy of language that is directly relevant to this study concerns the interrelationships within this family of concepts alluded to by Hobbes: what is the nature of the relationship between speech and reason implied by the identity of the Greek name for each? Specifically, is it logic that constitutes the commonality? Is speech "rational" because it can be logical—and only because and to the extent it is logical? Or is the rationality of human speech more than mere logic? And if its embodiment of rationality is more than its logicality, what is the nature of this "more"?

There were conflicting currents and ambiguities in classical philosophy regarding these questions. On the one hand, Plato and Aristotle both seemed attracted to the idea that language achieved its rational potency at least partly from its capacity to embody and trade upon the structure of logic and mathematics. On the other hand, Plato recognized that the power of dialectic—approachable only through mathematics—was neither identical with nor reducible to mathematical reasoning. Similarly, it seemed clear to Aristotle that attaining good definitions of words—the building blocks of language—required intellectual procedures that were fundamentally different from mathematical or logical ones. The definitional process outlined in the *Posterior Analytics*, for example, was more akin to the perceptual consolidation of *gestalten* than to mathematical axiomatization. Any philosophy of essences and substantial forms could never fully assimilate language to logic.

The axis of the seventeenth century's revolt against classical philosophy, however, was the rejection of substantialism. As the intellectual revolutionaries of that period saw it, it was precisely the bondage of the tradition to verbal essentialism that accounted for its confusions and impotencies. The philosophical and scientific failures of Scholasticism, according to its critics, stemmed from its systematic abuse of language. And one of the major abuses was the proliferation and reliance upon terms referring to entities and quiddities, faculties and properties. "Vain philosophy" involved "insignificant speech" and "empty words." Philosophical advance would thus come by way of linguistic purification.

This purification was to proceed in two ways. First, the terms whose emptiness had been smoked out by the assault upon essentialist illusions would be banished from philosophical discourse. Second, once this terminological purgation had taken place, the meaningful speech that remained would be clarified by a careful analysis that linked each term with an unambiguous objective referent. These accomplishments would have the therapeutic consequence of disempowering metaphysical charlatans; and they would simultaneously open up the prospect of developing an ideal language freed from all obscurity. Descartes speculated, for example, that a successful analysis of the simple ideas that lay behind language would permit the construction of "a universal language very easy to learn, speak, and to write," a language that would "represent matters so clearly that it would be impossible to go wrong."[19]

This philosophical quest for a logically perfect language received new impetus and inspiration in the early years of the twentieth century from achievements in the field of formal logic, especially those of Frege, Russell, and Whitehead. In their *Principia Mathematica*, Russell and Whitehead had constructed a system of logic that was more powerful and extensive than any that had preceded their efforts. The basic goal of the work was to clarify, unify, and simplify mathematical logic by deriving all of mathematics from a very small number of purely logical axioms. When this accomplishment was placed into a larger philosophical context, it seemed to Russell to offer the promise of achieving what his Enlightenment precursors had only hoped for. Namely, it seemed to Russell that what the *Principia* offered was the skeleton of Descartes's "universal language." Writing of the *Principia*, Russell said: "It is a language that has only syntax and no vocabulary whatsoever. . . . It aims at being that sort of language that, if you add a vocabulary, would be a logically perfect language."[20] Because Russell's philosophical atomism seemed, like the corpuscularism of his predecessors, to suggest that relating linguistic primitives to the simples of the world would be unproblematic, at least in principle, the attainment of a philosophically ideal language with empirical content seemed a possibility.

At work here were three related fundamental notions: a conception of language, a philosophical program, and a latent metaphysic. The model of language basic to the whole project essentially equated language and logic, the only difference being that a language needed at some point to connect with the world whereas a logic could remain self-contained. Despite this difference—despite the fact, that is, that a language possessed semantic reference whereas a logic need only be syntax—the structure of each was considered the same. A "good" language, one devoid of insignificant terms or faulty inferences, was conceived as a logical system of truth-functions based upon atomic propositions that were the equivalent of logical primitives. A language, in short, was seen as a logical calculus, even if its logical structure might often be concealed and sometimes distorted by the imperfections and conventions of real-world speech.

The philosophical program generated by this conception of language was a refined version of Hobbes's "resolution" and Descartes's "analysis," now given a linguistic focus. It centered around the clarification of grammar by means of reductive analysis. The assumption was that most philosophical conundrums grew out of systematically misleading linguistic conventions. These conventions became misleading because they obscured or distorted the true logical form of the propositions they sought to express. The task of the philosopher, then, was to dissipate this linguistically induced confusion by revealing the proper logical form of problematic assertions. This linguistic analysis was "reductive" in its operations, in the sense that it achieved its goals by reducing the misleading complex propositions to their simple—and therefore clear—constituents.

The metaphysic that sustained this view of language and this philosophical program was monistic and corpuscular. Oftentimes, this underlying metaphysic was simply assumed rather than displayed. It appeared in view, in a rather desultory fashion, whenever the adherents of reductive analysis attempted to characterize the content of the linguistic simples. Russell's explications of logical atomism, for example, also reflected these metaphysical presuppositions, when he spoke about the "ultimate simples out of which the world is built . . . [that] have a kind of reality not belonging to anything else."[21] At bottom, as J. O. Urmson has rightly observed, what was at work here was the traditional empiricist metaphysic that assumed the world to be a concatenation of ontologically discrete bits and pieces of material things.[22] Even later, when logical atomism was superceded by logical positivism, with its disclaimer concerning all metaphysical commitments, this empiricist metaphysic remained influential.

Russell not only coauthored the logical treatise that served as an inspiration to the whole development of the logical empiricist program; he also produced what was taken to be a paradigmatic example of the reductive analysis he and his followers expected to be so philosophically potent. Philosophers had puzzled over the nature of nonexistent entities that occasionally appeared in otherwise meaningful propositions, such as "The king of France is bald." What is the referent of this sentence's subject? We seem neither to be able to say that it exists nor to say that it is nothing: it does not exist because France has no king, but the sentence must refer to something. What Russell demonstrated was that the apparent dilemma could be evaded by translating the problematic sentences into others that were syntactically more cumbersome but logically more simple and precise. Pleased and impressed by this success in resolving a nagging philosophical perplexity, adherents of the analytical program anticipated that the same method of logical reduction would resolve other long-standing philosophical issues in the same manner.

The classic exposition of the conception of language associated with this program was provided by a sometime student of Russell's, namely Wittgenstein, in his *Tractatus Logico-Philosophicus*. The basic supposition of this highly influential, aphoristic little treatise was that, to borrow Russell's introductory characterization, "The essential business of language is to assert or deny facts."[23] Language, in short, is representational. And its constituent parts are functionally akin to proper names, correlated on a one-to-one basis with the particular facts that compose the world. Language is thus a "picture" of reality. Wittgenstein's theory of language is, in its fundamentals, then, pretty much the same as Augustine's. What he adds is the empiricist addendum that "objects are simple,"[24] and he assimilates these simples to logical primitives. Thus the "logical space" of an ideal language would replicate the factual space of the world. If all atomic facts were known and named, consequently, molecular or complex facts could be logically inferred from them. Thus language is, ideally, tantamount to a truth-functional calculus that mirrors the world.

Although Wittgenstein did not concur with Russell in all respects, his theory of language went hand in hand with Russell's attempt to conceive his *Principia* as the skeleton of a perfect language and with Russell's account of the analytical task of philosophy. Natural science produces true propositions, and "philosophy is not one of the natural sciences." The role of philosophy is not to assert but to elucidate. "Most of the propositions and questions of philosophers arise from our failure to understand the logic of our language." And philosophy should remedy these failures by "the logical clarification of thoughts." Since language is properly logical, philosophy should elucidate it by displaying its logical form. "All philosophy is," then, "a critique of language" in the same sense that Russell had critiqued our language by "showing that the apparent logical form of a proposition need not be its real one."[25]

This was in 1921. Despite the usual disagreements among philosophers in the ensuing decade, these related notions that language is a representational truth-functional calculus and that linguistic clarification via logical reduction should be the main business of philosophy dominated the analytic movement in Great Britain and logical empiricism on the Continent. Shortly before the onset of World War II, however, doubts about these conceptions surfaced within a number of influential articles authored by leading participants in the analytic tradition. And by 1950, when academic philosophy resumed following the interregnum of the war years, it is safe to say that the nature of the analytic enterprise and the associated conception of language had both been transformed quite markedly. Philosophers still sought to resolve conceptual confusion through linguistic analysis, but "analysis" no longer referred exclusively to logical reduction; and language was recognized to be more complex and varied than the model of a pictorial calculus allowed. What had happened, and why?

The problems that led to this transformation were already presaged in the *Tractatus*. Even as he articulated in a sharp and dogmatic form the view of meaningful language as limited to descriptive assertions, Wittgenstein realized that his statements of this doctrine were paradoxical and anomalous. That is, Wittgenstein's propositions about language were themselves neither tautologous nor empirical, although they asserted that only tautologies or empirical propositions were meaningful speech. The contents of the *Tractatus*, then, were left in the same kind of uncomfortable position as the claim "all generalizations are false"; just as this proposition contradicts itself, the claims of the *Tractatus* rendered themselves meaningless. Apparently more self-aware than

Hume, whose famous similar assertion consigning to the flames all statements that were not mathematical propositions or factual assertions placed him in the same situation, Wittgenstein had at least faced up to his problem. In the concluding paragraphs of the *Tractatus,* Wittgenstein acknowledged that "anyone who understands me eventually recognizes [my propositions] as nonsensical, when he has used them—as steps—to climb up beyond them. He must, so to speak, throw away the ladder after he has climbed up it."[26] Even as he enthusiastically forwarded Wittgenstein's ideas for consideration, then, Russell confessed to having "a certain sense of intellectual discomfort" arising from "the fact that, after all, Mr. Wittgenstein manages to say a good deal about what cannot be said."[27]

Immediately following this remark, as he groped about for an escape from this paradox, Russell made an offhand suggestion that turned out to be prescient. "Possibly," he wrote, "there may be some loophole through a hierarchy of languages, or by some other exit."[28] During the 1930s, in any case, some of the most thoughtful analytic philosophers began to move in this general direction—not toward establishing a hierarchy of languages necessarily, but at least toward a recognition of a variety of types of legitimate speech. And they did so, in part, precisely by reflecting upon the nature and role of the verification principle—a principle that had to be embodied in propositions sharing the paradoxical status of Wittgenstein's pronouncements about meaningful speech.

In a notable article written in 1938, for example, C. L. Stevenson pondered the meaning of the corollary of the verification principle: "metaphysics is without meaning."[29] This dictum, he concluded, constituted what he termed a "persuasive definition." The point of such definitions, Stevenson argued, is "emotive" and prescriptive: they seek to mandate acceptable linguistic practice, and in so doing they carry emotive force. Such persuasive definitions, however, continued Stevenson, are by no means entirely arbitrary or groundless. Instead, they allude to and rely upon certain similarities or differences in the "objective" world, to which they refer. Thus, wrote Stevenson, the statement that "metaphysics is without meaning" is like the statement of nineteenth-century critics that "Pope is not a poet." Both statements refer to real-world distinctions—in the former case to distinctions between scientific and metaphysical assertions, and in the latter case to distinctions between Pope's verses and those of a Shakespeare or a Milton; and both statements make recommendations for the understanding and deployment of a term—in the former case "meaning," and in the latter case, "poet"—based upon the recognition of the differences alluded to. Not only was Stevenson's argument illuminating *vis à vis* the verifiability principle, but it was also pregnant with important implications for the understanding of language and for the understanding and conduct of philosophical analysis. Concerning language, Stevenson's argument—in parallel with the similar argument of John Wisdom's "Metaphysics and Verification"[30]—implied that the point of an assertion involves its function and not merely its reference; and it likewise implied that there might be a plurality of meaningful speech types corresponding to the variety of functions that different assertions perform. Accepting these implications, in short, required that philosophers develop a more complex and more tolerant conception of language than the one with which they had been working.

Concerning the nature of philosophical analysis, what was interesting was not so much what Stevenson said as what he did. That is, he had himself "analyzed" the meaning of a perplexing and potentially misleading statement, and he had done so in a most illuminating way. His analysis, however, had not involved a reduction of the problematic utterance to hidden and simple constituent logical components. Instead, Stevenson's analytical method clarified the meaning of certain propositions by pointing to their function. He had not looked for the *parts* of the problematic claim, but had looked for its *use*. And in so doing, he had—in line with John Wisdom's argument in "Philosophical Perplexity," which appeared at about the same time[31]—not so much solved a problem as dissolved the problem; he had, that is, not provided an acceptable answer to a valid question, but he had instead demonstrated how and why the question (i.e., "is metaphysics meaningful?") led to confusion by its misleading linguistic assimilation of several different issues.

Stevenson's achievement and Wisdom's suggestion were especially significant because the program of reductive analysis was stagnating. The expectations that more and more philosophical puzzles would be resolved by the same process of logical reduction Russell had directed at "The king of France is bald" had not been fulfilled. Philosophers were forced to realize, then, that Russell's achievement had not been to take a decisive step toward the discovery of the fundamental elements of a single truth-functional linguistic calculus. Instead, he had escaped an apparent philosophical dilemma by recognizing a systematically misleading linguistic usage. In his particular case, the misuse involved a logical confusion; but all potentially confusing misuses of language were not so narrowly and exclusively logical. What was generalizable about Russell's analytical method, in short, was its genus rather than its species: Russell's logical clarification of language was only one form of avoiding linguistically induced puzzles by recalling language to its proper functions. And while Russell's belief that he had his hands on a metaphysically potent weapon for the reduction of language to its logical constituents was compatible with—and seemed a warrant for—the conception of language as a truth-functional calculus, the broader conception of philosophical analysis was not so compatible. Indeed, the new understanding of analysis seemed clearly to imply that language must involve a multiplicity of forms and functions.

These themes and reorientations were consolidated and given a highly influential, albeit not very systematic, expression in Wittgenstein's *Philosophical Investigations*. In this work, published shortly after World War II, Wittgenstein was involved in cajoling and teasing himself out of his earlier bewitchment by the abstract and idealized conception of language as a calculus. It is exceptionally instructive, in fact, to do what Wittgenstein suggested in his preface—namely, to juxtapose the *Investigations* with the *Tractatus*, because the ideas of the later work can "be seen in the right light only by contrast with and against the background of my old way of thinking."[32]

The stark contrast between the two books is immediately apparent in their radically different form as well as in their substance. The *Tractatus* is composed of flat and terse declarative aphorisms, piled one on top of another: "The world is all that is the case"; "What is the case—a fact—is the existence of states of affairs"; etc. This style reflected the combined influence of Wittgenstein's certitude ("The truth of the thoughts that are here set forth seems to me unassailable and definitive. I therefore believe myself to have found, on all essential points, the final solution of the problems"), his thesis that "what can be said at all can be said clearly,"[33] and his metaphysical and linguistic corpuscularism, which construed both language and reality to be composed of discrete atomic propositions and objects. (It is a style ably mimicked by a student who wrote on the title page of a library copy of the *Tractatus*: "For weeks, this book and its author were my life. Now I am finished. I want to watch Batman.")

The style of *Philosophical Investigations* is quite different. There are still aphoristic declarations in this later work, to be sure, but they are mixed in with a panoply of queries, puzzles, analogies, and thought-experiments. Just as one of Wittgenstein's colleagues had prompted his doubts about his earlier conception of language as a pictorial calculus by making an irreverent gesture, and asking "What is the logical form of that?" Wittgenstein raises in his *Philosophical Investigations* a whole host of problems and puzzles designed to disconcert those who share what he now sees as his previous confusion. As if he were baiting his former self, for instance, Wittgenstein demands: "Think of exclamations alone, with their completely different functions. Water! Away! Ow! Help! Fine! No! Are you inclined still to call these words 'names of objects'?"[34]

The conception of language that emerges from the pages of *Philosophical Investigations* represents a clear departure from the Augustinian and positivist conceptions of language as logically linked names of objects. Several specific contrasts on key issues stand out as manifesting the significant shift that has taken place. In the first place, Wittgenstein abandons a central contention of the *Tractatus* to the effect that "the general form of propositions is: This is how things are." Reflecting on his previous commitment to that idea, Wittgenstein concludes that he had been captive to his preconceptions rather than looking accurately at language: "That is the kind of proposition that one repeats to oneself countless times. One thinks that one is tracing the outline of the thing's nature over and over again, and one is merely tracing round the frame through which we look at it."[35] No longer captive to the illusion that "picturing" is the sole function of language, Wittgenstein instead now not only recognizes but insists upon the irreducible multiplicity of linguistic functions. Language does not merely picture; it performs. And it performs in many ways. "But how many kinds of sentences are there?" Wittgenstein asks. "There are *countless* kinds: countless different kinds of use of what we call 'symbols,' 'words,' 'sentences.' And this multiplicity is not something fixed, given once for all; but new types of language, new language-games, as we may say, come into existence, and others become obsolete and get forgotten." "The term 'language-game'," Wittgenstein continues, "is meant to bring into prominence the fact that the *speaking* of language is part of an activity, or of a form of life." And, after reviewing examples of multiple language-games, Wittgenstein remarks again upon his earlier folly: "It is interesting to compare the multiplicity of the tools in language and of the ways they are used, the multiplicity of kinds of word and sentence, with what logicians have said about the structure of language. (Including the author of the *Tractatus Logico-Philosophicus*.)"[36]

Correlatively, Wittgenstein now insists that words are not simply names whose meanings are determined by the objects to which they refer. The process of ostensive definition is not so unproblematic as the pictorial conception of language assumed. Instead, it is systematically ambiguous. One cannot adequately define any term simply by pointing at something. For the listener must somehow "catch on to" what aspect of the phenomenon pointed at is being indicated. Even in the simplest instance, for example, one might think that "red" meant fruit or edibles if someone pointed to an apple and said: "This is red." As Wittgenstein puts it, then, "An ostensive definition can be variously interpreted in *every* case."[37]

Although simple cases of confusion arising from the systematic ambiguity of ostensive definition might be fairly easily resolved, the difficulties multiply in more complex cases. Consider, for instance, pointing to a piece of ultracontemporary furniture and saying "this is a table," pointing to a playing card and saying "this is a trump," or pointing to a piece of rumpled green paper and saying "this is money." In each case, the word being defined has a meaning that is context relative. The context is a framework of human activities and purposes. And the listener can apprehend the word's meaning only if he already grasps the context—only if, in other words, he can already understand the language-game within which the word functions. "So one might say," concludes Wittgenstein, that "the ostensive definition explains the use—the meaning—of the word when the overall role of the word in language is clear. . . . One has already to know (or to be able to do) something in order to be capable of asking a thing's name."[38]

Language is not a calculus; "language is an instrument."[39] The words within languages and the concepts they embody are likewise instruments or tools. They do not passively register or represent static things. Instead, they designate functions and in doing so are themselves functional. Especially striking in their functionality are what later came to be called "performative" utterances, such as "I promise." But all words do things in the context of "language-games" that arise within "forms of life." Their meanings thus are, in the now well-worn phrase, their use.

It is therefore misleading to imagine that all language is somehow an imperfect approximation of an ideal language that would simply represent reality without ambiguity or obscurity. "If you say that our languages only approximate to [calculi which have fixed rules] you are on the brink of a misunderstanding. For then it may look as if what we were talking about were an ideal language. As if our logic were, so to speak, a logic for a vacuum." And later, "our clear and simple language-games are not preparatory studies for a future regularization of language—as it were first approximations, ignoring friction and air resistance."[40]

Philosophical analysis, therefore, cannot accurately or properly be construed as the reduction of "complex" and hence confusing real-world languages to a language of logically linked "simples." Philosophical analysis does indeed try to remedy linguistically induced confusion. "Philosophy is a battle against the bewitchment of our intelligence by means of language." It attempts to eliminate as far as possible "bumps that the understanding has got by running its head up against the limits of language."[41] But this therapeutic process cannot consist solely or even predominantly of "resolution." It all depends on wherein the confusion lies in language; and it is a great mistake to suppose that the confusion generally arises from "unanalyzed" "complex" terms. Imagine, says Wittgenstein, two language-games, (a) and (b). In game (a) composite objects (brooms, chairs, tables, etc.) have names, and in game (b) only the parts are given names. "To say that a sentence in (b) is an 'analyzed' form of one in (a) readily seduces us into thinking that the former is the more fundamental form; that it alone shows what is meant by the other, and so on. For example, we think: If you have only the unanalyzed form you miss the analysis; but if you know the analyzed form that gives you everything. But can I not say that an aspect of the matter is lost on you in the *latter* case as well as the former?"[42] For example, "Suppose that, instead of saying 'Bring me the broom;' you said 'Bring me the broomstick and the brush that is fitted on it!'—Isn't the answer: 'Do you want the broom? Why do you put it so oddly?' "[43]

In some cases, to be sure, philosophical analysis may remedy linguistically induced confusion by reducing misleading complex propositions to their logically more simple components, as Russell did in the paradigmatic instance cited earlier. But this logically reductive analytical process is not properly generalizable as the essence of what linguistic analysis is all about. It is merely one example—appropriate in a small set of particular cases—of the wider method of resolving "grammatical" confusion by recalling language to its proper usage within the form of life that generated it in the first place. We are recurrently tempted to make words function out of context and thereby lead ourselves astray into a thicket of tangled concepts. As Wittgenstein put it, "philosophical problems arise when language goes on a holiday" or "when language is like an engine idling."[44] The proper therapeutic tack in each case is to direct the grammatically ensnared sufferer to "look at the use" of his terms, to recognize their appropriate function, and to restore them to the setting of the language-games from which they arose in the first place.

It was never part of Wittgenstein's intent to provide a "theory of language" in any explicit or systematic sense of that phrase. Instead, he was quite content to pursue more modest goals in the service of resolving problems that seemed immediately pressing to him. Specifically, he sought to dispel his own bewitchment by the misleading mirage of a single, perfect, purely descriptive linguistic calculus. He wanted to impress upon us that language instead is a complex of multiple and various language-games that develop out of a variety of human activities. And he sought to redefine philosophical analysis in light of this revised outlook upon language.

It seems reasonably clear, nevertheless, that the reorientation of philosophical analysis in which his work—along with that of precursors such as Stevenson and Wisdom and successors such as J. L. Austin and John Searle—played such an important role rests upon assumptions about human speech and language that depart from the parallel assumptions that informed the conceptions of philosophy and linguistic analysis it displaced.

The essence of the shift in orientation and assumptions that has taken place is manifested in the titles of leading books in the different periods. In 1934 Carnap focused upon *The Logical Syntax of Language*. Three decades later, J. L. Austin focused upon *How To Do Things with Words* (1962) and John Searle focused his inquiry into the nature of language upon *Speech Acts* (1969). The earlier orientation presumed that a language was a logical calculus, almost always imperfectly incarnated in actual practice, whose function was to mirror a world of objects. The key to capturing the essence of language and to perfecting its deployment, therefore, lay in the clarification of syntax. Once the syntax of language was freed from needless obscurity and logical confusion, it was assumed, problems of semantics would largely disappear—because linguistic "referring" was conceived as equivalent to primitive and unproblematic pointing at things. The pragmatics of language use were not seen as logically relevant to an understanding of language per se. They were of interest to sociologists rather than to philosophers of language, except insofar as they were a potent source of linguistic confusions.

Today that orientation has been virtually turned upside down. The internal logic of a language system is still deemed important to understand, but it is safe to say that no one any longer assumes that such a logical explication will clarify the nature of language or guarantee its felicitous deployment. Language is conceived not as a self-contained logical system that one can unproblematically append to things or insert into practice like a technical mechanism. Instead, it is seen as a set of conventional rule-governed symbolic practices that serve as the vehicle of human communicative action. To understand it, we must attend not simply to syntax but to semantics, and the latter is recognized to be complex and problematic: linguistic "meaning," we might say, is now understood as a gerund rather than as a property. Words do not possess meanings like ships have barnacles. Rather, people mean things—i.e., communicate information of various kinds—by deploying words as symbolic instruments. It follows, moreover, that we cannot understand linguistic meanings without paying careful attention to linguistic pragmatics—i.e., by looking at the language-games in which words play roles. One cannot grasp the meaning of any linguistic expression without understanding the network of intentions and purposes that inform it.

Thus the patterns of activity that generate language now are front and center in linguistic analysis and the philosophy of language. In the words of John Searle, "the unit of linguistic communication is not, as has generally been supposed, the symbol, word or sentence, but rather the production or issuance of the symbol or word or sentence in the performance of the speech act." It follows, then, that "a study of the meaning of sentences is not in principle distinct from a study of speech acts. Properly construed, they are the same study."[45] The pragmatic dimension of language that was earlier deemed devoid of philosophic interest now becomes crucial. The philosopher of language cannot consign the exploration of the ways language is used to other disciplines, such as sociology and anthropology. Instead, it would hardly be overstating the case to say that the philosopher of language must, of logical necessity and not from idiosyncratic curiosity, be something of a sociologist or anthropologist. He or she must, in order to understand his or her subject matter, understand the forms of life it expresses.

Conclusion

The course of the philosophy of language over the past several decades thus mimics the course of the philosophy of science during the same period. Before, the life of both science and language was believed to be logic; today, the life of both is seen as experience. Before, the center of attention was syntax; today, the focus tends to be on pragmatics. Before, the crucial intellectual feat presumed to be involved in both language and science was inference; today, it is judgment. Before, the goal was to obtain an abstract snapshot of the finished products of science and language. Today, the goal is to provide a concrete moving picture of the evolution of scientific programs and language-games.

As interesting as these developments have been, our account of them has not been intended as an exercise in intellectual history. Our survey has been far too cursory to contribute much along these lines; and in any case, our central concern lies elsewhere. The relevance of these sketches should become clear, however, when they are placed into the context of our original observation that logic, science ("ologies"), and language (*logos* as "word") provide us with the fundamental reference points for our conception of rationality. If that is the case, then it follows *prima facie* that significant parallel changes in our conception of scientific inquiry and linguistic communication—such as those we have reviewed here—not only invite us but require us to reflect upon the implications of these changes for our understanding of human reason.

Chapter Three **Post-Positivist Praxis: The Constitution of Rational Enterprises**

What is common to recent developments in the philosophy of science and the philosophy of language is a shifting, or at least a broadening, of analytical attention from syntax to semantics and from semantics to pragmatics. That is, whereas priority had previously been given to matters of the internal logic of languages or scientific theories, some attention to problems of "reference," and little or no attention to the forms of life from which these arose, the balance of concern has now shifted. More attention is now given to what are recognized as more complex problems of meaning; and it has become more and more widely recognized that a sophisticated understanding of meaning in theory and language cannot be divorced from the practical intentions that produce them.

The pivotal question *vis à vis* my central contention that recent developments in our understanding of science and language should lead to a parallel change in our understanding of what human reason is all about, therefore, becomes this: are there identifiable patterns in the pragmatics of science and language that seem essential to the successful conduct of these enterprises? And if so, what are they?

Posing these questions amounts to conducting within the context of post-positivist conceptions of language and of science a quasi-Kantian form of inquiry with a quasi-Hegelian intent. That is, we need to perform a "transcendental deduction"—although one not encumbered by Kant's specific metaphysical assumptions—on our revised conceptions of language and science, with the hope of discovering the shape of "reason in history"—although again not in a manner predetermined by Hegel's specific metaphysical assumptions.

In this chapter, then, I want to argue that such an investigation can in fact discern a physiology of rational practice within the successful conduct of scientific inquiry and linguistic communication; that the basic patterns are similar in each case; and that this physiology of successful scientific and linguistic practice is a manifestation of the intrinsic "politics" of practical reason. This post-positivist conception of practical reason, in turn, will serve as a reference point for the central questions of the chapters that follow: what is the nature and the possible extent of reason in politics? and what implications follow for our understanding of legitimate and felicitous democratic governance?

The Scientific Enterprise and the Republic of Science

In his transcendental critique of human knowledge, Kant sought to answer the question: are there necessary conditions of possible knowledge, and if so, what are they? The proper way to answer that question, Kant assumed, was to take those intellectual achievements that seemed to him, and to others, to qualify as the paradigmatic cases of valid knowledge and to try to identify reflectively the underlying conditions that make this knowledge possible. For Kant, this approach required that he look for the grounds of possibility of logic, mathematics, and Newtonian natural science. And his conclusion was that this knowledge was made possible only by the functioning of synthetic a priori categories of understanding organized and deployed by the activity of a transcendental unity of apperception.

The answer Kant gave to the problem he posed, we can appreciate in hindsight, was heavily structured and ultimately vitiated by the constraints of his own metaphysical assumptions and by the limitations of the science of his own day. Kant was both a Cartesian dualist and a Newtonian mechanist. His substantive epistemology, therefore, was predicated on the model of an ahistorical, individual mind cognizing equally ahistorical mechanistic phenomena. For us in the twentieth century, living as we do in a temporalized universe and seeing scientific knowledge as evolving rather than fixed, Kant's solution no longer can seem fully convincing.

Nonetheless, the question Kant posed and the way he approached it remain determinative, I would argue, for anyone seeking to understand and define human reason. Unless we are to be content with a purely stipulative and dogmatic conception of human reason, we have no choice except to proceed as Kant did. That is, we must first identify the best instances of what we are willing to accredit as valid knowledge; and then we must try to identify the necessary conditions of these successful feats of cognition.

The notion of "necessary conditions," however, is somewhat ambiguous. There are many different types of "conditions" that govern cognitive activity, and one looking for the necessary conditions of successful knowing might look in a corresponding number of different directions. In Kant's own case, "necessary conditions" tended to be construed as "indispensable fundamental concepts." Thus his inquiry turned into a quest for the most basic concepts without which Newtonian theories of nature would be impossible.

Our own inquiry into the necessary conditions of knowledge must be oriented somewhat differently. Recognizing as we now do that the definitive basis of scientific knowledge cannot be a fixed set of substantive concepts—since all the concepts informing scientific theory may be subject to change as that science evolves—we must look elsewhere. What seems more constant—and hence definitive of the rational enterprise of scientific inquiry—than the continuously evolving substantive concepts produced by the various scientific disciplines are the methods, procedures, and institutions characteristic of the enterprise. Our version of Kant's question, then, should be: are there procedural and institutional conditions apparently indispensable to successful scientific inquiry, and if so, what are they?

Remembering that the best contemporary attempts to understand scientific inquiry have found it necessary to shift from a narrow focus on scientific syntax (i.e., the logical structure of scientific theories) to a concern with pragmatics, we cannot construe "procedural" here in the narrow sense that so often has characterized homilies on "the scientific method." These attempts to specify the essence of scientific procedure in terms of Cartesian *regulae* have always been quite barren. Confined a priori to specifiable rules, these accounts can only consist of the clear but limited-in-utility rules of logical inference together with broad but vague methodological admonitions such as "look for all available evidence." Nor should the necessary procedural conditions in question be construed to refer to specific experimental techniques, because these also are contingent intellectual tools that change with technological innovations and shifting problem areas—and hence are not universal defining features of scientific rationality itself.

To find the "necessary conditions" of successful scientific practice, we have to look not at a specific repertoire of substantive concepts nor at formal rules of logical inference nor at specific experimental techniques. However heretical such a suggestion might be to the philosophic tradition that has identified science with *theoria*, we are best advised to take the pragmatic turn in the philosophy of science with utter seriousness and to look instead at the politics and sociology of the scientific enterprise.

Like all social enterprises, the conduct of scientific inquiry is governed by a network of organizing and regulating conventions and institutions. These conventions and institutions, in turn, are informed and sustained by a corresponding set of mores, values, and beliefs. These institutions and sustaining mores are not, evidence would suggest, peripheral to scientific practice. Instead, they are essentially constitutive of the successful pursuit of scientific knowledge. It is no mere accident that wherever and whenever these institutions atrophy or these mores wither, the scientific enterprise is seriously damaged—even threatened with extinction.

Even in our society, heavily scientific in orientation, we are often insufficiently cognizant of these "social bases" of scientific practice. There are two principal reasons for our inattention to this important phenomenon, one of them psychological and the other doctrinal. The psychological factor at work is the same one that led to Burke's comment that a widespread preoccupation with political theory was generally a sign of a troubled society. Conversely, successful practice diverts attention from a concern with first principles: why examine underlying presuppositions of an enterprise that is functioning superlatively? The doctrinal source of our relative inattention to the constitutive pragmatics of science is the ironically dogmatic and unempirical approach to epistemology of our dominant empiricist philosophy. Rather than basing its account of human knowing upon careful empirical examination of successful learning, empiricism offers an account generated theoretically from its basic metaphysical suppositions. Because these suppositions are atemporal and Democritean, this empiricist account proceeds in terms of ahistorical and value-free individual minds passively receiving the impress of brute facts. However implausible this account may be—as Hume unwittingly demonstrated—it has systematically diverted attention from the activities of communally organized intellects that constitute real-world scientific inquiry.

In times of crisis, however, when the conventional institutions or tacitly operative mores of science come under direct attack, we are forced to recognize and defend that which we usually simply take for granted. Two of the best accounts we have, therefore, appeared as responses to the Nazi and Soviet attempts to transform the pragmatics of scientific practice in accordance with their ideological precepts and in the service of their political goals. One of these was provided by Robert Merton and the other by Michael Polanyi. The convergence of their accounts is especially noteworthy, since Merton was an American sociologist who was generally positivistic in his understanding of scientific knowledge and Polanyi was a Hungarian expatriate scientist-turned-philosopher who was antipositivistic in his philosophy of science.

Faced with the Nazi condemnation of "Jewish physics" and the Soviet proscription of "bourgeois genetics" and observing the tensions and irrationalities induced by the attempt of both totalitarian regimes to subvert the norms and governance of science, Merton focused on what he termed the "ethos of science," but he also identified some of the procedural correlates of these mores. Polanyi focused on the patterns of governance, but he also remarked upon the beliefs that informed these patterns. Their accounts complement each other and together provide a helpful topography of the constitution of rational enterprises.[1]

The central features of this "republic of science," to borrow Polanyi's phrase, could be said to be: an animating consensus, criteria of citizenship and attendant modes of participation, and criteria and procedures for decision making. The presence and interplay of all these elements are necessary for the successful conduct of scientific enterprises, and the distortion of any of them imposes its costs. If the violation of the standards and deviation from procedures is sufficiently great, the enterprise may by crippled or destroyed altogether. Political regimes that covet the fruit of scientific discovery but are for some reason unwilling to tolerate the constitutive norms and institutions of science find themselves in a dilemma. They cannot have it both ways. When they impose their external constraints or criteria on the practice of science, they wind up with scientific decay or with Lysenko-type quackery. Yet the acceptance and tacit validation of the scientific ethos may threaten their regime in other ways.

Successful scientific practice depends in the first place upon the presence and the general acceptance of a common actuating goal. This goal is the attainment of scientific truth—the quest to make contact with patterns of natural reality. The animating force of this goal depends logically, also, upon the general acceptance of the belief that "objective" reality exists and is capable of apprehension by the human mind. The scientific enterprise cannot flourish in cultures, for example, that consider nature to be a transient illusion or the product of imaginative fabrication or too sacred to investigate. Nor can it flourish in cultures that presume human cognitive powers to be radically defective or illegitimate.

The actuating force of a common purpose introduces into the politics of science an element of what Merton calls, in quotation marks, "communism." By "communism" Merton refers to several aspects of the scientific ethos and procedures. First, it refers to the "common heritage" upon which all scientists trade as a guide and resource for their own research. Second, it refers to the collaborative nature of the scientific enterprise—to "the essentially cooperative and cumulative quality of scientific achievement." Third, it refers to the way in which scientific discoveries "do not enter into the exclusive possession of the discoverer and his heirs," but instead are generally treated as a form of "common property." And finally, it refers to the mandate that one scientist communicate and share his data and ideas with his fellow scientists: "The institutional conception of science as part of the public domain is linked with the imperative for communication of findings. Secrecy is the antithesis of this norm; full and open communication its enactment."[2] Whenever particular scientific findings have military uses or commercial possibilities, the need or temptation to sequester or appropriate these findings creates serious tensions with the ethics and traditional practices of the scientific community.

The constitutive status of science's common purpose generates the first criterion for citizenship in the republic of science: recognition and acceptance of the common purpose. The scientific community is a sect rather than a church. Members of the community are consciously "dedicated," as Polanyi puts it, to its larger purposes. "The devotion of all scientists to the ideals of scientific work may be regarded as the General Will governing the society of scientists." It is not a variable or arbitrary will, however. "It is seen to differ from any other will by the fact that it cannot vary its own purpose."[3]

The "dedication" required of the individual scientist is not sainthood. It is commendable if the individual scientist has Kierkegaard's "purity of heart," willing only one thing, and that the advance of knowledge. But this total dedication would be a work of supererogatory virtue and not a requisite for membership. The individual scientist, Polanyi argues, "must feel under obligation to uphold the ideals of science and be guided by this obligation . . . otherwise science would die."[4] But he or she is not required to abjure all particular interests and purposes, even in the pursuit of the goals of science. Individual scientists may be, and often are, motivated by vanity or ambition. But that is acceptable, provided that these particular ambitions be subordinated functionally to the common goal of the enterprise.

Merton makes this point—which is of real importance *vis à vis* the applicability of norms of rational enterprises to the political realm—quite explicitly. His correlate to what Polyani terms "dedication" is "disinterestedness." "Science, as is the case with the professions in general," he writes, "includes disinterestedness as a basic institutional element." But this mandate of the scientific ethos should not be confused with selflessness: "Disinterestedness is not to be equated with altruism nor interested action with egoism. Such equivalences confuse institutional and motivational levels of analysis. A passion for knowledge, idle curiosity, altruistic concern with the benefit to humanity and a host of other special motives have been attributed to the scientist. *The quest for distinctive motives appears to have been misdirected. It is rather a distinctive pattern of institutional control of a wide range of motives which characterizes the behavior of scientists.*"[5]

Apart from this demand for disinterestedness or dedication, admission to the republic of science is open and nondiscriminatory. The logic of rational enterprises makes them the original "equal opportunity employer." As Merton puts it, "objectivity precludes particularism." Hence "universalism" is another tenet of the scientific ethos. And one of the corollaries of universalism is "the demand that careers be open to talents. The rationale is provided by the institutional goal. To restrict scientific careers on grounds other than lack of competence is to prejudice the furtherance of knowledge. Free access to scientific pursuits is a functional imperative."[6]

This nondiscriminatory openness of admission to the scientific enterprise mandated by universalism does not entail complete egalitarianism, however, as Merton's allusion to "competence" intimates. As Polanyi observes, "there are differences in rank between scientists"; and "there is a hierarchy of influence."[7] Not everyone contributes equally to the advance of the scientific enterprise, and it would be counterproductive for these differentials in ability and judgment not to be recognized. The resources of science would be squandered, and progress retarded, if the most competent and knowledgeable were not accorded strategic priority. In this respect, the scientific enterprise is a meritocracy. It is important to note, however, that stringent limitations are placed upon both the incidence and the functions of a scientific hierarchy. In the first place, it is only a "natural" elite that is acceptable—like the kind Thomas Jefferson deemed important for a democracy. Priority of place derived from favoritism may occur in scientific enterprises, because scientists are not immune to nepotistic impulses, but it is clearly illegitimate in principle and it is effectively discouraged by procedures of impersonal review. Next, any permissible elements of hierarchy in the scientific enterprise are contingent in the sense that differences in rank "are of secondary importance: everyone's position is sovereign."[8] And they are contingent in the sense that they depend entirely on the consent of the other citizens of the polis. A high-ranking scientist may exercise power only because he or she can exert influence—only because of "the fact that his or her opinion is valued and asked for."[9] It follows, also, that the hierarchy is characterized by mobility. Institutional inertia and rigidities—for example those attending to academic tenure—may impede this mobility to some extent. But it is clear that an individual scientist's rank and influence may wax and wane significantly over time.

Scientific universalism also involves the imposition of certain procedural restraints on scientific decision making. It imposes impartiality of adjudication. Particularistic or ascriptive attributes are in principle irrelevant to scientific decisions. As Merton writes: "The acceptance or rejection of claims entering the lists of science is not to depend on the personal or social attributes of their protagonist; his race, nationality, religion, class and personal qualities are as such irrelevant."[10] Hence the imposition of particularistic criteria is rigorously discouraged by a variety of procedural devices such as the demand that scientific findings be subject to independent and impersonal testing and replication or the practice of anonymous review of scholarly articles submitted for publication.

Besides the exclusion of particularism—and hence of political purposes that dictate particularism—other procedural rules are intrinsic to scientific enterprises. As Merton terms it, scientific inquiry requires "organized skepticism." Science does involve "accepted truths." But the very warrant for the acceptance entails recognition that the "truths" must always be potentially subject to challenge and test—to being hauled before the bar of reason. And that recognition requires the establishment of procedural norms, obligations, and restraints that make that kind of challenge and test possible.

Chief among these procedural norms, obligations, and restraints are those of publicity, fairness, and toleration. "Publicity" here means simply that the bar of reason is an open court. Its deliberations meet the Wilsonian criteria of open covenants, openly arrived at. It is always permissible for someone to demand that a given contention or previously accepted truth be subjected to public scrutiny. To be sure, someone making that demand may arouse little interest and may encounter difficulty in obtaining an adequate forum for a hearing—especially if he or she has little standing in the scientific community, if the "truth" challenged seems well validated by past testing, and/or if the challenger can offer little in the way of *prima facie* warrants for undertaking the investigation. Nevertheless, it is never acceptable to reject demands for testing out of hand or to insist that such tests be conducted in an exclusionary manner.

Scientific toleration thus requires, first, the protection and even encouragement of dissent. The protection of dissent does not, in scientific enterprises, constitute license for willful obstructionism or mindless revolt. It is expected that challenges to scientific conventional wisdom reflect some respect for the weight of scientific tradition—some grasp of the fact that the truths the revolutionary would challenge did not themselves appear on the scene arbitrarily but were instead themselves validated, even if tentatively, by the very testing procedures the revolutionary would now invoke. A rational challenge involves recognition that the truths under attack were themselves rationally generated. Subject to that legitimate condition, however, the scientific community must always accord protection to dissenters if it is not to stifle scientific originality and with it scientific progress. As Polanyi puts it, "The professional standards of science must impose a framework of discipline and at the same time encourage rebellion against it. They must demand that in order to be taken seriously, an investigation should largely conform to the currently predominant beliefs about the nature of things, while it must allow that in order to be original it might have to go to some extent against these. Thus the authority of scientific opinion enforces the teachings of science in general, for the very purpose of fostering their subversion in the particular."[11]

Scientific toleration also means the willingness to listen to the arguments of an opponent. The obligation to attend to the ideas of others in a rational enterprise arises out of what might be termed "rational humility"—the recognition of the contingency and fallibility of even the best knowledge of the day—and out of "rational hope"—the anticipation of future understanding of things yet unknown. Mill expressed this facet of the scientific ethos in one of his arguments for liberty of thought and discussion: "since the general or prevailing opinion on any subject is rarely or never the whole truth, it is only by the collision of adverse opinions that the remainder of the truth has any chance of being supplied."[12] This obligation is sometimes onerous. As Polanyi notes, "it is irritating to open our mind wide to a spate of specious argument on the off-chance of catching a grain of truth in it."[13] But it is an obligation incumbent upon citizens of the republic of science.

The procedural norm of "fairness," finally, does not in this context refer to some Rawlsian-type rules of allocation. Rather it refers to obligations of self-restraint in argumentation. It is incumbent on participants in a rational discussion to present their case as "objectively" as possible. This demand does not entail, as conventional scientistic mythology sometimes has it, the total elimination of all elements of personal perspective and human passion from knowledge claims: without the passion for truth we would have no science, and with no situatedness in a historically specific location we would have no base for our knowledge, no "where" from which to know. What fairness does require is the effort to identify, acknowledge, and quarantine any extraneous partisan emotions and biases that accompany and possibly motivate our view. These biases and interests may be important to us, but they do not validate and may distort the ideational content they permeate. As Polanyi writes: "To be objective we must sort out facts, opinions, and emotions and present them separately, in this order. . . . It is a painful discipline . . . but fairness requires this, and also that . . . the limitations of our knowledge and our natural bias be frankly acknowledged."[14]

The final distinctive and characteristic feature of the scientific polity that commands attention is its system of authority. The scientific community must organize itself not only to adjudicate between contending theories but also to allocate its resources. Decisions have to be made under conditions of moderate scarcity. The decisions need to be prudent, and they need to be legitimate. The manner in which the necessary "authoritative allocation of values" is made is essentially the same across the range of scientific disciplines; it is a system only marginally influenced by external political authorities; and it has been markedly successful in advancing the ends of the enterprise.

The ultimate source of authority in the scientific enterprise could be said to be reason itself. In rendering judgment, it is always the "force of the better argument" that is supposed to prevail. When disagreement is present, the various parties to the controversy are permitted and obligated to "back up" their views by giving reasons for them. What constitutes relevant reason-giving may vary from case to case; but it is clear that it involves adducing evidence, providing explanations, and invoking the common purposes and heritage of the scientific community. The invocation of force and appeal to partisan interests, conversely, would be deemed irrelevant and improper.

Sovereignty in this system is dispersed among all of the citizenry of the scientific republic. Rousseau's designation of the whole people as "the Sovereign" seems largely appropriate in scientific governance. Each member of the society is answerable for his or her actions and judgments to all of his or her peers. As Merton notes, moreover, it is this "ultimate accountability of scientists to their compeers" that effectively translates "the norm of disinterestedness into practice."[15] The final court of appeal is to the tribunal of public opinion. In the scientific enterprise, this sovereign tribunal functions in a way that approximates in both method and results what Condorcet had hoped for in a larger setting. It is "independent of human coercion [and] powerful by virtue of its size." It operates "with equal strength on all men at the same time [and] ensures a more certain and more durable power over their minds." It is a tribunal "whose scrutiny is difficult to elude and whose verdict it is impossible to evade."[16]

The sovereignty of scientific public opinion works reliably, however, only because it is an informed opinion and only insofar as it does not become corrupt. It is a form of "opinion" because it involves judgment. It does not possess the cognitive hardness Plato ascribed to *episteme*. But it also is not mere *doxa*, the kind of untutored and ill-grounded opining that Plato deprecated as a dangerous guide. The members of the scientific community have sufficient background, understanding, and grasp of the issues to make judgments that are neither arbitrary nor idiosyncratic. The process of appeal to the scientific tribunal, moreover, would be corrupted if it were not chastened by the collective conscience of science—by an operative allegiance to the constitutive purposes and sustaining ethos of the enterprise. As Polanyi cautions, "if each scientist set to work every morning with the intention of doing the best bit of safe charlatanry which would just help him into a good post, there would soon exist no effective standards by which such deception could be detected. A community of scientists in which each would act only with an eye to please scientific opinion would find no scientific opinion to please."[17] Part of Condorcet's utopianism, one can conjecture, stemmed from his failure to appreciate the grounds for and the weight of this cautionary note.

Because all scientists are not equal in experience, expertise, or rank, some hierarchic features can be found operative in the function of scientific authority. Established and respected scientists exercise some control over the work of apprentices, and their voices carry more weight in the adjudication of scientific controversies. This element of hierarchic authority, however, must in order to remain true to the purposes and ethos of science strive to be self-abrogating. It is a poor scientific mentor, although there are many of them, who would make his or her students into intellectual clones, attempting in effect to mediate forever the contact between the students' minds and objective reality. Instead, the exemplary scientific master is one who would foster the students' abilities to render independent judgments on their own authority. For only in that way will the students become full contributing participants in the cooperative enterprise, and only from the proliferation of such autonomous contributors will science continue to prosper.

Authority in the scientific republic is characterized by "looseness," dispersion, and reciprocity. It is "loose" in the sense that it does not insist upon the acceptance of all the specific concrete details of current scientific orthodoxy. Respect for the integrity of the individual scientific conscience and respect for the right to dissent on matters of particular doctrine preclude a tighter form of authority. Acceptance of the fundamentals of the scientific ethos, acquiescence in the goals of the enterprise, and attachment to the common heritage may be obligatory; but no one is excommunicated for deviance on particular concrete cases of belief or practice. Polanyi characterizes this aspect of the scientific enterprise as an adherence to a "general" rather than a "specific" pattern of authority. The former, he writes, lays down "general suppositions" whereas the latter "imposes conclusions."[18] There is a Protestant spirit to the republic of science: it is a "priesthood of all believers."

The dispersion of scientific authority is thus linked with its looseness or generality. Authority is not concentrated or centralized but is parceled out among multiple centers of expertise. No single authority is empowered to lay down the law for all to obey. Individual scientists exercise a shared authority in their areas of special competence, and they know enough about adjacent disciplinary domains to develop a sense of who relevant authorities are in these areas. The system is one of overlap among differentiated but connected centers of authority, complementarity, and reciprocal respect. Because no single authoritative individual or institution exerts hegemony over all others, some degree of mutual trust—confidence in the authoritativeness of others' judgments—is necessary for the system to cohere. When one sector of a scientific discipline believes the views and practices of another sector to have been corrupted by extrascientific interests—for instance, as in the recent contretemps between Soviet psychiatry and the world psychiatric community—the collaborative unity of the discipline is thoroughly disrupted.

To summarize, then, the republic of science embodies a distinctive system of authority that seems essential to its successful operation. It is an authority that is vested ultimately in the entire scientific community. It relies upon the force of the better argument. It is dispersed among different segments of the community that both complement and check each other. It aims at its own self-abolition, which it can for practical reasons never fully accomplish. The epic confrontation between Reason and Authority that Condorcet depicted in his *Progress of the Human Mind*, therefore, is somewhat misleading even though it captures something important. Condorcet saw quite astutely that the sovereignty of reason proclaimed by the Enlightenment and embodied in the scientific enterprise invalidated traditional forms of authority, at least as far as the life of the mind is concerned. Besides being too sanguine about the unproblematic extension of this form of governance to the larger public sphere, however, Condorcet's depiction obscured the fact that scientific praxis transforms authority rather than abolishing it. The successful coordination of scientific endeavors—given the limitations of individual energies and awareness—still requires a functioning system of authority. It is, however, a rational system, one based on competence, good reasons, and trust rather than one based on position, force, and mindless obedience.

The Polis of Rational Discourse

Reflection reveals, then, that the scientific enterprise is characterized by certain "necessary conventions." By "conventions" here we mean procedures that govern the conduct of the enterprise, and by "necessary" we mean so intimately connected to the functional logic of the enterprise and so distinctively conducive to its success as to be deemed "essential" to it—not in a Platonic but in a colloquial sense. These conventions are tantamount to the constitution of the scientific polis. They include standards of participation, rules of conduct, and modes of authority. To the extent that we are willing to acknowledge scientific conduct to be an exemplar of rational activity—as suggested by the etymological connection in "ology"—we have grounds to believe that these procedures can be taken as definitive of rational praxis.

This tentative conclusion would be bolstered, presumably, if parallel reflection on the conduct of that other etymologically indicated exemplar of human rationality—*logos*, or speech—produced a similar outcome. In this section, I want to argue that this is in fact the case: that reflection reveals the existence of certain "necessary conditions" of successful speech-acts, that these procedural conventions can be consolidated into a conception of the "polity of speech," and that this polity is strikingly and nonadventitiously isomorphic with the republic of science.

At first blush, the larger philosophical implications of a post-Wittgensteinian view of language might seem to be irrationalist. That is, Wittgenstein's insistence upon "leaving everything as it is" and his insistence that meanings of words are exhaustively determined by their uses could seem to be a reprise of Humean skeptical conventionalism and methodological conservatism in a linguistic mode. Just as Hume had insisted—*contra* Enlightenment hopes for the direct and decisive apprehension of reality by reason—that no standards of truth or reason were available beyond what had proved to be useful conventions, so Wittgenstein insisted—*contra* Enlightenment faith in a nascent perfect language—that no standards for correct usage of words were available beyond what had proved functional in conventional language-games.

One of the first serious attempts to adduce the implications of Wittgenstein's later philosophy for social theory, for example—Peter Winch's *Idea of a Social Science*—seemed to issue into a form of historicist relativism.[19] In this provocative study, Winch deftly appropriates Wittgenstein's insights to criticize positivistic accounts of social science in many quarters—from Mill's *Logic of the Moral Sciences* to Pareto to R. S. Lynd. Winch argues convincingly that the attempt to assimilate the practice of social science to empirical-analytic models of natural science depends upon the uncritical acceptance of the belief in unproblematical "ostensive definition" that Wittgenstein destroys in his *Philosophical Investigations*. Since social phenomena are not simply extended things, however, but rather are meaningful actions, their apprehension requires the feat of hermeneutic "catching on to" that Wittgenstein described. To know what a social event *is*, the social scientist must have some understanding of the form of life that gives it meaning. To suppose otherwise is to imagine that—as Wittgenstein showed to be impossible—one could understand the meaning of a word without a prior understanding of the language-game in which it functioned. In effect, Winch appropriated Wittgenstein to show that *Verstehen* is not a questionable process[20] but rather a hermeneutic achievement whose accomplishment is essential to social science.

Winch likewise demonstrated the distortions consequent upon a too facile imposition of interpretative concepts derived from one form of life upon other forms of life. This kind of wrenching of concepts out of their context amounts to the kind of "language going on a holiday" that Wittgenstein saw as productive of much philosophic confusion. In the case of social science, what it produces tends to be reductive and ethnocentric distortions of other cultures. The Western social scientist, for example, who interprets certain practices of other cultures as primitive and delusionary simulacra of practices in his or her own culture may be guilty of making what philosophers term a "category mistake." And that same social scientist will be immune to appreciating the source of his or her error, because he or she insists upon misconceiving a hermeneutic act as an empirical observation.

Winch carries this critique to what seems to be a relativistic conclusion.[21] Relying upon Wittgenstein's admonition that philosophy must "leave everything as it is" and upon Wittgenstein's insistence on the irreducible pluralism of language-games, Winch argues that both philosophy and social theory must be purely elucidatory and not appraisive. The critical task of philosophy is purely negative: "to deflate the pretensions of any form of inquiry to enshrine the essence of intelligibility as such, to possess the key to reality."[22]

It must remain neutral in the sense that "to take an uncommitted view of . . . competing conceptions is peculiarly the task of philosophy." Because "any worthwhile study of society must be philosophical in character," this injunction to remain noncommittal carries a parallel lesson for social theory. The social scientist must bear in mind not only the philosophical folly but also the moral impropriety of interpreting social events in terms not derived from those invokable by the participants. Every form of life "has criteria of intelligibility peculiar to itself," Winch asserts.[23] Actions can be "logical or illogical" only within the context of these criteria of intelligibility. And hence it is not only naively arrogant but actually nonsensical for a social scientist to apply the criteria of one language-game to describe and by implication appraise the conduct of another language-game. What counts as "agreement or disagreement with reality," Winch argues—as a lesson of the *Philosophical Investigations*—"takes on as many different forms as there are different uses of language."[24] And no one possesses the right to insist upon the hegemony of his or her own language or has the resources to step outside of a language to adjudicate among competing language-games/cultures/interpretations of reality.

Such, then, is the relativistic terminus of Wittgenstein's later philosophy of language when it is assumed that no language-game can be reduced to another or assessed by criteria other than its own. It is possible, however, to avoid the unattractive choice between acquiescing in this irrationalist conventionalism on the one hand or falling back into positivistic contradictions and illusions on the other if a different set of implications of Wittgenstein's perspective are pursued. Instead of taking each language-game as an irreducible monad, impervious to external translation or assessment, suppose it is asked: what are the necessary conditions for the successful conduct of language-games? What are the implicit rules binding upon and the commitments made by all those who would participate in these language-games? Can we identify the *conditiones sine quibus non* of successful speech acts? If these conditions— the rules of a meta-language game, as it were—could be specified, the devastating "pragmatic" critique Wittgenstein and others levelled against objectivist conceptions of language could be accepted without lapsing into irrationalism. Rationality in speech could not, to be sure, inhere in the eternally valid lineaments of a single perfect language. But it would not be necessary to jettison all canons of rationality. Instead, the power and discipline of reason would be seen to inhere in the capabilities possessed by and the constraints imposed upon all competent users of human language.

It is important to recognize at the outset, however, that this line of attack is promising only so long as it is directed at a specific subset of language-games. The attempt to generalize about the implicit understandings inherent in the whole gamut of human speech acts is surely doomed to futility. In this respect, Wittgenstein is undoubtedly correct to insist that different language-games possess only "family resemblance" and not universal common features.

The attempt to find pragmatic counterparts of Kant's conditions of possible knowledge by reflecting upon the conditions of successful speech acts has possibilities only if we confine our attention to cognitively oriented speech. Some speech is merely expressive, differing only in degree from shouts, cries, moans, or laughter. Other speech is purely instrumental, oriented toward manipulation or coercion. Some speech is intentionally deceptive, some purely strategic. The understandings implicit in these widely divergent forms of verbal activity are disparate, even contradictory in key respects. If we focus our investigation entirely upon what we can term "rational discourse," however, a clearer and more consistent pattern of necessary conditions of felicitous speech acts emerges. When Jürgen Habermas writes, for example, that "a general theory of speech actions would thus describe exactly that fundamental system of rules that adult subjects master to the extent that they fulfill the conditions for a happy employment of sentences in utterances, no matter to which particular language the sentences may belong and in which accidental contexts the utterances may be embedded" or speaks of a search for "pragmatic rules that shape the infrastructure of speech situations in general,"[25] he speaks too broadly in a way that invites misunderstanding and easy refutation. Instead, the whole project of a "universal pragmatics" makes sense only in the context of a more specific type of communication—a type indicated by some of Habermas's other formulations of the scope of his investigation. What is really at issue here are "the fundamental norms of rational speech",[26] the necessary conditions of communication oriented toward reaching the truth, the implicit assumptions "that each of us must intuitively make when we want to participate seriously in argumentation." More simply, what we want to identify are the essential features of "communicative rationality"[27] as embodied in human speech acts.

Delimiting our inquiry in this way is neither improper nor crippling.

Human speech acts are relevant to our inquiry, after all, only insofar as they exemplify the power of reason at work. It was the capacity of words to contribute to the rational apprehension of the order of the world—not the brute fact of verbal sounds per se—that led the Greeks to use the name *logos* for both reason and speech. It is entirely appropriate to our fundamental concern with developing a theory of rationality, then, to direct our attention to the implicit constitutive norms of cognitively oriented discourse.

To look for the constitutive universal conditions of rational speech acts amounts to asking a question characteristic of the Continental tradition's philosophy of consciousness in the context of subject matter more characteristic of the Anglo-American tradition's philosophy of language. It is not surprising, then, that the most suggestive inquiries along these lines have been carried on by two German philosophers who are conversant with trends in Anglo-American linguistic analysis: Jürgen Habermas and Karl-Otto Apel. Apel calls the line of inquiry in question "transcendental hermeneutics" and develops it by drawing implications from Wittgenstein's later philosophy in line with the spirit of Charles Sanders Peirce. Habermas calls his inquiry "universal pragmatics" (more lately, the "rational reconstruction" of universal competences) and develops it by using ideas taken from Austin and Searle to expand Chomsky's theory of linguistic universals in a pragmatic direction. Their conclusions converge upon a theory of communicative competence with normative implications.

As Apel observes,[28] one corollary of Wittgenstein's analysis of meaning-in-language is the discrediting of methodological solipsism. Language-games are not the creation of solitary individuals. Instead, they are sets of logically related linguistic practices generated by and embedded within social "forms of life." These practices are "rule-governed," regulated by the conventions and understandings implicit in the form of life underlying them. The "logic" of a language-game is a function of the rules that constitute a form of life. Any participant in a language-game, in turn, must understand and generally abide by the rules of the game: if he or she cannot understand the rules he or she cannot make himself or herself intelligible; and if he or she will not abide by them, he or she cannot maintain credibility.

The possibility of successful language-games thus depends upon the general capability of human beings to grasp and acquiesce in the rules governing linguistic conventions. This capability, Apel argues, amounts to a tacit apprehension of the "meta-rules" that are presupposed by all rational speech. These meta-rules are not those that fall within the ambit of particular language-games. Instead, they are the necessary rules that make it possible to organize and conduct language-games in general. These are rules "that cannot be first established by 'conventions,' but rather that make 'conventions' possible at all: for instance, the norm of respecting rules in the social context, and this implies—amongst other things—the norm of fair and truthful (veracious) discussion."[29]

In parallel fashion, Habermas investigates the structure of the "performative" dimension of linguistic competence. As Searle and Austin have ably argued, the meaning of linguistic utterances is not exhausted by their propositional content. We know what these utterances mean only by understanding not only their content but also what Austin termed their "illocutionary force"—that is, by knowing what it was the speaker intended to *do* with the words he spoke.[30] We must know, for example, whether the speaker is using his words in order to promise, to condemn, to offer, to legitimate, to worship, to bargain, or whatever. And to know that, we must understand the conventions of the form of life within which the speaker's intention makes sense.

It is Habermas's contention, then, that there is a discernible pattern to and a rational basis for the illocutionary force of utterances made in the context of truth-oriented speech acts. Truth-oriented language-games seek "to achieve a new definition of the situation which all participants can share."[31] Anyone who would participate in such a language-game must recognize and acquiesce in certain entry conditions for that participation. For any speech act to count as a legitimate contribution to rational discourse, it must implicitly raise what Habermas calls "universal validity claims" and be prepared to vindicate them. Specifically, any utterance in such a language-game claims to: embody a comprehensible expression, carry a sincere intention, communicate a true proposition, and accept legitimate norms.[32] A player in the game of rational discourse, in short, claims for his or her verbal contributions intelligibility, truthfulness, truth, and rightness. He or she accepts the propriety of challenge to any of these claims, and he or she supposes that he or she can and will provide appropriate grounding for his or her assertions in response to any such challenge. Those who understand these tacit requisites of rational speech can be said to be "communicatively competent."

These norms of communicative competence can be said to compose the constitution of the polis of rational discourse. They can be thematized further by inquiring into the perfect setting for their embodiment. The resultant model is logically equivalent to the "perfect market" of the economists: just as rational economic exchange could appear in pure form only under certain background conditions—full mobility of resources, complete price information, and so on—so could rational discourse appear in pure form only in a certain kind of setting. Habermas speaks of this perfect market of rational discourse as the "ideal speech situation." A fully rational economic exchange is one that occurs when no admixture of ignorance corrupts anyone's accurate perception of his or her interest and no admixture of force disturbs action pursuant to this perception. Likewise, a "rational consensus" could be said to emerge from rational discourse only when no outside influences prevent each participant from knowing and expressing his or her own mind.

Fully articulated, the ideal polis of rational discourse bears a clear and striking resemblance to the republic of science. Each embodies the same pattern of interrelated consensus, authority, liberty, and participation. The ideal speech situation is constituted by a common commitment to attaining a rational consensus. This is the *telos* of the enterprise. It is a dialogic version of Kant's "rational will"—an outcome in which the wills of the participants are determined by criteria appropriate to rational beings. The fundamental decision rule in the polity of ideal speech is "accept the force of the better argument." This is the operative principle of authority. The entry rules governing the ideal speech situation—like those of a perfect economic market—are liberal and egalitarian. Anyone who accepts the constitutive goal and the rules of the game is a welcome participant. And every participant must have free access to all dialogic roles. The procedural rules of the polity of rational discourse are dictated by its ends and its principle of authority. Each participant, for all his or her freedoms, is under a dual procedural obligation. On the one hand, he or she is obliged to offer "rational grounds" for his or her contentions: he or she must stand ready to "give reasons" when asked. And each participant has an obligation to listen to the other speakers. Otherwise, he or she would not be subject to the basic norm of "listening to reason."

Conclusion: The Renaissance of Practical Reason

It seems justifiable to conclude, then, that the philosophy of science and the philosophy of language—when reconstructed from a particular point of view, at least—have followed essentially the same path in the past several decades.

At the outset of this period, most philosophers of science and philosophers of language pursued a dream continuous with the philosophical hopes of the Enlightenment—hopes that, in turn, had deep roots in the ideals of classical philosophy. Both science and language aspired to the perfection of classical *theoria*. An ideal language and ideal scientific theory would both be perfectly luminous mirrors of objective reality. They would be clear and distinct, verifiably true, and unsullied by the contingencies of time, place, or personality. They would constitute and convey "positive" knowledge—the *theoria* of a de-essentialized universe.

The attempt to consummate this quest for an ideal language and a positive science encountered significant difficulties. Indeed, these difficulties seem to be insuperable. Upon reflection, they indicate the fundamentally utopian character of the whole project. The belief that human knowledge—as contrasted with some mythical knowledge of a contemplative deity—can attain the status of *theoria* turns out to be philosophically incoherent. Attaining the perfection of *theoria* for science and language can seem a reasonable goal only so long as the ineluctable constitutive role of the knowing subject is systematically repressed or radically idealized. The hopelessly disintegrated ego of Hume's epistemology and the hopelessly elevated ego of Cartesian epistemology, that is, are not adventitious imperfections in the search for a modern version of classical *theoria*: instead, between them they reveal both the incoherence of the project and the locus of the incoherence.

Only scientists produce science. Only speakers produce language. These propositions read like truisms, but the classic and modern quests for positive knowledge treated their content as accidental. Contemporary philosophy of science and philosophy of language, in contrast, have at least tacitly acknowledged the essentiality of these facts of life. Careful inquiry into the logic of both science and language has found itself forced to broaden its scope—from syntax alone to semantic linkages and on to pragmatic contexts. The "logic" of science, as contrasted with logic *in* science, now has to be put in quotation marks. It is a "logic-in-use," an internally consistent structure of investigation and not merely formal logic. Similarly, when a linguistic analyst speaks of the "logic" of a language-game, he or she is referring not to a formal calculus to be found within it but to the systematic and coherently patterned network of meanings created and integrated by the overall "point"—the purposes and intentions—of the game.

The rationality of science and language, consequently, can no longer be persuasively characterized in terms of formal logic alone. These enterprises do not run on mechanical deductions but on human savvy. The source of their accomplishments is not the ability to draw abstract inferences so much as it is the capacity to make sound judgments in the context of improving our perceptions of the world and our communications about it. Rationality is not defined by standards of pure content so much as by norms of proper and efficacious procedure.

From this perspective, the striking convergence between the analysis of scientific and linguistic pragmatics is not surprising. The remarkable congruence between Merton's and Polanyi's account of the republic of science and Habermas's and Apel's delineation of the ideal speech situation is not so remarkable after all. These parallels instead simply manifest the recognition of what we can call "the politics at the heart of reason." They represent an apprehension of the institutional dynamics essential to rational praxis.

This reformulation and reinvigoration of the idea of rational praxis implicit in recent philosophy invites—even requires—rethinking the relationship of rationality and politics. The several centuries-long refinement of critical rationalism's research program rendered our conception of this relationship increasingly problematic. The domain of what counted as "rational" was gradually constricted to the point that its relevance to political norms seemed highly questionable. Reason turned its head from politics entirely in order to cultivate its own allegedly pure theoretical garden. Or else it required of "rationalism in politics" a self-arrogating claim to certitude that made it dangerous and delusionary.

Recognizing the pragmatic dimension of rationality—the "politics in reason"—changes this picture quite dramatically. It simultaneously enlarges the range of rationality, jettisons demands for and claims of certitude as a hallmark of reason, shifts the focus of norms of rationality from content to process, and substitutes a paradigm of a communal dialogue for the paradigm of a logical soliloquy. This reorientation undermines some of the most influential accounts of political rationality produced by modern philosophy. It explains why the utopian rationalism of early liberalism was doomed to disappointment, based as it was on the application to politics of a mistakenly elevated notion of reason's capacity to produce certitude and moral unanimity. It likewise undermines the technocratic rationalist's conception of politics as expert manipulation, based as it is upon an exclusively instrumental conception of reason together with the mirage of certitude it shares with liberal utopianism. It also reveals the "economizing" rationalism of laissez-faire individualism and of uncritical pluralism as unwarrantedly narrow, since these philosophies confine practical reason to means-ends calculations in the service of monologically articulated self-interest. Finally, although this philosophical reorientation does not by itself mandate a rejection of the "decisionist" relativism that identifies liberal toleration with moral skepticism and positions liberalism on the edge of the slippery slope to nihilism, it does offer philosophical resources for transcending the limitations of this conception of liberalism.

What the recognition of the politics in reason offers us, constructively, is an avenue for vindicating the essential intuition of the Enlightenment—the intuition that the life of reason is defined by norms of behavior that also play a crucial role in creating a good society. It provides us with points of reference for regrounding the ideals of liberalism in a philosophy of reason. The conception of practical reason that is pivotal for our constructive task is both old and new. It remains true to the classical idea that disciplined cognitive activity is central to felicitous and virtuous conduct. But the semi-instrumentalism, the quasi-deductivism, and the contextual essentialism of Aristotle's formulation are set aside in favor of a conception that answers better to our contemporary understanding of the world and of scientific and communicative achievements. The conception of liberalism that emerges, I argue, is likewise both old and new. It assumes a more complex form in accordance with the more sophisticated form of rationalism that informs it. In doing so, it incorporates and synthesizes several political themes that have tended to compete rather than to cohere with liberalism. Yet it is faithful to the most fundamental beliefs and aspirations of the liberal tradition—to the belief in the efficacy and autonomy of reason and to the aspiration for a society that is open, free, participatory, and dedicated to pursuit of the human good.

Chapter Four **Politics as a Rational Enterprise**

The central lesson of the preceding chapters is that the myth of *theoria* must be abandoned. However productive that myth has been in some respects—inspiring the quest for ever greater rigor, ever greater precision, ever greater demonstrability of our knowledge—it postulates a goal of epistemic perfection that lies beyond human reach. It presupposes a static ontology, whether of Aristotelian forms or of Democritean bodies, and timeless knowers. And despite its virtues as myth, the depiction of knowledge as *theoria* has inflicted real costs. It has given us a misleading account of scientific conduct and of linguistic communication. When taken as a norm for political practice, moreover—which both classical and modern rationalists urged—the myth of *theoria* has been more destructive than creative. It has produced a modern version of "rationalism in politics" that generates a highly unattractive pair of politically disparate but logically linked alternatives: neo-Comtean fantasies of truth-bearers on the throne and post-Humean confinements of reason to instrumentalist servitude.

Abandoning the myth of *theoria*, however, by no means necessitates abandoning the faith of reason. That argument—that as goes *theoria* so goes reason—has been made from diametrically opposed quarters. On the one hand, that claim is raised by defenders of positivistic orthodoxy who try to universalize their own Cartesian anxiety as a tactical expedient. They conjure an "after us, the deluge" vision of future disasters allegedly consequent upon a failure to hold fast to the hard simplicities of objectivism. As they would have it, we must either pull up the philosophical drawbridges and stand with them in defense of their version of rationalism or else we are surrendering to the barbarians—both intellectual and political—howling at the walls of civilization. On the other hand, the same tight linkage of rationalism and the myth of *theoria* is insisted upon to opposite effect by philosophical irrationalists and political anarchists who seem to delight in stoking the positivists' alarm. They offer what they depict as a liberating invitation to dance upon the grave of "repressive" Reason—reason being for them what God was to Feuerbach: a reified idol of the imagination that enslaves its worshipers.

In fact, neither the nightmare vision of positivistic orthodoxy nor the utopian dream of the dadaists is convincing. Both rest squarely upon the identification of reason with *theoria*. If that identification is rejected, then neither the horrific nor the intoxicating conclusion is compelling. And in truth, the equation of reason and *theoria* does not hold. Both arguments misconstrue or ignore the implications of recent philosophy of science and of language. For the lesson of recent developments in these fields is not the relinquishment of standards of rationality but rather the recovery of its practical dimension. The lesson is not that there is no structure to rational inquiry, but rather that to grasp this structure we must look beyond mere logic and recognize its constitutive pragmatics. At the heart of reason we find neither abstract deduction nor a void. Instead, we find a characteristic pattern of procedures and institutions we have chosen to call the "politics in reason." Whether these procedures and institutions are sufficiently "internal" to rational inquiry to warrant inclusion in the very definition of rationality is largely beside the point. It is sufficient to appreciate that the characteristic pragmatics of rational inquiry qualify as necessary conditions for and constituent features of the life of rational enterprises.

To grant that there is a "politics in reason" does not mean *ipso facto*, however, that there is an important role for reason in politics. "Politics" means something different in the two instances here: in the first case, it refers to procedural dynamics, and in the second case it refers to the social regulation of behavior and authoritative allocation of goods. It would be a faulty argument grounded in semantic confusion to say that simply because there is a politics (i.e., constitutive pragmatics) of reason there must be a place for reason in politics (i.e., the governance of human affairs). Abandoning the myth of *theoria* in no way obliterates the important distinctions between what traditionally have been termed "theoretical" undertakings that pursue truth and the "practical" undertaking to order social life. Procedures that are absolutely essential in the one undertaking might be wholly inapplicable in the context of the other.

Our questions, then, are these: are the norms of conduct apparently essential to effectual cognitive activity in science and language also applicable and valid in political activity? Is the constitution of rational enterprises relevant to the tasks of organizing and regulating human activity? Is it meaningful to speak of rationality in politics; and if so, what does it mean? Is it possible for political practices in some respects to be rational? And even if it is logically and empirically possible for politics to be conducted "in a rational manner," is that desirable and why?

It was observed earlier that all conceptions of "rational behavior" and hence all conceptions of "rationality in politics" are produced by analogical reasoning. Anyone promoting such a conception must argue that patterns and strategies of behavior similar to those successful in cognitive enterprises are appropriate and productive in other contexts as well. Making such a claim requires identifying the most important similarities and differences between the different enterprises that bear upon the propriety of adapting the methods of one to problems of the other. And it requires designating what the similarity of the methods in the different contexts consists in. Finally, arguing for the normative validity of such a conception, in common with all normative argumentation, requires that the proposed standard of behavior be linked in a compelling way with what the listener is willing to accredit as humanly desirable. The argument that follows, then, assumes these analogical and rhetorical forms together with the attendant limitations. It can, therefore, hope only to persuade rather than to compel. Because these limitations are intrinsic to all such arguments, however, they can be acknowledged without apology.

The questions at hand and the forms of argument appropriate to them, then, are the same as those found in all attempts to establish a place for rationality in politics. What distinguishes our inquiry from the parallel inquiry of classic political rationalists such as Plato, Hegel, Kant, Condorcet, and the others is not the form of inquiry but the substantive reference point from which we take our bearings. When Plato asked about the role of reason in politics he had in mind a conception of reason as quasi-geometric dialectical intuition. Hobbes took as his starting point his understanding of reason as calculative foresight. Comte started his inquiry with the idea that reason was fundamentally a capacity to apprehend laws of historical development. Hegel had in mind the dialectical unfolding of divine self-consciousness. And Condorcet, Locke, Weber, Mill, and the others all had their own models of rationality to deploy upon the political stage. The conclusions reached in each case, then, were partly a function of the specific analogical judgments rendered in the process of adapting procedures and powers alleged to be characteristic of cognitive activity to the domain of politics; but they were even more significantly a function of the varying conceptions of rationality with which the theorists began.

Our own reference point is the process-centered conception of rational practice we have found characteristic of and essential to the successful pursuit of scientific knowledge and linguistic communication. It is the pattern of rational practice exhibited by science and language and reflectively articulated in Polanyi's and Merton's "republic of science" and in Habermas's and Apel's "ideal speech situation." Our question is whether there is a useful and valid place in politics for a form of practice that centers around participatory and open dialogue directed to solving problems standing in the way of common goals—a form of practice that accords to its participants the rights and expects of them the obligations logically pursuant to the status of partners in this kind of dialogue.

I argue that we should give a qualified affirmative answer to this question. The conception of rational practice derived from recent philosophy of science and of language is adaptable to politics, albeit with some inevasible limitations that need to be acknowledged. The type of politics warranted by this philosophically recast version of rationalism turns out to be a particular conception of democratic liberalism—one that bears close family resemblance to the liberalism of the seventeenth and eighteenth centuries, but also one that reveals these earlier versions of liberal rationalism as simplistic and utopian. For the rationality of democratic liberalism on our conception appears as more complex, more catholic, more contingent, and more fragile than early liberal theorists understood. And finally, I argue that this recent version of democratic liberal rationalism can be deemed "valid"—that is, worthy of our acceptance as a norm—on the grounds that it is practically efficacious and morally legitimate.

The Ends of Rational Politics: Consensus and the Common Good

Any enterprise amenable to being conducted in a rational manner must have some constitutive end or goal that imposes a coherent pattern upon its component functions. In the case of science and language, it is the common goal of apprehending the truth—about the world or about each other's meaning—that performs this role. Any claim that politics can be conducted—at least in some respects—as a rational enterprise, then, must be able to specify the common purpose underlying a rational society.

This necessity represents an immediate difficulty that skeptics about rationality in politics are quick to point out. A political society, they argue, unlike the republic of science or the ideal speech situation, has no specifiable common goal capable of playing this role. It is impossible for the disparate and contending individuals who compose a political society to focus their activities on a common purpose, and hence the applicability of rational procedures to political organizations breaks down at the outset. If not impossible, this argument continues, the specification of such a constitutive common goal would necessarily be illiberal in two senses: a common goal can be presumed to exist only on the basis of illiberal philosophical presuppositions, and a common goal can be made to exist only by illiberal political methods. That is, only philosophical dogmatists believe that human beings have been given a common end by nature and that they know what it is. Only political authoritarians are willing to impose a common end on people. And neither dogmatism nor authoritarianism can be deemed rational or liberal.

It is easy to see the force of these objections. They are accurate and telling objections to some traditional conceptions of the common good and to some historically important attempts to implement them. Theocracies and totalitarian regimes in fact have embodied the objectionable claims and produced the objectionable policies that prompt these skeptical demurrers. Nonetheless, these objections are too all-encompassing. Contrary to the universal doubt they express, it is possible to have a conception of the common good that is compatible with liberal premises and that is sufficiently robust to provide the focal point for rationality in politics.

The skeptical argument that the good has no constitutive role in a liberal regime is ultimately the product of a misleading either/or choice thrust upon us by the myth of *theoria*. If it is in fact true, as Locke asserted in one of his letters, that "what comes short of certainty . . . may not be called knowledge,"[1] then the good must not be knowable. For only fools and fanatics delude themselves that they possess or could possibly possess a certain and final knowledge of the human good.

On this either/or account, then, the liberal position becomes that of Hobbes. The good is radically individualized and seen as an object of taste rather than of knowledge. Hobbes amends Aristotle's observation that all of a human being's voluntary actions aim at some good by adding the words "to himself."[2] And he concludes that "every man . . . calleth that which pleaseth and is delightful to himself, good; and that evil which displeaseth him."[3] And this account, in turn, leads to the conception of liberal society as an *entente-not-so-cordiale*, a problematic conception that led Hobbes to opt for a strong sovereign power and that has plagued excessively individualistic theories of liberalism to this date.

When the myth of *theoria* and its attendant calculative ideal of knowledge is set aside, however, the choices are not so stark and unattractive. It is no longer necessarily a matter of opting between patently unwarranted claims of moral certitude on the one hand and pyrrhonism on the other. Instead, it becomes possible to conceive of the good as imperfectly knowable in a way that is epistemically parallel to the truth—as that conception functions within scientific inquiry and linguistic communication. And this conception of an imperfectly knowable good turns out to be in keeping with less skeptical and subjectivist views of the relationship between liberalism and the human good. For, if one considers Locke's *Second Treatise* and *Some Thoughts concerning Education* rather than the more theoretical account in his *Essay*, and if one considers Mill's political treatises rather than his *Logic*, it seems clear that they both believed that a liberal society was oriented toward attaining a genuine—but only imperfectly knowable—common good.

The human good is human flourishing—the felicitous exercise of human capabilities and the satisfaction of legitimate human wants and needs. The political common good, therefore, is whatever permits and facilitates the flourishing of the lives of a society's members. It is of course possible for philosophers and common folk alike to differ in their views about *what* human flourishing consists in. And it is obvious that people often disagree about what political institutions and policies are best calculated to promote the flourishing of citizens' lives.

In this respect, however, the conception of the good is quite similar to the conception of the truth as it functions in the context of scientific inquiry and linguistic communication. For "the truth" is our apprehension of the structure of our world, and the scientifically true is whatever permits and facilitates this intelligibility of the world to our knowing minds. Scientists and philosophers nonetheless may and in fact do differ among themselves as to *what* this intelligibility consists in. For example, some argue for a correspondence theory of truth, others for a coherence theory, and so on. These disagreements over what "the truth" consists in at some theoretical level do not, however, lead to abandonment of the assumption that science aims to uncover the truth. Nor does it impede the idea of the truth from functioning as the *telos* of scientific activity. For whatever truth may consist in, in the day-to-day conduct of scientific inquiry the search for the truth proceeds through efforts to remove impediments to our understanding. Whatever scientific truth may be in the abstract, it is approximated in the concrete work of scientists through attention to solving specific problems. The working scientist does not ask "what is truth?" and then set out *de novo* to attain it. He or she asks "what are the current gaps or conundrums that seem to impede our understanding?" and then sets out to remedy these flaws.

In like manner, disagreements over what "the good" consists in need not impede the idea of the good from functioning as the *telos* of a political society. For whatever the good may be in some abstract sense, in the day-to-day life of society the quest for the common good proceeds through efforts to remove impediments to the flourishing of the lives of the members of society. Whatever the human good may be in the abstract, it is approximated in the concrete through attention to solving specific problems. Political leaders and citizens do not need to ask constantly "what is the common good?" Instead they ask "what are the current obstacles to the flourishing of our lives individually and collectively?" and then set out to remove them.

The distinguished legal philosopher Edmond Cahn has argued, I think persuasively, that the ideal of justice is not apprehended directly. Instead, certain actions or circumstances—such as irrationally inequitable treatment—arouse our sense of injustice. Only by a kind of *ex post facto* reflection do we arrive at a more constructive conception of what justice consists in.[4] The same can be said of our knowledge of the human good. What we perceive is not some directly intuited abstract model of the good life. Rather we come to understand the human good only by encountering and reflecting upon what is frustrating, alienating, constraining, divisive, and debilitating. Only in the rearview mirror, as it were, do we begin to understand the shape and dimensions of the positive human good. When pragmatists tell us that the good—like the truth—is "what works," they provide an inadequate philosophical criterion apart from further specifications. But they are correct epistemically speaking: it is only by finding out what does not work *vis à vis* human flourishing that we come to know what is good.

The human good can thus be known only through experience. Mill is therefore correct when he argues that different plans of life may be conceived as "experiments of living." Only by trying out different modes of life can we make reasonable judgments about the best way to live. We have to experiment ourselves, and we can gain vicarious experience from observing the lives of others. The "verdict of the only competent judges" as to what is humanly fulfilling, then, is the judgment of those who have the benefit of comparative experience.[5]

It also follows from this account that our knowledge of the good is fallible and imperfect. Indeed, Mill arrives at the "experiments of living" notion from his observations about the fallibility of our knowledge regarding human action, analogizing it in this respect to our opinions. Not even the most romantic seeker after all possible human experience, after all, could even remotely approach achieving an acquaintance with all possible or even all existing modes of experience. Hence all judgments about the human good are based on partial evidence and are accordingly quite imperfect.

Moreover, because human beings differ in their capacities, tastes, and inclinations, any reasonable conception of the human good must be somewhat flexible and pluralistic. One does not have to agree with Robert Nozick's conclusions to appreciate the force of his observation about human diversity. Consider, he suggests, the characters of (among others) Wittgenstein, Yogi Berra, Picasso, Thoreau, Einstein, Henry Ford, Sir Edmund Hillary, Ralph Ellison, Bobby Fischer, and Emma Goldman. "Is there really *one* kind of life," he asks, "which is best for each of these people?"[6] Clearly not. Although our common humanity provides some constant features to the human good, the particulars of what such widely divergent people will find to be a good life will surely vary. And any compelling conception of the human good must be sufficiently capacious to encompass this variety.

Finally, because historical circumstances are constantly changing, the particulars of the human good can never be specified once and for all. Some growing room must be accommodated. The fact that we can read Greek tragedies from over two thousand years ago with profound sympathy and appreciation suggests that the dimensions of human life do not fluctuate greatly in some fundamental respects as time passes. But the needs and wants of twentieth-century people living in large-scale industrialized societies are not identical with those of the people who lived in fourth-century B.C. Hellenic city-states. And our descendants will undoubtedly have requirements of a good life that we cannot ourselves imagine.

A conception of the human good commensurate with the facts of historical existence and with the capabilities and limitations of human knowledge, in sum, must take this form. It must be pragmatic in the sense of being irreducibly tied to problem-solving feats of intelligence. It must be experimental and therefore fallibilistic. It must be pluralistic and open to emendation in the light of changing historical circumstances. These features add up to what could be called an open-textured theory of the good.

An open-textured conception of the human good is not dogmatic but explicitly antidogmatic. It cannot be used as the basis for a closed or authoritarian society, but instead has more liberal implications. It serves not as a substantive a priori answer to the questions politics addresses, but rather as the orienting question for a free and humane political project. It is a question—"what is our common good and how do we achieve it?"—that is capable of functioning in an analogous way to the question "what is true?" in the theoretical disciplines. For as Dudley Shapere has recently argued, whatever truth *is* it *functions* as an "intelligible framework for problem-solving."[7] Just so the common good *vis à vis* the politics of a rationally conducted society. It functions also as an intelligible framework for solving the problems of our common life. We do not postulate in advance what the common good is and then enforce it. We seek to know and create our common good by solving the difficulties that afflict us.

The standard philosophical arguments invoked by deontological liberals to undermine the contention that liberal democratic practice should focus on the common good are useful but flawed. They explain why no political society, even with the best will in the world, could ever make all of its decisions simply by achieving a rational consensus about the common good—unless that society were characterized by a religious and moral unanimity that is highly unlikely. But these arguments go too far both in their pessimism about the role of the good and in their parallel optimism about the viability of rules of neutral justice as an alternative. And this faulty argument is in turn largely the product of an untenable epistemological dichotomy.

Consider, to take a paradigmatic example, the argument of John Rawls in his Dewey lectures. Conceptions of the good, Rawls argues, are not cognitively meaningless preferences. However, they are grounded in moral, religious, and philosophical beliefs. These moral, religious, and philosophical doctrines in turn—even if they admit of truth and falsity—do not admit of rational adjudication: "on such doctrines reasoned and uncoerced agreement is not to be expected." This inadjudicability arises because these doctrines are grounded in metaphysical notions that are beyond the reach of evidence. Indeed, the metaphysical depth of the differences renders their rational discussion and evaluation difficult or impossible because it generates "not only diverse moral and political doctrines, but also conflicting ways of evaluating arguments and evidence when they try to reconcile these oppositions."[8]

In contrast to this metaphysical quagmire surrounding conceptions of the good life, Rawls then argues, discussions about justice can be based on more solid ground. Even persons who hold divergent conceptions of the good can reach agreement on principles of justice, because these principles can be derived from "forms of reasoning accepted by common sense, including the procedures of science when generally accepted." The appropriate strategy for ordering a liberal society thus is shaped by this epistemological distinction. Principles of justice can be based on commonly accepted views, whereas "opposing religious, philosophical and moral convictions, as well as diverse conceptions of the good" cannot be agreed upon or adjudicated. Hence a liberal society should be grounded in commonly accepted principles of justice that are "appropriately impartial"[9] among conceptions of the good.

Rawls's solution to the dilemma he poses does not stand close examination, however, for conceptions of justice cannot in fact be as successfully insulated from moral and metaphysical disagreements as he imagines. The "common sense" Rawls relies upon is not only culturally specific, as he has himself explicitly recognized in his recent work, but also involves tacit metaphysical commitments. The debates surrounding *A Theory of Justice* have made that evident. It would be equally evident were Rawls to confront, say, a believer in the doctrine of *karma*. For the doctrine of *karma* is an account of just deserts that conflicts with

Rawls's "difference principle"; but it also is a metaphysical and religious conception as impervious to definitive rational refutation as any conception of the human good.

Nor for that matter can conceptions of justice be so neatly severed from the influence of conceptions of the good. If justice consists in according people their due, and if their deservingness is determined in some measure by the worth of their actions, then conceptions of justice are at least partly determined by conceptions of the good. Rawls obscures this relationship because his theory of justice renders desert irrelevant. But that claim—that desert is irrelevant to distributive justice—is itself dependent upon a contestable metaphysic of human action.

Were Rawls correct concerning the incapacity of reason *vis à vis* the good, therefore, liberal society would seem to have no choice but to fall back upon purely self-interested contractual bargaining for its basis. No luminous principles of justice ascertainable by common sense are available to provide a framework of order that transcends self-interest. But liberals need not revert to Hobbesian logic entirely, for if Rawls is too optimistic about our ability to discern consensual principles of justice he is also unnecessarily pessimistic concerning the possibility of reasoned agreement about what is good.

Undeniably, full agreement on the nature of the good life is a chimera. The metaphysical and religious dimension of conceptions of the good that lie beyond definitive rational adjudication will always frustrate that hope. The human good, however, is not—as Rawls's argument seems to imply—a single lump encapsulated by metaphysics. Like human life itself, what is good has many dimensions and multiple components. What is good in economic pursuits is not exactly what is good in football or what is good in love or what is good in worship. Therefore, even if religious and metaphysical differences may prevent me from achieving full agreement about the good life in all its dimensions with all my fellow citizens in a pluralistic liberal society, we can still engage in rational discussion and reach some accord regarding some important features of our common good. My Presbyterianism does not entirely incapacitate me from meaningful discussion and potential agreement with my fundamentalist neighbor concerning the need for passing a municipal bond referendum, or from discussion and possible agreement with my Sikh neighbor concerning the desirability of adding computer instruction to our public school curriculum, or from discussion and possible agreement with my agnostic neighbor concerning the best zoning strategy for our city to follow. Locke drew the line too sharply between the things of this world and the things of heaven in his *Letter concerning Toleration* as he sought to explain the possibility of circumscribing a domain for politics that did not trench on ultimate concerns. But Rawls and other neutralists go to the other extreme in connecting them too inextricably. Even if some of the ultimate religious and moral convictions that divide people lie beyond rational determination, that difficulty does not vitiate entirely the possibility of rational dialogue and consensus on more specific and limited aspects of the human good.

Liberal *Homonoia*: Fraternity in a Rational Society

The constitutive role of the human good in the rational society creates among its citizens a limited but significant form of *homonoia*, or likemindedness. And it is this particular form of political concord that provides the appropriate philosophical basis for the liberal conception of fraternity. Traditional societies have generally taken for granted a substantial element of *homonoia* among their membership. The leading philosopher of *homonoia* was Aristotle, citizen of one of the Greek citystates, which were in a sense little church-states. They were animated, at least in their self-estimation, by a common conception of the good and by a civil religion that embodied this conception. The assumption was that this kind of agreement upon fundamental moral precepts and beliefs was requisite to a viable polity. Centuries later, when Europe was confronted with the crumbling of doctrinal *homonoia* within post-Reformation Christianity, this same assumption led to the policy of *cuius regio, eius religio*. The notion that a stable political society could be composed of groups who diverged on basic moral and religious precepts seemed wildly unrealistic.

The role of *homonoia* in tolerant and pluralistic liberal society has been, in contrast, variable and controversial. On the one hand, fraternity was included with liberty and equality on the rhetorical masthead of Enlightenment liberalism. Rousseau spoke of the necessity for some form of civic religion. And some theorists of democracy have spoken of the need for some underlying consensus to sustain democratic society. On the other hand, thoroughgoing contractualist conceptions of liberal society and relativistic theories of democracy seem to dispense with *homonoia* altogether.

Individuals in a contract society relate only through specific mutual agreements based on self-interest. They cooperate sporadically in an instrumental fashion, but they need not be united in any significant manner by mutual devotion to a larger public interest or set of ideals. "I'll scratch your back if you'll scratch mine" is all that is needed in the way of principles. Similarly, citizen relations in a democracy conceived along relativistic lines are based simply on mutual forbearance: "I'll leave you alone if you'll leave me alone." Toleration may be based on respect, but it can also be grounded in simple indifference. *Homonoia* is not required.

Homonoia is the public and political version of friendship. It is, in Aristotle's words, "friendship between the citizens of a state, its province being the interests and concerns of life." The bases of friendship, Aristotle also observes, are several. It may be based on utility, or pleasure, or on common devotion to some good. Friendships based upon utility and pleasure, in turn, have to be seen as inferior to the latter kind. For friendships based upon utility or pleasure "are grounded on an inessential factor."[10] Friends who come together only for the usefulness or pleasure derived from their association are friends *per accidens*. Such friendships are therefore evanescent. When the immediate profit for which the friendship was created and valued disappears, the friendship dissolves as well.

After its earlier ideals and enthusiasm waned, liberalism has tended to adopt only the inferior version of friendship—that based on utility—as part of its conception of society. Liberal society is pluralistic and market oriented. Its citizens do not share a conception of the good, but pursue many individual goods. They come together only out of utility—out of mutual self-interest. Any larger conception of *homonoia* tends to be viewed with suspicion, since it would seem to undermine the legitimacy of religious and social pluralism, perhaps even challenging the principle of toleration.

If a liberal society is understood to be a rational enterprise oriented toward the good of its citizens, however, it becomes possible to see it as incorporating a limited form of *homonoia* that is compatible with toleration and pluralism. This limited form of *homonoia* corresponds to and is grounded in the open-textured theory of the good. The participants in politics as a rational enterprise, that is, are joined and united in a common devotion to achieving the human good—for themselves and for the society as a whole. But this common devotion to the human good is compatible with a tolerance for competing concrete conceptions of the good, just as the rational enterprise of science can tolerate competing conceptions of truth.

The citizens of a rational society do not possess the *homonoia* of "compact" societies that have, in effect, an official religion. (Complete *homonoia* in any case is surely only an ideal type—a limiting condition that is never actually achieved by autonomous and fractious human beings. But it is more closely approached in church-states that embody a single official conception of the good life for human beings.) Cognizant of the open-ended and experimental status of the good—and equally aware of our cognitive frailty when it comes to moral knowledge—a rational society must abandon the goal of full *homonoia* as a legitimate aspiration. Nevertheless, it need not go to the other extreme of abandoning *homonoia* altogether in capitulation to radical *heteronoia*—a society of strangers and enemies. For the participants in politics as a rational enterprise do share a common orientation to achieving the human good, however difficult it may be to know exactly what the best life consists in and however various the modes of human flourishing may be. The citizens of a rational society do not share in detail a common mind about what the good may be. But what they do share is a common aspiration to create and sustain a society in which all are able to achieve to the greatest possible extent what they find to be the good life for themselves.

The *homonoia* of the rational society is thus limited in its scope. It cannot achieve the full unity of mind of the classical conception of political concord. But it is nonetheless a real form of political friendship that unites its citizens in a common enterprise and allows them to relate to one another in a fraternal manner. They may not be blood brothers united by a common oath, but neither are they reduced to making "living together" mean "grazing together like a herd of cattle."[11]

A liberalism that takes seriously its early aspiration to be a form of society based upon rationality, therefore, has grounds for resisting its reduction into a market society composed of adversaries. It need not acquiesce in Burke's charge that liberal society amounts to "nothing better than a partnership agreement in a trade of pepper and coffee, calico, or tobacco, or some other such low concern, to be taken up only for a little temporary interest, and to be dissolved by the fancy of the parties."[12] Instead, within the limitations that attend our knowledge of what is good, a liberal society that conducts itself according to the norms of rational practice is a partnership of citizens united in their quest to build a social order conducive to human flourishing.

The Conversation of Democracy: Practical Discourse and the Public Sphere

The central institution of a rational society is intimately associated with the *homonoia* that is one of its elements. For friendship and discourse go together. As Aristotle wrote, immediately prior to his comment that human "living together" is not the same as grazing together like cattle: "A man ought to have a sympathetic consciousness of his friend's existence, which may be attained by associating with him and conversing and exchanging ideas with him."[13] The relationship here is causally reciprocal: friendship expresses itself in the exchange of ideas, the sharing of consciousness; and conversely, the sharing of thoughts through speech is essential to the growth of friendship.

This linkage of friendship and public speech was central to the Greek conception of the *polis* and was also vital to the functioning of democratic institutions in the Greek city-states. Hannah Arendt reminded us of this facet of Greek political thought and stated it well: "For the Greeks the essence of friendship consisted in discourse. They held that only the constant interchange of talk united citizens in a polis. . . . [In their view] the common world . . . remains 'inhuman' in a very literal sense unless it is constantly talked about by human beings."[14] If we are to take seriously the conception of rational practice as a framework for the legitimate and effective conduct of public affairs, we have a great deal to learn from the Greeks in this respect.

The central institution of a rational society is precisely what the Athenian *agora*, the "ideal speech situation," and the republic of science have in common: a free dialogue among equal participants oriented toward their common purpose. Rationality finds its embodiment here not in abstract logic or calculation, but in the concrete *logos* of real human speech. All rational politics, then, is in a literal and general sense "parliamentary," a political adjective derived from the verb "parler," to speak. The validation of "free speech"—of a particular sort—and its deployment during crucial stages of the decision-making process is the hallmark of a rational society.

This claim appropriates the intuitive truth that served as the basis for Condorcet's depiction of the epic struggle between Reason and Authority. Condorcet's own rationalism was primitive and utopian, believing as he did that truth was simple and scientific method infallible. As a consequence, he seemed to believe, erroneously, that authority was dispensable and that its elimination could produce a politics of perfectibility. For his simplistic rationalism and liberal perfectionism, Condorcet has been dismissed with some justice as a naive visionary whose expectations for the future were mocked by history. But however imperfectly expressed, at the heart of Condorcet's vision was an accurate and important conceptual distinction between two kinds of politics: one that imposes its ends upon its subjects and one that provides an institutional framework within which citizens determine the ends of their society by reasoning together.

The heart of a rational polity is what William Lee Miller has termed "the conversation of democracy." As Miller writes, "The governing of a free people is a work of deliberation, of conversation, of discussion, of debate and argument, and even persuasion. That assumes that citizens can speak and listen and think and sometimes be persuaded. It is not fashionable to say so, but it is nevertheless true that despite all the irrationality and self-interest in it, it rests at last upon the reason and the conscience of citizens, upon a public that develops a mind and a will."[15]

In authoritarian regimes, ancient or modern, speech is always kept on a leash. It is an instrument of predetermined order, not an organizing principle for the determination of what social order shall mean. Public speech in such regimes is not the medium of the tribunal of reason, but is instead a vehicle of celebration and admonition. Authoritative outcomes are not produced out of rational dialogue; instead, authorities use speech to convey and implement their orders.

It was part of fascist ideology, to note the extreme case, to disparage in explicit terms the role accorded to rational discourse by liberal democratic regimes. Parliamentary deliberations, Hitler wrote in *Mein Kampf*, were merely the babble of irresponsibles. Most members of a parliament, he said, "are present only to collect their attendance fees, and certainly not to be illuminated by the wisdom of this or that fellow 'representative of the people.'" Even less, he insisted, could the general citizenry be considered capable of rational deliberation: "The people in their overwhelming majority are so feminine by nature and attitude that sober reasoning determines their thoughts and actions far less than emotion and feeling." An appropriate educational system should not so much try to remedy this situation, but accept it as natural, for "the training of mental abilities is only secondary" to its mission. The only speech that counts, then, is not the written word but the "magic power of the spoken word." And the reason for this evaluation is that the spoken word can essentially bypass the mind altogether and "move the masses" by "a storm of hot passion."[16]

Speech in such a polity, in short, does not function as rational discourse. It serves not to engage the mind but to ignite the passions. It is not a part of discursive will formation, and it is not educative; instead it seeks "to force a doctrine on the whole people."[17] More prosaic authoritarian regimes, such as those imposed by military bureaucracies, may be less fervent and candid in their view of democratic conversation, but they too must keep speech on a leash. In such settings, it is always the principal institutions of rational discourse and public deliberation that are most constrained—parliaments, the press, and universities.

What we call "authoritarian" regimes, then, could be said to follow in the pattern of Sparta rather than Athens. Public order is founded more upon fearful obedience than rational assent. For in Sparta, also, speech functioned only within this limited context: "Thus in Sparta speech could never become the political tool it was elsewhere, or take shape as discussion, argumentation, rebuttal. In place of Peitho, the force of persuasion, as an instrument of the law, the Lacedaemonians extolled the power of Phobos, that fear which made all citizens bow in obedience. They boasted of relishing only brevity in speeches, and of preferring sentitious and pithy turns of phrase to the subtleties of debate. For them speech was still *rhetrai*, those quasi-oracular laws to which they submitted without discussion and which they refused to expose to public scrutiny by writing them down."[18]

On the basis of this characterization, the way might seem open to interpreting the clash of contemporary superpowers as an updated version of the clash between Athens and Sparta. And at one level, that of concrete behavior, that characterization may not be terribly far afield. Communist societies have emphasized social solidarity and relied more on Phobos than upon Peitho to organize their citizenry. And Western liberal democracies are home to almost an excess of public speech and deliberation—in legislatures, newspapers, journals, tabloids, television, colleges, and universities. The confusions and deformations occasioned by a postivistic conception of rationality, however, introduces a paradoxical twist to this account at a level of theoretical self-understanding. For the behaviorally Spartan Marxist societies have depicted themselves as the historical embodiment of reason, while most recent liberal theorists have found no place in their view of liberal democracy for practical discourse of the traditional sort—that is, for rational deliberation about the human good. One implication of my argument here is that both of these accounts are faulty: that communist societies have been more Spartan than rational and that rationality is a more integral part of healthy liberal societies than is often appreciated. Correlatively, the dramatic changes under way in Eastern Europe represent in part a rational rebellion against Spartan closure.

The difficulty with the Marxist conception of rationality in politics (and I refer here to the self-justification of extant Marxist societies rather than to, say, neo-Marxist theoretical accounts) has been that it is heir to Condorcet's delusion about "simple truths and infallible methods." And it transformed that delusion from a hopeful account of the future into a self-congratulatory account of the past. As Jürgen Habermas has helped to remind us,[19] Marx was unable to disentangle himself from the epistemological inadequacies of positivism. And his orthodox followers, from Engels onward, have if anything compounded that error. In this positivistic myth, then, Marx appeared as the practitioner of an infallible method that generated a definitive science of history and society. Once accomplished, of course, there was nothing left to do but to transform this theoretical truth into practice. Reason's work was effectively complete, and the future belonged to the bureaucrats.

The ironic result of the positivistic myth of "scientific socialism," then, has been a form of society that is functionally almost indistinguishable from the kind of society that Condorcet thought reason would render obsolete. Delete the references to church and crown, and Condorcet's complaint about pre-Enlightenment Europe becomes uncannily descriptive of Marxist regimes: "It was rather to holy books [and] revered authors . . . that people turned for rules and precedents by which they could guide their conduct. There was no question of examining a principle in its own right: it was always a matter of interpreting, discussing, attacking, supporting one set of quotations by appeal to another. A proposition was accepted not because it was true, but because it was written in such-and-such a book. . . . In this way the authority of men was everywhere substituted for the authority of reason."[20] Only the holy books were different. When reason's work is considered to be done, it functions as dogma and eventuates in the same slavish political practices it was supposed to demolish.

If right-wing positivism has produced the Komitet Gosudarstvennoi

Bezopasnosti (KGB) as the new vicars of Reason, the left-wing positivism more characteristic of Anglo-American culture has left reason bereft of a political role. Right-wing positivists believe that normative truths are scientifically ascertainable and thereby hypostatize political reason. Left-wing positivists believe that practical norms are cognitively empty because they cannot be scientifically known and thereby undermine rationality in politics. For if it be true that all ethical statements are merely commendatory expressions of emotion, the content of political speech must be very thin. Whatever the role and significance of political conversation, it cannot on this account encompass practical discourse—deliberation about the human good and how to achieve it—at all.

The political implication of ethical emotivism is to debunk or unmask those who purportedly engage in moral discourse. If they enter such a conversation sincerely, they must be deluded about the meaning of their assertions. Or else they are hypocritical, engaging for strategic reasons in what they know to be meaningless prattle. Once the emotivist message had sunk in, the confused would be de-mystified and the hypocrites unmasked. Both, presumably, should then be silenced and the conversation of democracy brought to an end.

Political speech, even on this account, would not disappear entirely, of course. But it would have to consist entirely in strategic communication—in bargaining. The political goals of each speaker would be a predetermined function of his or her individual passion. They would figure in the discourse only as the tacit motivating force behind the tactical offers or threats being made. A democratic legislature would become a "parley-ment," its speech shrunken to the discussion of terms with enemies. To reverse Clausewitz's aphorism, politics becomes war by other means. Given a sanguine interpretation, the outcome of the parley becomes the pluralist "equilibrium." Given a less cheerful cast, it is a sublimated Hobbesian free-for-all. The shrinking of democratic discourse thus eventuates in a shrunken conception of democratic governance.

The metaethical dispute over the nature and meaningfulness of ethical statements, therefore, has political implications. To sustain the conversation of democracy as a significant part of democratic practice rather than as an epiphenomenal gloss over it, one must have an intelligible and convincing conception of practical discourse. Because such a conception seems to be both embryonic and controversial in contemporary philosophy, it would be foolish and presumptuous to attempt this feat here. However, it is possible to provide a very brief outline of practical discourse sufficient for our purposes.

Practical reason is directed toward the determination of what is humanly good and how that rationally desirable end should be pursued. Rational discussion about these concerns thus originates with assertions by some of the participants in answer to the practical question: what is to be done? The first stage of practical discourse, therefore, is an open forum in which all the answers anyone wishes to propose to that question are articulated and acknowledged.

Presumably, only on rare and happy occasions will all parties to the conversation speak with one voice in prescribing a course of action. Hearing different policy recommendations, participants in practical dialogue will demand warrants or reasons on behalf of the various proposals. The warrants for claims of practical reasons, of course, are not deductive inferences from purely descriptive assertions. Hume was surely correct that "ought" conclusions cannot be deduced from "is" premises. But to demand "proofs" of this sort is simply to misconstrue practical reasoning. To provide a warrant for a practical prescription, one must explain how it contributes to the fruition of human life. Such an explanation is the necessary first step to justification in the context of practical discourse, since, as Charles Taylor has observed, "to say of something that it fulfills human needs, wants, or purposes, always constitutes a *prima facie* reason for calling it 'good.'"[21]

To argue that a given policy will contribute to the attainment of human needs, wants, and purposes in turn involves two constituent elements—one causal and the other hermeneutic. Causally, a sound practical argument must provide a plausible explanation of the empirical linkage between the desired course of action and the human ends it is designed to achieve. Hermeneutically, a sound practical argument must provide an interpretation of human existence within which the wants, needs, and purposes alluded to make sense.

Both of these constituents of a practical argument, of course, are contestable. They do not admit of demonstration. But neither kind of claim is arbitrary or cognitively empty. The causal claims may seem least problematic. However, casual explanations involve theoretical judgment, and future causal paths are inherently speculative. Many notable practical ideological disputes, as a consequence, significantly involve divergent judgments on causal questions, such as: "does poverty cause crime?" "is the collapse of capitalism inevitable?" "is a strong

government necessary for social peace?" and so on. As for the hermeneutic account of human life that sustains the designation of human
needs, wants, and purposes, the possibility of divergent judgment
seems obvious. So here, perhaps, the important point to insist upon is
that all practically relevant hermeneutic accounts do not disappear into
the mists of metaphysics or the vagaries of religious belief. An interpretation of human existence that, with Freud, insists that the capacity
for love and for work are essential to human flourishing, for example,
may cohere with many metaphysical and religious points of view.

Once the warrants for a proposed course of action have been adduced, the argument is open to challenge by other parties to the dialogue. Critics may try to undermine an argument by giving reasons to
doubt the explanatory framework that sustains and informs it. Marx's
critique of classical economics, for example, to the extent that it was
successful undermined the practical case for a market society. Alternatively, critics may seek to override an argument by contending that its
purposes are valid but nonetheless less essential or important than other
purposes that clash with it. The argument on behalf of curtailing free
speech in cases of "clear and present danger" would be an example of
this kind of argument.

After all relevant arguments have been made and criticized, several
outcomes are possible. First, one argument may prove to be more
persuasive than all other contenders. Such an univocal result is unlikely, but it can and does happen. Perhaps one position was simply
grounded in better economics, or perhaps it more adequately captured
the logical policy implications of generally accepted values, or perhaps
it grew from a more comprehensive appreciation of the relevant circumstances, or perhaps it was able to prove that important rights were
involved that trumped more mundane considerations. However rare,
all of us can probably recall several occasions of practical disputation
among family, friends, or colleagues that saw such a result.

At other times, several contending arguments may lead toward a
synthesis in which the various concerns of the parties are, as a Hegelian
would say, *aufgehoben* in a creative fashion. "Compromise" is an inadequate term to characterize such outcomes. For a compromise is a me-
dian outcome between two positions that oppose each other along a
single continuum. A compromise is when you want two thousand
dollars for your used car; I want to pay only one thousand; and we agree
on a price of fifteen hundred. In many policy disputes that generate
practical dialogue, however, the discussion may reveal not a zero-sum

conflict of this sort, but rather contention between different legitimate concerns that pull in divergent directions. With a little thought, it may prove possible in such instances to devise a strategy, hitherto unanticipated, that can satisfy the major legitimate concerns of the contending parties. One possible example of such an outcome would be the creation of "magnet schools" in public school districts undergoing reorganization. Whether or not these schools prove desirable and workable in the long run, they clearly represent a creative attempt to accommodate those who give priority to school desegregation and those who give priority to quality education. The goals are not contradictory, but they may conflict in given cases. The magnet school approach, whether successful or not, seeks to satisfy both concerns by desegregating and beefing up curriculum at the same time.

Finally, neither persuasion nor creative synthesis may prove possible, and the practical dialogue ends with conflicting interests or principles that can neither be adjudicated nor reconciled. Unless the parties to the dispute decide to resort to force, however, the conversation then does not simply terminate, but instead it shifts its focus. When a mutually acceptable policy has not been generated by the discourse, the parties then must decide on the best way to deal with their persistent disagreement. For even given the specific irreconcilable issues that divide them, the participants in the dialogue have a common interest in preventing the disagreement from disrupting their peace, their security, or their freedom. Locke's *Letter concerning Toleration* and Milton Friedman's argument that market-choice mechanisms permit "unanimity without conformity" are good examples of practical arguments that address this issue. Or if tolerant pluralism is not a viable solution to the dilemma of irreconcilable and inadjudicable conflicts—if a single outcome is mandatory—the focus of practical dialogue becomes the appropriate decision-rules to employ. In particular, the discussion at this point in a democracy tends to be directed toward devising the most satisfactory voting system possible. Obviously, interested parties will be biased in favor of voting rules that enhance their chances to win. But general interests and widely shared values remain as criteria for rational discussion and choice—for example, the common interest in social stability and the widely shared principle of equality. John Stuart Mill's argument on behalf of proportional representation in *Considerations on Representative Government*, however unavailing, makes a good example of a contribution to practical dialogue at this state of discussion.

Practical dialogue directed toward identifying and implementing the common good thus does not *supplant* resort to the ballot, even in the most rationally organized society we can imagine. Voting and public deliberations employing practical reason are not alternative modes of decision making, but complementary ones. The notion that seems implied in Jürgen Habermas's account of the rational society that practical discourse in an ideal speech situation would always produce a rational consensus is surely unrealistic. But equally inadequate is the widespread notion that democratic decision making begins with and is exhausted by voting. The former account recognizes the elements of reason and unity in healthy group decisions but neglects the elements of will and plurality. The latter account inappropriately and unnecessarily makes will and plurality the whole story.

The Discipline of Reason: The Political Power of Practical Discourse

Political theorists have given us widely divergent estimates of the political power of reason. In Condorcet's essay on *The Progress of the Human Mind*, Reason (with a capital *R*) is depicted as a kind of autonomous force that engages in an ultimately successful epic struggle with the forces of unreason (i.e., Authority). In Hegel, this conception is metaphysically radicalized, and Reason is portrayed as the ultimately determinative sovereign power within history, a power that cunningly uses the mundane motivation of mankind to fulfill its own purposes. At the other extreme, skeptics and "realists" often depict politics as a battleground of individual interests in which reason figures only in the guise of "rationalization" as a hypocritical cover for selfish appetite.

The truth lies between these extremes. Reason is neither sovereign nor impotent in politics. Reason is not sovereign because it is neither a transcendent entity nor an autonomous power. Rationality is not an independent superhuman force, but a human capacity that may or may not be employed. On the other hand, when rationality becomes operative in political affairs, it is not merely subservient to interests. For the logic of practical discourse exercises an important shaping force on the issues it confronts. Practical reason is not like a cab that people can enter and exit at their convenience. Instead, those who become party to practical dialogue find themselves subject to the discipline of reason—a discipline that may dismay individuals but that has a salutary effect on the *polis*.

Where the conversation of democracy—public, institutionalized practical reasoning together about the common good—is vital, it benefits the body politic in several important ways. In the first place, vital practical discourse improves the grounds of political decision. Second, it forces upon the citizenry a "moral point of view" by demanding and enforcing "objectivity" in practical disputes. Finally, it helps to create, sustain, and define a democratic moral community. In so doing, the effective institutionalization of practical discourse helps to mitigate difficulties of democratic governance that have concerned thoughtful commentators such as John Stuart Mill and Rousseau.

The demands and dynamics of practical discourse enhance political decision making in several ways. For one thing, every participant in the dialogue is faced with the necessity of articulating his or her own political purposes and views. To do that, an individual must lift himself or herself above the level of habitual or instinctive behavior and become more fully cognizant of his or her genuine needs and purposes. Each participant is forced from prereflective torpor into leading a more "examined life." The various inchoate desires that motivate us have to be reconciled and integrated into some coherent pattern that amounts to what Mill and Rawls have characterized as a "plan of life." Simply by virtue of what must be done to participate in practical discourse, each party to it must become a deliberative being—a "rational animal." Everyone who acquires the awareness level sufficient to participate in practical discourse, in effect, has to accomplish within himself or herself precisely the sort of character transformation Rousseau attributes to the passage from the state of nature to the civil state. One "who so far had considered only himself finds that he is forced to act on different principles and to consult his reason before listening to his inclinations."[22]

At the same time that he or she is forced to render his or her own goals coherent and intelligible, one who engages in practical discourse also is forced to broaden his or her appreciation of the needs and purposes of others. In discourse, one not only must speak but must listen as well. Participants in practical discourse do not have the luxury of moral solipsism. The presence and needs of others are forced upon them and must be taken into account as they reflect upon the bearing of their own purposes in the context of a real world that must be shared and rendered mutually habitable.

In short, no party to practical discourse can remain submerged in the pleasure principle. The reality principle intrudes in the form of other people's words. The reality principle also receives a boost from the capacity of practical discourse to enforce some degree of foresight upon the participants. In rationally evaluating conflicting policy recommendations, it becomes necessary to take the longer-run consequences of the policies into account. There is, of course, no guarantee that this heightening of rational awareness will take place, because if all participants have an interest in ignoring the future—as in some issues of intergenerational justice, for example—a conspiracy of the short-sighted may well occur. Usually, however, practical reflection forces people to a greater awareness of eventual effects of different courses of action than they would otherwise have had. In this respect, practical discourse serves the same salutary function Hobbes ascribed to his "civil science." That is, it provides a useful corrective to the myopia induced in human beings by their immediate passions and interests.

The necessity of giving reasons in practical discourse also forces each participant to search for principles relevant to his or her concerns. Claims based upon principle carry more weight than do simple expressions of wants and needs. The latter are not without their own moral weight, of course, recalling Taylor's observation that contribution to the fulfillment of human purposes constitutes a *prima facie* case for calling something "good." Claims based upon more general principles, however, usually trump claims that are not capable of being so grounded. Hence the conduct of vital practical discourse tends to make those who join in it not only more reflective and more farsighted but more principled as well. It does not, of course, create regenerate or altruistic motivations outright. That accomplishment comes only from moral conviction, moral habituation, and possibly grace. But it puts everyone involved under the necessity of finding generalized principles of right to legitimate the goals they deem desirable.

Finally, the constitutive logic of practical discourse in effect forces an "objective" point of view upon those who participate in it. Statements of subjective whim or idiosyncratic preference carry little weight in practical justification. Instead, in order to attempt to justify an evaluation, prescription, or policy proposal, a speaker in practical discourse must provide "backing" by relating his or her proposal to general rather than to particular interests. It is hard to improve on David Hume's depiction of this intrinsic generalizing dynamic of moral discourse. "The more we converse with mankind . . . the more shall we be familiarized to these general preferences and distinctions, without which our conversation and discourse could scarcely be rendered intelligible to each other. Every man's interest is peculiar to himself, and the aversions and desires, which result from it, cannot be supposed to affect others in a like degree. General language, therefore, being formed for general use, must be molded on some more general views, and must affix the epithets of praise or blame, in conformity to sentiments, which arise from the general interests of the community."[23]

More recently, Kurt Baier relied upon the generalizing force of practical discourse to explain how it is that "moral talk is impossible for consistent egoists."[24] The logic of practical discourse forces participants to assume "the moral point of view": their prescriptions must be based on principle, must be meant for everybody, and must be for the good of everyone alike. Hence the language of egoism, predicated upon categories and distinctions grounded in particular interests, simply cannot meet the conceptual entrance requirements of practical dialogue. Following Baier's analysis, John Rawls has incorporated these features of practical discourse into what he calls "the formal constraints of the principle of right." Given the inherent nature of moral talk, Rawls argues, any principles that admit to justification must, among other things, be general, universal, and capable of public acknowledgement.[25] And, like Baier, Rawls concludes that because of these properties of moral speech, when it comes to talk about what should be done, the straightforward egoist is rendered mute.

This is why what Sissela Bok terms the "test of publicity"[26] is not an empty formalism. Anyone who enters the public forum, whatever his or her actual motives, must speak the language of common interests and general principles. We are all familiar with the manifestations of this requirement, even if we reflect too little upon its significance. When it was proposed to end the tax deductibility of the so-called three-martini lunch, for example, restaurateurs were understandably concerned that enactment of the change would cost them revenue. Privately, this was their obvious motivation for campaigning against the loss of that tax break. In public, however, their argumentation could not be merely a declaration of group interest. Instead, they had to invoke concerns that were arguably relevant to the general interest—for example, the potential loss of jobs and heightened unemployment payments from the public treasury—and try to link them with the policy issue at hand. It would be easy to dismiss the resulting public discourse as somewhat hypocritical, with its invocation of the common good in the service of self-interested goals. But that criticism would be beside the point. The point is not the purity of heart of the parties to public practical discourse, but rather the effect that discourse has upon the framing of political conflicts, upon deliberation about the issue at stake, and upon the awareness and behavior of the participants. For the requisite ground rules of such discourse—implicit in the logic of practical reasoning—result in the transformation of what begins as a clash of private interests into a question of the public good. The interested contributors to public deliberations may not in fact want the debate to be focused in this manner. But they have no choice.

The power of institutionalized practical discourse in effect works upon individual disputants much like the famed invisible hand allegedly works in economics. Although their desires may be selfish, their speech acts are constrained to be directed toward the general good. In the realm of overt behavior, to be sure, individuals may ignore the force of the better argument to pursue individual interest over general good. But the impact of this invisible hand in the realm of speech is considerable, nonetheless. It keeps the common good in constant view. It stimulates the adducing of good reasons for policy choices. It enhances the role and improves the judgment of disinterested neutrals in politics. It helps to create a public consciousness. And it causes the morally serious and public-spirited members of society to temper their individual desires in behalf of more inclusive goals and more general values.

For these reasons, the commitment to vital practical discourse operates as a counterforce against the potentially self-destructive centrifugal tendencies that inhere in any liberal polity. Based as they are on consent and individual autonomy, liberal societies necessarily accord at least tacit legitimacy to "selfish" desires. Without the countervailing effect of some centripetal forces, however, the unfettered pursuit of individual interest threatens at least a plunge into the swamp of possessive individualism and possibly even, if Hobbes was right, into an anarchy of each against all.

John Stuart Mill worried about the fissiparous tendencies of free societies in the last chapter of his *A System of Logic*. "The strongest propensities of uncultivated human nature (being the purely selfish ones, and those of a sympathetic character which partake most of the nature of selfishness) evidently tend in themselves to disunite mankind, not to unite them—to make them rivals, not confederates." As a consequence, he argued, "social existence is only possible by a disciplining of those more powerful propensities, which consists in subordinating them to a common system of opinions."[27]

Under the influence of a Comtean belief that scientific progress would bring with it increasing unanimity in political viewpoints, Mill overestimated the degree to which a "common system of opinions" would likely prevail in advanced societies. To the extent that the force of ideas can be effectual in constraining passions, however, practical dialogue contributes toward the "disciplining of those more powerful propensities" that Mill deemed a necessity. In practical discourse, the passions have to justify themselves subordinate to a linguistically in- duced generalized frame of reference. The inherent logic of practical discourse thus in effect enforces Rawls's "formal constraints of the principle of right." The passions may, of course, rebel against this discipline of practical reason—because reason is not a police power— but not with impunity. For in a society where the norms of rationality prevail, desires incapable of rational defense lose their legitimacy—and with it, much of their force.

The Community of Discourse

The "objectivity" that rationality forces upon participants in practical dialogue is, therefore, highly salutary in a free society. The individual preferences that liberal premises enfranchise are inhibited from actu- alizing their destructive potential. Moreover, the institutionalization of practical discourse not only exerts a useful constraint on the disunifying propensities that concerned Mill; it also contributes in a more direct way to the creation of a democratic moral community.

For resolutely individualistic versions of liberalism, of course, the creation of a democratic moral community is a nonproblem. On these accounts, the exhaustive *raison d'être* of liberal democracy is to enable individuals to be as free as possible to pursue their individual purposes. Other people seem to figure into this pursuit only problematically— only, that is, as potential obstacles. The inhabitants of a liberal society are essentially competitors—rivals for space, for resources, for power. The role of the state is simply to referee the contest. The only bonds between citizens are contractual in nature, formed by agreements based on the self-interest of the parties involved.

Not only conservatives and socialists, but other liberals, have rightly protested the inadequacy of this individualistic account of the good society. Conservatives such as Carlyle and Burke lamented that liberal individualism reduced the relationship between human beings to a mere "cash nexus" and that it reduced society to "nothing better than a partnership agreement" in a commercial enterprise. And Marx bemoaned the alienating effects of denying that we are "species beings." However, to retain fraternity, conservatives have seemed willing to abjure equality and the Marxists to sacrifice liberty. The former have aspired to recover community in hierarchical form, and the latter have incarnated community in a totalitarian manner.

Among democratic theorists, neither Mill nor Rousseau was content with the individualistic liberals' abandonment of democratic community. For both of them, some component of social unity was essential to democracy. Yet their accounts of what that unity should consist in and their notions of how it could come about are distinctly questionable.

The basis of community (although he is more apt to call it "unity") in Mill, as we saw in an earlier chapter, was the utilitarian standard backed up by a "powerful natural sentiment" that he believed "advancing civilization" made stronger; the desire "to be in unity with our fellow creatures." The trouble with this formulation is twofold. In the first place, the scenario of an increasingly powerful human desire for unity is a free-floating piece of utopian optimism, unsustained by careful logic and invalidated by experience. And second, the utilitarian norm of greatest good for the greatest number provides a defective account of what human community should be. Perhaps it was not accidental or inconsequential that Mill spoke more of unity than community, for the utilitarian principle proceeds on the mythic supposition that society is one aggregate body whose happiness can be computed and hence maximized as a single sum. The result is that, as Rawls puts it succinctly, "utilitarianism does not take seriously the distinction between persons." In its conception of society, "separate individuals are thought of as so many different lines along which rights and duties are to be assigned and scarce means of satisfaction allocated in accordance with rules so as to give the greatest fulfillment of wants."[28] But persons are in fact distinct, and they are not merely abstract "lines" along which rights, duties, and goods may be distributed. And society is not formed by the coagulation of individual cells into an aggregate whole, but instead arises from the interaction of distinctive and autonomous persons.

Consequently, the conception of community embedded in utilitarian premises is faulty.

Rousseau's solution to the problem of community in democracy is equally problematic and subject to dangerous interpretation. Rousseau was properly unimpressed by the notion that an aggregation of purely self-interest maximizing particular wills could add up to an acceptable form of democratic society. His constructive account, like that of Mill, however, embodies an excessively unitary conception of a democratic community. The whole (society) seems not simply to transcend and transform the parts (individual citizens) but rather to subsume them altogether. The members of the society created by the social contract are, as Rousseau insists, elevated from merely natural and private creatures into civil and social persons. In the process, however, they seem to lose—despite Rousseau's protestations to the contrary—both the autonomy of their wills and the integrity of their own moral judgment. When outvoted, for example, the citizen of Rousseau's democracy is supposed to conclude that he or she was "mistaken" and that "if his particular opinion had carried the day he should have achieved the opposite of what was his will." And when individuals are compelled to submit to conventions established by the Sovereign, they are held to "obey no one but their own will." Thus the social compact "gives the body politic absolute power over all its members" and it requires "the total alienation of each associate, together with all his rights, to the whole community."[29]

Implicit in the constitutive dialogue of the rational society is a conception of democratic community that is superior to both individualistic reductivism and to the excessively unitary conceptions of Rousseau and utilitarianism. For participants in practical discourse are united by a common enterprise and are bound by obligations that constrain their self-interest; but they remain distinct persons who retain their integrity and autonomy.

Democratic citizens who confront and interact with each other in the *agora* to reason together about what should be done are not monads who relate in purely contractual fashion. They bargain, but are not mere bargainers—for the *agora* is more than a marketplace. Bargaining occurs at the limits of rational consensus and does not simply substitute for discussion of how common purposes may best be served. The parties to a practical dialogue, moreover, are not mere adversaries. They may have conflicting opinions and divergent interests. But they are not simply opponents in a zero-sum game. Instead, they are united in a common quest to ascertain what the public interest may require and to find policies that maximize the general welfare. There is always tension and opposition in practical discourse, for if unanimity were natural and spontaneous there would be little need for discussion; but there is not enmity, so long as the bonds of dialogue hold.

A condition and, reciprocally, a product of serious dialogue, more-over, is respect for the other parties to the conversation. Respect here does not mean admiration, necessarily; nor does it require affection. It simply means the recognition of the other as in some sense a moral entity and to some degree an equal. To engage in practical dialogue with someone implies attributing to that person the status of a rational being. We can reason only with those who have the mental capacity to entertain and articulate ideas and who have the seriousness of purpose to submit those ideas for rational evaluation. Since these respect-worthy attributes are the same ones upon which we base our own self-regard as a moral being, recognizing those qualities in another person at the same time implies accepting him or her as an equal—at least in certain fundamental ways. More will be said later about the equality of citizens of a rational society. For the moment, the point simply is that persons in dialogue are not the isolated, self-sufficient, and self-aggrandizing monads of straightforward individualism. Instead, they are members of a genuine community bound by ties of mutual obliga-tion and respect.

A community of discourse is not, however, a collectivist unity. Par-ties to practical dialogue are joined in common pursuit of the human good; they share their thoughts and concerns; they also share obliga-tions engendered by the requisites of intelligible speech oriented to-ward the truth. But they are under no necessity to alienate themselves totally to the community, as Rousseau demands. Nor are they sub-sumed into the utilitarian "macro-person." The very notion of dialogue presupposes separate existences. In the act of speaking to another, one implicitly distinguishes one's own identity from that of his or her audience. "I say" is a declaration of autonomy as well as a mode of communication and relationship.

Participants in rational discourse, moreover, are not bound to sur-render the integrity of their judgment. Unlike Rousseau's citizen, who is supposed to conclude that he or she was mistaken if the preponderant judgment runs against him or her, one who accepts the conventions of rational discourse may be permitted to persist in his or her views. In the scientific community, for example, so long as the evidentiary basis and the theoretical logic behind the prevailing consensus is not absolutely overwhelming, rational dissent is possible and generally respected. In practical discourse, of course, such a decisive outcome of deliberation is rare. It is entirely appropriate, therefore, for members of a society grounded in practical discourse to continue the argument in hopes of carrying the battle another day. The preponderant judgment must be respected, but no one need confess error simply because he or she holds a minority view.

A human community constituted by practical discourse is a real-world approximation of what Kant termed a "realm of ends." It is, to borrow Kant's phrase, "a systematic linking of rational beings."[30] In Kant's formulation, the practical reason involved was "pure" universalizing form applied a priori to the will independent of all experience. The "linking" among the rational beings in the realm of ends was therefore abstract and indirect. It consisted in their common relationship to and determination by the objective laws of pure practical reason. And because it was essentially logical rather than experimental, moral discourse could be monologic. To know what to do, one should "ask oneself" whether he or she could will that his or her maxim should be a general law.

The "realm of ends" formed by mutual commitment to the norms and institutions of practical discourse, in contrast, is concrete and dialogic. Rather than attempting to escape heteronomy and rise above experience, it uses the experience of its members as a crucial resource. It relies on Aristotle's *phronesis* rather than on pure reason. And rather than speaking with themselves about the potential universalizability of maxims guiding their actions, the parties to practical dialogue "reason *together*." They talk and listen to each *other*, since the desires and perceptions of all participants figure into the determination of the common good. The hallmark of the relationship among serious and sincere parties to practical dialogue, likewise, is what Kant designates as the proper attitude of rational beings for each other: respect. But whereas for Kant "respect for a person is properly only respect for the law of which he gives us an example,"[31] in the society constituted by practical dialogue respect is directed toward the persons themselves. They deserve and elicit respect because of the moral status they achieve through their acceptance of the discipline of discourse. For it is only through this acceptance that human beings achieve the "rational will" that is the appropriate object of moral respect.

Conclusion

A society that conducts its affairs as a rational enterprise, in sum, is characterized by this complex of functionally interrelated systemic components. It is a community of autonomous persons oriented toward the understanding and attainment of their common and individual human good. The members of this community possess a liberal form of *homonoia* that corresponds to the open texture of the human good they seek. And the central institutional feature of the enterprise is practical discourse that not only seeks to define the common good but that forces upon those who participate in it an implicit acknowledgment of the formal constraints of the principle of right.

This is a conception of good political practice that should hold appeal to liberals in the tradition of Locke and Mill and to communitarians in the tradition of civic republicanism alike. For it is a conception that embodies the concern of Locke and Mill for the larger common weal as it likewise incorporates their insistence—as I argue in the next chapter—upon the fundamental liberty, equality, and integrity of individual citizens. And it is a conception that embodies the communitarians' concerns for community and common good while providing the grounds—as I also argue in the next chapter—for a coherent conception of civic virtue.

The conception of politics as a rational enterprise likewise avoids falling into the standard difficulties visited upon both liberalism and communitarianism by their usual philosophical bedfellows.

Contemporary liberalism is generally associated with philosophies of utility or philosophies of right. The former make it difficult to preserve the integrity of individual citizens and at the same time inflicts upon liberalism a dogmatic and reductive (to the extent that it is not hopelessly ambiguous) conception of the good. Philosophies of right, on the other hand, have protected individual liberties but made it exceptionally difficult to understand or validate any larger conception of constitutive political community; and they have, for correlative reasons, been excessively skeptical about any animating role of the human good in liberal politics. Politics as a rational enterprise, in contrast, sustains both individual integrity and community; and it gives the common good a central role in politics while leaving it open-textured enough to ratify liberal concerns for tolerance and pluralism.

The current tendency of the communitarian perspective on politics, on the other hand, has been toward a reliance upon the normative validity of conventional "shared understandings" that threatens to deprive the communitarian ideal of critical force. This difficulty appears most strikingly, perhaps, in sections of Walzer's *Spheres of Justice,* in which he feels obligated to explain why the norm of shared understandings might not legitimate a caste society.[32] In parallel, communitarians who like Sandel juxtapose "situated selves" and "constitutive communities" to the "unencumbered selves" and purely instrumental societies of rights-based liberalism have some real difficulty explaining how this line of criticism does not lead to a relativistic and conventionalist outcome. Like Walzer, Sandel does not intend this conclusion. But it is clearly a somewhat awkward argument to criticize deontological theories by invoking the normativity of "situated principles of justice" and then insisting that these constitutive situations can themselves be subject to moral judgment. From where? By reference to what?

The conception of politics as a rational enterprise, I believe, can be of assistance to communitarians at precisely this point. It is a normative conception that incorporates and validates the central communitarian concerns about community and common good. It not only sustains the claim that "when politics goes well, we can know a good in common that we cannot know alone";[33] but it also explains how that is possible. And it provides the communitarian argument with fundamental critical standards that seem problematic on the "shared understandings" account. For it is not any and all communities that are normative, but only communities whose practices adhere to the constitution of rational enterprises—only communities that, for example, accept the discipline of reason and respect the autonomy of their members.

When we consider the implications of the model of a community of rational practice for the rights, privileges, and obligations of its individual citizens, moreover, we find that the communitarian and republican concern with civic virtue receives a logical basis. Yet it does so without in any way jeopardizing the deontological liberal's insistence upon the sanctity of individual civil rights. For citizenship in a rational republic involves a complex pattern of related rights and duties. Having examined in this chapter the central systemic features of politics as a rational enterprise, then, we now turn to look at what this form of politics means at the level of the individual citizen.

We have seen that citizenship in the republic of reason makes one a participant in a democratic moral community, a community character-ized by a specific and limited form of *homonoia*. It is possible, moreover, to go somewhat farther in specifying the elements of citizenship in a rational society. For individuals in societies are like words in language-games. Every language-game, as Wittgenstein has impressed upon us, has its own "logic." "Logic" here means not formal demonstration; instead, it means the structural and functional "fit" between an orga-nized ensemble and its constituent parts. Each word acquires its mean-ing from its "use"—i.e., from the role it plays within the larger pattern of speech acts. We can understand what words mean, then, only after we know the point of the game. Conversely, if we understand the overall structure of a language-game, we can make some inferences about its constituent elements.

For example, if someone who had never heard of football were told the overall structure and logic of the game, he or she would be able to draw some inferences about the tasks and roles of individual players. If the point of the game is to advance a ball over a goal line despite the physical opposition of the defense, it seems apparent that the game will generate ball carriers, blockers, and tacklers. It is "in the nature of the game." Given the point and fundamental institutions of a rational society, likewise, it is possible to make certain inferences about the role demands incumbent on its "players." Given the nature of a republic of reason, we can make some reasonable inferences about the rights, privileges, and obligations of its citizens.

Citizenship in a rational society, it turns out, incorporates some of the most important liberal norms. In this respect, the intuition at the heart of early liberalism concerning the congruence between rational practice and liberal values seems vindicated. At the same time, it is only a particular variant of liberalism that seems congruent with the structure of a rational society. Citizens of a rational society, for example, cannot be dogmatic libertarians, moral pyrrhonists, or possessive individualists. Their rights and privileges arise in the context of obligations incumbent upon them. Those obligations, moreover, seem very similar in character to the norms of civic virtue championed by civic republicans. The full pattern of citizenship in the republic of reason, therefore, encourages us again to look at the relationship between liberalism and civic republicanism as one of complementarity rather than opposition.

Participation

Participation, as a norm of good practice, has had a somewhat checkered career in the histories of both political liberalism and political rationalism. When the phrase "participatory democracy" gained currency a couple of decades back, its adherents could find sustenance from some traditional theories of liberal democracy; but it also was true that they were placing emphasis on a norm of political practice that had been ignored or subordinated by other and recent versions of liberalism.

Lockean liberalism gave little mention to participation. The necessities of good government, as depicted in the *Second Treatise*, were consent, representation, respect for individual rights, and concern for the general good. The important thing for the individual was that his or her rights be protected and his or her interests represented in the councils of state.

It was principally Rousseau and Mill who insisted that adequate representation alone was not sufficient to the purposes of democracy. Rousseau chided the English for believing they were free. They were free, he said, only at election time; and after that they lapsed into slavery. In a healthy state, the people did not leave things to designated representatives. Instead, they participated directly in public affairs. "In a well-ordered city every man flies to the assemblies."[1]

Mill, without buying into the myth of the general will, agreed that active participation by the citizenry in public affairs was an essential feature of the "ideally best polity." Participation, Mill argued, was necessary for two reasons. In the first place, the politically passive are forever in danger of having their interests neglected. Every person is alone the best guardian of his or her own rights and interests. Hence these rights and interests "are only secure from being disregarded, when the person interested is himself able, and habitually disposed, to stand up for them." Second, Mill believed that the "principal element" of good government was "the improvement of the people themselves. "Improvement" for Mill meant, in turn, the development of intelligence and the moral capacities. And political participation was conducive to both. It was conducive to the improvement of the people's intellect, because "the only sufficient incitement to mental exertion, in any but a few minds in a generation, is the prospect of some practical use to be made of the results"; and the political consequences of public participation provide this practical incentive. Likewise, the moral capacities of individual citizens are enlarged by participation in public affairs, because it becomes necessary for an active participant to "weigh interests not his own, to be guided . . . by another rule than his private partialities, and to apply, at every turn, principles and maxims which have for their reason of existence the general good."[2]

The pluralist and libertarian conceptions of liberal democracy that have been dominant recently, at least in this country, have basically abandoned the notion that citizen participation in public affairs is somehow essential to a good society. Indeed, these theories of liberalism tend to undermine the notion of participation altogether; for in the libertarian view all legitimate interests are private, and in the pluralist view extensive participation can be dangerous. The libertarian liberalism of a Robert Nozick or of *laissez-faire* economists such as Milton Friedman in effect strips Locke of his concern for natural law or common good and takes what is left as the liberal ideal. Legitimate politics, on this account, is simply an institutional device for the maximization of private interests. "Participation" here can only mean the same thing as the "rational" pursuit of self-interest. There is no legitimate public sphere for any more expansive form of participation to inhabit. The pluralist conception of democracy is more in the tradition of Hume's utilitarian conservatism than of Mill. Like Hume, the pluralists are "realists," wanting to keep their ideals close enough to current actualities to maintain credibility. And also like Hume, they take stability and moderation—rather than, like Mill, individual improvement—as the decisive tests of a good polity. Participation, therefore, loses its standing; for participation seems clearly less essential to system stability and moderation than it is to individual development. Indeed, participation can be seen as potentially unsettling if it is too extensive. Widespread political mobilization often creates serious pressure on a liberal regime. Moreover, given the demonstrably low levels of knowledge and the apparently questionable devotion to liberal verities on the part of much of the populace, a certain amount of nonparticipation may be seen as a very good thing. Some apathy may be quite welcome.[3]

Political rationalism, like the liberalism with which it is sometimes associated, has similarly run in different directions on the issue of participation. Although they did not explicitly make it a functional centerpiece of their political theories, some early modern rationalists held views that were conducive to the idea that increasing political participation could be expected with the advance of enlightenment. For these rationalists, reason was characterized by simplicity, clarity, and hence accessibility. Thus it could seem plausible to suppose, as Descartes once predicted, that the peasant of the future would exceed present-day philosophers in his capacity to apprehend the truth. On that supposition, it would seem logical to imagine that political participation would be beneficial and that it could increase as rational competency spread throughout the populace. On the other hand, by the nineteenth century earlier beliefs in the simplicity of reason and the consequent accessibility of truth were being questioned. And once it was concluded that the rational capacity to understand scientific discoveries was limited to the few, rationalism could and did lead to a new form of political elitism that consigned the general citizenry to passive obedience. "Can it be supposed," asked Comte, "that the most important and the most delicate conceptions, and those which by their complexity are accessible to only a small number of highly prepared understandings are to be abandoned to the arbitrary and variable decisions of the least competent minds?" Of course not. Thus "spontaneous subordination . . . becomes the type of all wise social coordination."[4] Participation, for most of the populace, on this account is exhausted by followership.

The logic of our post-positivist conception of liberal rationalism lends support—and additional philosophical backing—to Mill's insistence upon the importance of participation in a good society. Several considerations suggest the logical linkage between the norm of participation and the conception of politics as a rational enterprise. The underlying basis of the linkage can be stated succinctly in the words of Jürgen Habermas: "In a process of enlightenment, there can only be participants."[5]

In the creation of a political society, human beings are—as Hobbes put it in his introduction to *Leviathan*—both the matter and the artificer. The point of a rational society is to understand and, as best as possible, achieve the common good. The "matter" in such a task is the wants, needs, and desires of the people. And a crucial part of the creative ("artificing") process is attaining a sound judgment about the content of the common good. Citizen participation, then, is essential on both sides of this process.

Concrete conceptions of the common good are not obtainable a priori. Instead, we can gain some estimation of the common good only experimentally and empirically. The relevant "data" from which to generate a warranted conception of the general good are the aspirations and needs of a society's members. The common good may, as Rousseau insisted, not be simply an additive sum of all the individual interests in a society. But any account of the common good not grounded in the real concerns and interests of the citizenry would clearly be illusory.

To know what the common good is, then, we must begin by ascertaining the wants and needs of the people. How can this be done? Surely, only by listening to what they say they want. Ultimately, as Mill was correct to insist, each individual is the best judge and guardian of his or her own best interests. Only those seeking an excuse for despotism invoke the notion of false consciousness in such a way as to deny that, eventually, claims about a person's "best interest" have to be validated by that person himself or herself. A rational society, therefore, must rely upon the free and full participation of citizens in its data-gathering process. Any interest that remains unarticulated is a datum lost.

The standard pluralist conception of liberal democracy, of course, would concede that "interest articulation" is a fundamental part of the policy process. But a rational society asks of its citizens participation in an additional way, as well. Not only their affective participation—their articulation of their wants—is demanded, but also their cognitive participation. For once the individual wants and needs of the citizenry have been canvassed, an act of judgment is called for. It is necessary at that point to reflect upon what the common good might be in light of the interests that have been articulated. The citizen of a rational society, in short, is asked to participate not only in the process of establishing the wants and needs of the community but also in an act of collective judgment.

Widespread participation in this process of collective judgment seems logically to be imperative in a rational society. Any plausible conception of the common good, especially in a large and diverse society, will necessarily be the product of an intellectual synthesis. By synthesis here I mean not a Hegelian synthesis allegedly created by the cunning of Reason. Rather I mean the kind of synthesis depicted by Karl Mannheim in *Ideology and Utopia*. As Mannheim wrote there, "all points of view in politics are but partial points of view because historical totality is always too comprehensive to be grasped by any one of the individual points of view which emerge out of it."[6] What Mannheim says of "historical totality" is certainly true, almost by definition, of the common good. Apprehending the common good requires a comprehensiveness of vision not available to single individuals or groups, who inevitably see social problems from a partial point of view. Only through the confrontation and juxtaposition of these partial points of view can a larger vision emerge that takes the various interests and perspectives into account. If participation in this process is limited, if all points of view are not adequately represented, the emergent synthesis will remain partial. Its depiction of the general good will be flawed, because it is not in fact general—some parts being left out of the picture.

It should not be supposed, of course, that the juxtaposition and confrontation of different viewpoints actually produces a single unequivocal comprehensive synthesis that all parties can accept. Mannheim seems to have fallen into this error by arguing that "politics as a science is for the first time possible"—a product of the "integration of many mutually complementary points of view."[7] But we have all experienced the enlarging of our conception of the common purpose of some group we belonged to when we heard other members of the group articulate their viewpoint. The point here is simply that the dynamics of this kind of "enlarging" are contingent upon adequate participation. Any viewpoint not stated is a perspective that is lost from the final assessment of what the general good requires.

Widespread participation is also essential in a rational society, finally, because it is, in Mill's words, a "school of public spirit." Participation draws individuals into a moral community and in the process civilizes them and makes them "rational beings." As the etymology of the term *idiot* indicates, the Greeks were sensitive to this impact on the individual of participation in public affairs. Anyone who never ventured into the *agora*, anyone whose life was exhausted in purely private pursuits, was seen as less than a whole human being. Participation in a rational society thus serves both the purposes of the society and enhances the welfare of its members at the same time.

Liberty

A rational society is impossible without extensive liberty. Civil liberties are not optional luxury items granted by the society out of largesse. Nor, on the other hand, are civil liberties possessed by individuals on the basis of some kind of a priori right or entitlement. Instead, a rational society must be a free society because freedom is a *conditio sine qua non* of its rationality.

It is not accidental but essential that specific freedoms are fundamental features of the prototypical rational societies of language and science. It is part of the definition of an "ideal speech situation" that the participants be free in several respects. And members of the scientific community likewise must be accorded the freedom to pursue their intimations of the truth if the scientific enterprise is to prosper.

The ideal speech situation, first, is necessarily an open forum. Communication would be constrained and distorted if anyone with something to say were precluded a priori from the conversation. Freedom of entry is thus a structural requisite of rationally organized discourse. For rational argumentation is designed to produce an outcome that is determined by the force of the superior argument. And that hope would be rendered dubious from the outset if some views were denied consideration. It is also a condition of truth-oriented speech that it be "sincere." As Habermas notes, in his account of the constitutive rules composing the infrastructure of the ideal speech situation, any speaker in rational discourse makes several implicit "validity claims." One of these claims is that the speech act is sincere—"truthfulness for the intentions expressed."[8] And for speech to be sincere in this sense, it must again be "free." One cannot be giving a truthful account of one's views if his or her expression of those views is skewed by outside forces.

Freedom is similarly a constituent feature of the republic of science.

Members of the scientific community, first, are given "academic freedom." They are free to conduct their research in line with their intimations of scientific truth. Second, institutional mechanisms such as journals and conferences try to ensure that all findings and theories of competent scientists receive a hearing by their fellows. And finally, each practicing scientist retains the liberty of scientific conscience: he or she can assent or not to the prevailing consensus on some matter on the basis of his or her own reading of the evidence. If his or her views are not generally accepted, most of the scientific community may head off in another direction. But the dissenter is not prohibited from trying to prove them wrong. The analysis of scientific inquiry and of communicative competence, then, lead to the same conclusion. Put simply, freedom of thought and speech is a necessary condition of rational practice.

A society that is organized around the rational pursuit of the human good, therefore, must be a free society. Each citizen of a rational society must be given the latitude to develop his or her own understanding of what is right and good. And each citizen must have the freedom to communicate that understanding to his or her fellow citizens, who in turn may share their own perceptions and have them tested by rational argumentation. Neither logic nor experience sustain the optimistic belief that the best ideas always emerge from the "free marketplace of ideas." But the results of an intellectual monopoly are almost invariably worse. Such progress as the fallible human mind can make depends on a dialectic of, to borrow Popper's phrase, conjecture and refutation. Censorship simply proscribes relevant conjectures and discourages the rational testing intrinsic to attempts at refutation. It is not accidental, then, that closed societies often generate substantively irrational doctrines, because the very fact of closure is a departure from procedural rationality. When force other than the force of the better argument distorts the free exercise of human judgment, outcomes such as Lysenkoism or Aryan physics are made possible.

Grounding the liberty of thought and discussion in the infrastructure of rational practice has somewhat different policy implications from grounding it in a putative right of the individual to "freedom of expression." For the point of free speech and discussion in a rational society is not the subjective gratification of the individual who likes to say what he or she pleases. Instead, the point is the essential contribution of free speech and discussion to the knowledge and attainment of the common good. What should have the absolute protection of a rational society, consequently, is the expression of thoughts and ideas. Where no ideational content is involved, the pleasure of free expression may be balanced against other interests. The liberty to manifest my feelings may be a good, but it is not the essential constituent element of rational practice that the liberty to communicate ideas is. If I want to say something about what I perceive to be true or good or right, in a rational society my protection should be absolute against those who could silence me. But if I want to express myself by dancing naked in the streets at midnight, that privilege may be granted or not depending upon how that "freedom of expression" impacts upon other legitimate interests.

The point of making this distinction between expression of ideas and expression of feeling is not to denigrate the value of the latter. Rather it is to base the protection of the former on stronger grounds. The libertarian case for the freedom of thought on grounds of individual entitlement sounds strong enough. "Entitlement" is an absolute term. But in fact, if individual entitlements are too broadly defined then they must in an imperfect and interdependent world end up by being balanced off against each other. If the basis of the protection of the free communication of ideas, however, is not one individual entitlement among other potentially conflicting entitlements but rather its distinctive and essential role in achieving the common good, a priority status is achieved. Expressing an idea is not one subjective pleasure to be traded off against other subjective pleasures. It is a *sine qua non* of rational practice and therefore cannot be balanced off against anything so long as the society wants to remain rational.

If freedom of expression in the broad sense does not, under the logic of rational practice, enjoy the same lofty status as the freedom to articulate ideas, a rational society nonetheless must be *prima facie* permissive in allowing individual citizens to lead their lives as they choose. The *prima facie* right to freedom of action enjoyed by citizens of a rational society is based on their status as rational beings and in recognition of the open-endedness and plurality of the human good. Rational beings must be, to some degree, autonomous agents. That does not mean that they must be radically autonomous in a Sartrean existentialist sense. They do not have the right to be bound only by rules they freely create. It does mean, however, that they are deliberative agents. They possess the capability to conceive, evaluate, and pursue goals. It is, then, commensurate with their nature and status that they be permitted to adopt their own "plan of life." This phrase has recently been invoked by Rawls, of course, in his theory of justice. But it is equally central to Mill's argument on behalf of individual liberty. In Mill's words, "he who lets the world . . . choose his plan of life for him has no need of any other faculty than the ape-like one of imitation."[9] Hence, to deny a citizen the *prima facie* right to determine his or her own plan of life is to deny his or her rationality; and no rational society can do that without self-contradiction.

The bias of a rational society toward freedom of individual action is also appropriate because of the nature of the human good—its constitutive *telos*. For the human good, as we observed in the previous chapter, is open textured, understood only through experience, and varies somewhat in individual cases because of differences in human tastes and talents. Whenever possible without infringing the rights and legitimate interests of others, therefore, a rational society will allow its citizens great latitude in what the Declaration of Independence somewhat reductively terms the "pursuit of happiness." The different plans of life generated by a rational but diverse citizenry amount to "experiments of living." Given the nature of the human good, it is proper to organize our life together so that "the worth of different modes of life should be proved practically, when anyone thinks fit to try them."[10]

The logic of rational practice in politics thus sustains Mill's argument in *On Liberty* but provides for it somewhat different—and I think more secure—philosophical foundations. As is well known, Mill chose to "forego any advantage which could be derived to my argument from the idea of abstract right as a thing independent of utility."[11] The difficulty with this posture, however, is that it seems to leave the status of individual liberty quite precarious if the utilitarian maxim is strictly applied. It seems quite conceivable that the suppression of some unpopular individuals' freedoms might result in more utils of pleasure to the suppressers than utils of pain to the constrained minority, simply because of the force of numbers. And in such an instance, utilitarian morality would seem to sanction the forfeiture rather than the protection of liberty.

Following the passage just cited, Mill seems to try to fend off such a possibility by interpreting "utility" in a way that transcends the Benthamite paradigm. The proper standard of action, he says, must be "utility in the largest sense, grounded on the permanent interests of man as a progressive being."[12] This step is in fact a necessary one if Mill is to succeed in what he sets out to do. However, Mill never really fills in this very abstract stipulation by specifying the nature or source of these "permanent interests." Moreover, with the key adjective "progressive" he seems to reach out rhetorically in the direction of Comte, where he would have been better advised to use the term "rational" and reach for support back to Aristotle or to Kant. For what gives liberty its priority in human life is its essential link with rational action and thence to human fulfillment.

Rights

Had Mill moved in this direction, moreover, he would not only have given his argument on behalf of liberty a firmer basis, he also might have realized that what he called "utility in the largest sense"—i.e., the common good of a rational society—was not incompatible with but complementary to "the idea of abstract right."

The idea of rights—whether "natural" rights or human rights—seems to be one of those conceptions we can neither live with nor live without. Like a cross between the abominable snowman and the phoenix, it is systematically elusive but impossible to kill. The Enlightenment-era constitutions of France and the United States placed rights at their center, only to have the whole idea dismissed by Bentham a few years later as "nonsense on stilts." More recently, one well-known theory of liberal democracy tells us that "the assumptions that made the idea of natural rights intellectually defensible have tended to dissolve in modern times";[13] but another begins by stipulating that "individuals have rights . . . so strong and far-reaching . . . that they raise the question of what, if anything, the state and its officials may do."[14]

Adherents of the doctrine of rights face two difficulties that their critics feed upon. First, it seems difficult to explain the basis of a claim of right if it is not grounded in explicit theology or in positive law. Second, it is difficult to specify the actual extent of specific concrete rights. Critics have noted, for example, that attempts to enumerate human rights—such as in the United Nations Universal Declaration of Human Rights (1948)—tend to turn into a wish list that confers the status of right upon almost every significant human goal. As a consequence, contradictory claims of right almost inevitably develop. Nozick's stipulated entitlement to holdings legitimately acquired, for example, is clearly not compatible with the claim of the United Nations

Universal Declaration that everyone has the right to an adequate standard of living.

The conception of a rational society cannot solve the latter kind of problem. The conferral of the status of right upon specific needs or claims is inevitably a product of casuistic judgment. Principles can supply only the base starting point for these judgments, involving as they do a complex assessment of circumstances and possibilities. The conception of a rational society does provide, however, a means of understanding the fundamental nature and basis of human rights in general. From the standpoint of a politics of rational practice, a right is quite simply a demand that can be predicated on the essential attributes of a rational being.

The basic argument here is the same as Kant's famous argument in section 2 of the *Metaphysic of Morals*, an argument given a contemporary rendering by Alan Gewirth in *Reason and Morality*.[15] The only difference is that Kant's argument was encumbered by his capitulation to Cartesian metaphysics and his consequent self-limitation of rationality to "pure reason." Because he alleged that his moral philosophy was not "held back by anything empirical," moreover, Kant claimed for his conclusions an epistemic status that in fact no moral argument can achieve. However, even if we reject Kant's admonition that we must not make our conception of right "dependent on the particular nature of human reason"[16] and insist instead that this is precisely what it is based upon, the structure of the argument—although not its putative status or its metaphysical basis—remains pretty much intact.

As we noted earlier, a rational being is purposive, deliberative, and autonomous. The voluntary actions of a rational animal are directed toward the attainment of some end. As part of his or her rationality, moreover, a rational actor has the capacity to consider different goals and to judge which of these possible ends is the best. He or she has the capacity for *proairesis*, "the deliberate desire of something within our power," a capacity that Aristotle saw as differentiating adult human beings from brutes and children.[17] And a rational animal is autonomous in the sense that he "knows himself at liberty to acquiesce or resist" the impulses of nature, a capacity that Rousseau saw as the distinctive feature of human beings.[18] Because of these faculties of deliberation, choice, and self-transcending reflection, moreover, a rational being has the ability to act on the basis of principles—in accordance with, as Kant put it, the concept of laws.[19]

Rational animals, then, do not "behave." They are not merely dependent variables in some great sociological mechanism. Instead they are responsible agents—persons who are answerable for what they do. To "hold someone liable" for his or her actions, however, is at the same time to accord him or her *respect*. Only those with *dignity*—with the standing of a moral being—can be declared "guilty." We may prod cattle with sticks to keep them in bounds, but the prodding is not punishment, not imposed penance, as it were. Cattle are not culpable, because they are not rational.

To accord individuals dignity and respect, as Kant insists, is to recognize them as "ends-in-themselves." This, then, is the fundamental basis of human rights in a rational society: every citizen, as a rational being, has a legitimate claim to be treated with respect, as an "end-in-himself or herself" and not merely as a means. What specific protections are entailed by this fundamental prohibition against treating rational animals as means may be subject to dispute. Indeed, how best to give concrete embodiment to this abstract principle should be one of the continuing items on the agenda of a rational society's dialogue. It seems reasonable to suppose that a rational animal could not exist in circumstances of total dependency on his or her immediate environment, for example, but whether and what kind of "private property right" that requirement entails is not entirely clear and may vary with changing circumstances.

Respect for human rights, then, is in a rational society not a categorical imperative—not a synthetic a priori mandate. But it is nonetheless a hypothetical imperative of great force. A rational society cannot deny human rights, it cannot treat its members as means rather than ends, on pain of logical self-contradiction and practical self-dissolution. A rational society requires rational persons as its constituency, simply as a functional necessity. Its most basic institutions presuppose rational participants. Hence, if a rational society were to treat its members as means rather than ends, if it did not respect them and accord them dignity, it would deprive them of the *conditio sine qua non* of their performance as citizens. Failure to recognize human rights turns people into mere subjects, and although an authoritarian state can subsist in that way, a rational society cannot.

Toleration

The *prima facie* bias toward liberty of a rational society, the open-endedness and plurality of the human good, and the rights that append to rational beings provide the grounds for another structural requisite of a rational society: toleration.

Liberals, it seems, have always known that they were supposed to be tolerant, but they have not always known exactly why. Liberalism has seen a number of justifications for toleration of different religious persuasions and moral perspectives. Some of these are supplementary to each other, but others—at least in their broader implications—seem to be in some tension with each other.

Locke's argument for toleration in his *Letter* was based on several kinds of considerations. Traditional doubts about the viability and propriety of toleration involved a belief that the enforcement of correct doctrine was necessary for political stability and for religious salvation. Locke confronted this belief with political, theological, moral, and epistemological arguments. Politically, he said, it was backwards to see religious dissent as a source of political subversion. Religious dissidents, he argued, become political dissidents not because they have different religious beliefs, but because they are persecuted. Enforced conformity in matters religious, then, is not the solution to previously subsisting subversive tendencies among religious dissenters, but rather the cause of these tendencies. Second, Locke invoked the doctrine of justification by faith to deny that my neighbor's apostasy would threaten my own salvation. "If any man err from the right way, it is his own misfortune, no injury to thee," wrote Locke. For the same reason—i.e., because "faith only and inward sincerity" are what "procure acceptance with God"—it is unavailing to force on someone a profession of faith that he or she in fact does not believe. Third, invoking epistemological views about the limitations of the mind that he was to expand in his *Essay*, Locke wrote that "every church is orthodox to itself" and that "the controversy between these churches about the truth of their doctrines and the purity of their worship is on both sides equal; nor is there any judge, either at Constantinople or elsewhere on earth by whose sentence it can be determined."[20] And finally, Locke pointed out that persecution even on "pretense of religion" was hardly compatible with Christian charity.

The toleration espoused by Locke, however, was limited in scope. It was, as some have termed it, "toleration on a leash." Several categories of people, including atheists, were not entitled to toleration. Moreover, Locke's epistemological fallibilism occurred in the context of his moral cognitivism; and his individualistic doctrine of justification by faith coexisted with his insistence on the significance of "the public good." Since Locke, the West has become increasingly secularized, and Western philosophers have generally become more skeptical about moral knowledge. The tendency within recent liberalism, therefore, has been not only to generalize toleration beyond the bounds Locke set for it but also to radicalize and secularize his arguments in its behalf.

Democratic relativism, for example, justifies toleration by radicalizing Locke's fallibilism with regard to moral truth. Locke believed that reason could tell us a lot about the good life, but that some disputes over esoteric niceties of theology were inadjudicable by the human mind. Relativists believe with Hobbes that "whatsoever is the object of any man's appetite or desire, that is it which he for his part calleth good."[21] Since there is no objective good, then, but only subjective appetite, it follows that no moral viewpoint or conception of the good life is better than any other. All such conceptions, being in fact expressions of subjective appetite, are not subject to justification and therefore have no warrant for hegemony. Toleration is simply a policy of live-and-let-live that seems appropriate on the basis of moral skepticism.

The libertarian strand of liberalism, similarly, secularizes and thereby radicalizes the individualism of Locke's doctrine of justification by faith. "The care of every man's soul belongs unto himself, and is to be left unto himself," Locke wrote in his *Letter.*[22] Exactly so, say the libertarians. Every tub should rest on its own bottom. Individuals have no positive obligations toward each other, but they do owe each other the toleration that is warranted by their right to run their own lives as they see fit. Toleration is the opposite face of individual entitlement.

These contemporary skeptical and libertarian arguments on behalf of toleration have their drawbacks, however. The unmitigated individualism of the libertarian account seems to ground toleration in mutual indifference. Toleration is just the positive face of a society of strangers. Libertarian toleration is Aristotle's cattle "grazing together" without getting in each other's way. It is better than oppression or fratricide, certainly; but it is an inadequate conception of a good society. Toleration is a political virtue that functions properly in concert with other political virtues. By excising toleration from this framework and elevating it to the paramount political virtue, the libertarian argument both distorts and overburdens it. A good society is tolerant, but a merely tolerant society is not good. Indeed, where mutual toleration is the only relationship among citizens, it ceases to be a virtue.

Grounding toleration in moral relativism is equally problematic. The difficulty here is that the argument "if relativism, then toleration" is logically incomplete. It does follow from value relativism that no one has *moral* grounds for imposing his or her views about the good life on others. Moral skepticism undermines intolerance based on moral certitude. But it cannot offer logical impediment to intolerance of other sorts. For if relativism denies that I have moral grounds for imposing my will or my ideas on you, it also provides no obstacle to my doing so out of a morally unadorned *libido dominandi*. Moral relativism may undermine the claims of fanatics, but it gives *carte blanche* to power-hungry cynics. In fact, a policy of toleration can be derived from a belief in moral relativism only when that belief is bolstered by other empirical or moral judgments. However, empirical judgments are always debatable, and the moral judgments are inadmissible on relativist premises.

Suppose, for example, that even if there are no cognitive grounds for enforcing uniformity of belief the political consequences of doctrinal *laissez-faire* are intolerable. Suppose that an unregulated multiplicity of moral or religious outlooks leads to anarchy and civil war. That, precisely, was what Hobbes believed on the basis of his experience with fractious post-Reformation sectarians in England. As a consequence, Hobbes drew from his own moral skepticism conclusions quite antithetical to a policy of toleration. "The actions of men proceed from their opinions," he argued. Adherence to contrary opinions leads to political conflict. Therefore, he concluded, "it belongeth to him that hath the sovereign power to be judge, or constitute all judges of opinion and doctrines, as a thing necessary to peace; thereby to prevent discord and civil war."[23] Hobbes's analysis of political dynamics can, of course, be disputed and his policy of censorship thereby called into question. The point, however, is that moral relativism alone is an insufficient basis for toleration.

Moral relativism by itself, rendering all norms cognitively groundless, can mandate no political practices—including the practice of toleration. Although moral skepticism undermines intolerance based on moral dogmatism, it requires assistance from some other quarter if toleration is to be more than an optional expedient. Only if people have rights, say, or if it is required by fraternity or by Christian charity can toleration be mandated as a matter of principle. The problem here, of course, is that relativism cannot avail itself of such supplementary argumentation without becoming self-contradictory. One cannot consistently maintain that all moral beliefs are subjective and relative but that people nonetheless have rights: either the claim that people have rights is itself relative and hence unsustainable, or else all moral claims are not relative.

It is not necessary, fortunately, to be a complete moral skeptic or to buy into the libertarian doctrine of individual entitlement in order to explain and justify toleration as a feature of the good society. A rational society is neither relativistic nor libertarian. It is oriented toward the recognition and attainment of the human good for its citizens. What we know about the nature of the human good, however, and what we know about the capabilities of the human understanding—taken in conjunction with the respect a rational society must accord its members—explains why toleration is a feature of a rational society.

A rational society must be tolerant, in the first place, because of the open-endedness and plurality of the human good. There may be constant elements in the good life that apply to all people at all times: love and justice, for example. The concrete expression and embodiment of even these constant features, nevertheless, will vary with respect to individual differences and changing historical circumstances. If love requires caring and caring for someone means promoting that person's welfare, than you cannot love a Yogi Berra like a Ralph Nader. Since people differ, you have to care for them in different ways. Similarly, what justice requires in circumstances of moderate scarcity may be different—or overridden entirely—in cases of dire need or great affluence. Plato believed that if a good society were to be created any change could only be a decline. But that belief was predicated upon his belief in a closed and finite cosmos. Unless we want to abandon what we have learned about history and evolution, we have to say that we know better. And since the world evolves, you cannot achieve the human good by using a cookie cutter. On principle, then, a rational society must—by acknowledging individual differences and historical variability—be a tolerant one. Insisting on conformity to preestablished patterns of living and believing will almost surely thwart the attainment of the human good in all its manifold and evolving embodiments.

The rational society, moreover, must acknowledge in principle the fallibility and corrigibility of all human knowledge. Even the most exact sciences, we now recognize, do not establish final and certain truths. Instead, even the most theoretical branches of inquiry proceed by a process of continual problem solving in the context of changeable research programs. And the result of this process of rational inquiry is not self-evident truth but warranted belief. It would be delusionary, then, to expect practical reason—i.e., our understanding of the human good—to achieve what the theoretical sciences cannot: namely, some final and perfect truth not subject to any challenge or any improvement. A rational society must be tolerant, therefore, not because it is dogmatically skeptical about values but because it acknowledges the contingency of all human knowledge, whether knowledge about the good or knowledge about atomic particles.

At the heart of Locke's argument on behalf of toleration was an intuition about the competency and the limitations of the human understanding with respect to moral knowledge. On the one hand, he clearly believed that reason could tell us some important things about what was good and right to do. As he wrote in the *Essay*, "the candle that is set up in us shines bright enough for all our purposes," shedding light upon "the conveniences of life and the information of virtue."[24] On the other hand, there were clearly limits to the extent of our ability to gain knowledge about moral and religious matters. A legitimate political society, therefore, could incorporate principles of natural law and conceptions of individual rights, but it nevertheless should tolerate a diversity of moral and religious persuasions among its citizens so long as these persuasions were not nihilistic or treasonous.

Locke encountered great difficulty, however, when he tried to articulate an explicit epistemological framework to sustain this intuitive conception.[25] For he claimed for moral knowledge a potential certainty that it never can in fact achieve, speaking of the possibility of obtaining "self-evident propositions . . . as uncontestable as those in mathematics" from which "the measures of right and wrong might be made out."[26] And while arguing that our knowledge of moral truths was empirically learned rather than innate, he grounded his account of empirical knowledge in a form of corpuscular sensationism that could not conceivably provide the wherewithal for moral learning.

The post-positivist conception of rational practice, when applied to the concerns of practical reason, helps to vindicate Locke's fundamental intuition about the propriety of toleration (in general outlines if not necessarily in concrete specifics) in a way that he himself could not do. Beguiled by the myth of *theoria* and demanding certitude as the sign of real knowledge, Locke could not give a coherent account of practical reasoning and ultimately left his doctrine defenseless before the onslaught of moral skepticism. Rather than dividing the world cognitively between a realm of translucent truth and a realm of darkness as Locke did, post-positivist rationalism places all our knowledge into the realm of genuine but imperfect knowledge—the realm of warranted belief that lies, as Richard Bernstein has put it, "beyond objectivism and relativism."[27] The spirit of a rational society, therefore, is what Judge Learned Hand called the spirit of a democratic society. It is tolerant, not because it thinks nothing is right, but because it is not too sure that it is right.

Equality

A political society organized as a rational enterprise is not intrinsically and necessarily egalitarian in the strongest sense of that term. Nevertheless, some very significant elements of equality are endemic to the dynamics of rationality. Just as a rational society is not libertarian but still mandates important liberties for its citizens, in like manner it does not necessarily imply full equality of condition among its citizens but still demands equality in a number of important respects.

The egalitarian features of a rational society are the consequence of the structural requisites of rational dialogue, the constitutive logic and language of moral discourse, and the characteristic mode of rational norms. Institutionalizing these aspects of rationality requires that citizens of a rational society be regarded as moral equals and that they be treated as equals. It requires both a fundamental equality among citizens and the equal protection of the laws.

The central institution of a rational society is rational practical dialogue. The framework of a rational dialogue—the speech situation it inhabits—is egalitarian both in its requisites and its consequences. In the first place, no a priori or invidious limitations upon entry into rational discourse are permissible. Anyone who accepts the canons and criteria of rational speech must be given access to the forum. Barring participation of interested parties delegitimates the dialogue, because exclusions of this sort politically manipulate the outcome. Rationality seeks an outcome based upon the force of the better argument, and no extrarational criteria for inclusion or exclusion are compatible with that intent. The dialogue of a rational society, therefore, requires institutionalized "equal opportunity." Habermas has made this point in the context of his "communicative ethics" by observing that no consensus can be rational unless there is a "symmetry of access" to the discourse that produces it.

A rational society must confer upon its citizens, then, a right of equal access. Otherwise, the dialogue upon which it bases its legitimacy is corrupted. The functioning of this institutionalized dialogue, moreover, works to create and reinforce moral equality among the participants. For it is possible to speak *to* other people in ways that connote inequality and/or an absence of moral relationship—by ordering, berating, or deceiving, for example. But it is not possible to speak *with* other people in a common search for the truth without conceding and manifesting their moral equality with you.

Partners in rational dialogue implicitly confer dignity upon each other. To speak seriously and meaningfully with someone is to grant them the status of rational being—someone who has ideas, who is concerned about the truth, and who must be persuaded and reasoned with rather than simply pushed about like a piece of furniture. And since what is recognized about the other in rational dialogue is what we know to be the grounds for our own claim to moral status—our autonomy, our intelligence, our responsibility—a fundamental moral equality is acknowledged at the same time.[28]

It is neither accidental nor arbitrary, therefore, that Bruce Ackerman designates "dialogic competence" as a necessary condition for membership in a liberal polity. For citizenship involves the possession of basic rights, rights are predicated upon respect, and engaging in dialogue engenders and requires the recognition of "each other's claim to self-respect." Because of these linkages, it is practically speaking not inaccurate to say that "the rights of a talking ape are more secure than those of the human vegetable."[29]

Similarly, it was not accidental that the rising importance of the *agora* in the Greek city-state brought with it a powerful impetus toward democratization. For the *agora* was the home of dialogue, and dialogue can occur only among people who are in a fundamental sense the moral equals of each other. The fact of mutual intelligibility and the mutual obligation to the norms of rational discussion display that equality as they presuppose it. Thus, in the Greek case, "those who contended with words, who opposed speech with speech, became in this hierarchic society a class of equals." Ultimately, the focus of politics upon discourse in the *agora* had the result of "opening to an ever-widening circle—and finally to the entire *demos*—access to the spiritual world reserved initially for an aristocracy of priests and warriors."[30] The logic of moral equality in a rational society is thus confirmed by practice. A rational society is also an egalitarian one.

If the procedural conditions of rational dialogue presuppose and enforce a basic equality of status among those who participate in it, the substantive logic of practical discourse equalizes in yet another way. As we saw in the previous chapter, the logic of practical discourse de-particularizes. One who enters into practical discourse must therefore shed his or her terminological egocentrism. "He must," in Hume's words, "depart from his private and particular situation, and must choose a point of view common to him with others."[31] To de-particularize, however, is to equalize. De-particularized language conceives the world from a common perspective; and to see in common, people must stand on equal footing. Similarly, the generalizing dynamics of practical discourse make it impossible to play favorites, because in generalizing one cannot be discriminatory. In the logic of practical discourse, everyone is treated as an equal. Where practical discourse is taken seriously, Rawls's veil of ignorance is not necessary to give the welfare of each person equal weight. The shroud of generality intrinsic to that discourse accomplishes the same thing. And since, as Ronald Dworkin has contended, the right to be treated as an equal is what the right of equal protection of the laws is all about,[32] it follows that an equal protection clause is a necessary part of the constitution of a rational society.

The enabling conditions of a rational society also set some limitations upon the permissible extent of economic inequality. Even where differentials in wealth are based on morally defensible considerations, economic inequality beyond a certain point would seem incompatible with politics as a rational enterprise. These limits cannot be precisely defined, but Rousseau stated the general criterion well: "no citizen shall ever be wealthy enough to buy another, and none poor enough to be forced to sell himself."[33] Economic inequality of such dimensions undermines the moral equality essential to unconstrained practical dialogue. It creates a society of masters and slaves rather than a society of free citizens, robbing those forced to sell themselves of the autonomy necessary to function as rational beings. The logic behind a rational society, then, coheres with the intuition of the republican tradition that extremes of wealth and poverty are destructive of free institutions.

Apart from these limitations on extreme disparities of wealth, it is not possible to specify the precise extent of permissible economic inequality in a rational society. It is clear that the distribution of economic resources would be made in accordance with general and nondiscrimina-tory rules directed toward justice and the general good. The rewards appropriate to differentials in ability, effort, and luck, however, must be determined like all policy issues: by practical dialogue among the citi-zenry and by whatever means of compromise and choice are used to resolve remaining areas of disagreement. The circumstances of human life make it impossible to arrive rationally at a definitive conception of social justice. Unconstrained moral discourse can disqualify some crite-ria of resource allocation—e.g., to each according to his threat advan-tage or to each according to whom he knows—as unjust. But no moral geometry will ever be capable of telling us with exactitude what kinds and degrees of the uneliminable differences among people should war-rant what kinds and degrees of differential return. What a book like John Rawls's *Theory of Justice* represents, from this perspective, is not a definitive standard of distributive justice incumbent on all rational people to accept, but rather one serious contribution to the practical discourse of a rational society through which a morally serious citizenry decide upon their allocative principles.

Finally, significant egalitarian consequences arise from the require-ment that a rational society be governed in accordance with the "rule of law." Since the "rule of law" is the mode of authority in a rational society, we will consider it under that heading, to which we now turn.

Authority

The ascendancy of reason in politics does not eliminate authority but instead transforms it. Participants in a rational enterprise hold their freedoms as an instrumental necessity for the attainment of the human good—since the autonomy of the mind is necessary for intellectual progress and the autonomy of the spirit is one constituent element of the human good. Thus, in a rational enterprise, the freedom of participants to do and think as they will is constrained by their obligation to do and think as they must.[34] The pattern of authority in a rational society is formed by the constraints and standards that the goal and methods of this enterprise place upon the actions of its members. The faithful observance of these constraints and standards constitutes civic virtue on the part of individual citizens. Of this more in a moment. First, a few implications can be drawn from the nature of a rational enterprise concerning its authority structure.

An authority structure can be said to consist of a criterion (or criteria), a mode of application, and a locus. In a rational society, the fundamental criterion for authoritative decisions is what Habermas appropriately has termed the force of the better argument. The mode through which authority is deployed is that of law. And the ultimate locus of authority is in informed and noncorrupt public opinion.

The ultimate source of authority in a rational enterprise is reason itself. We deploy reason in argumentation. It is, therefore, the force of the better argument that carries the weight of authority in a society organized as a rational enterprise. "Better argument" in the context of politics, in turn, means the most compelling account of the general good and of the best means of attaining it. In a society oriented toward the attainment of the common good, a good argument is one that can justify a policy as "what people would choose if they saw clearly, thought rationally, acted disinterestedly and benevolently."[35]

The "better argument," then, is one that gives a superior account of legitimate human wants and needs, of relevant circumstances and causal forces, of what fairness and benevolence would entail. Attempts to provide such accounts in a persuasive way are a form of casuistic practical argumentation that philosophers find hard to deal with (because it involves rhetorical appeal to our self-understanding and not simply the deployment of canons of logical inference). But it is a form of argument that all who are neither slaves nor tyrants engage in on a regular basis—whether deciding what the next family car should be, who we should hire, or who we should vote for in the next election.

The mode of authority in a rational enterprise is also distinctive. Because of the universalizing force that reason exerts upon the moral point of view, rational authority can only be exercised in the form of general imperatives. The process of practical discourse disenfranchises idiosyncratic perspectives and egocentric criteria; hence, any practical imperatives that emerge from this process will necessarily assume law-like generality in their expression. Strategic interaction in politics may proceed according to self-interest, allies, and enemies. But practical discourse knows only the needs and wants of human beings. Legitimate political rules in a rational society therefore can never take the form of "all friends of Ronald Reagan shall have this privilege while his enemies shall be burdened with that obligation." Instead, rational rules, to recall the language of Locke's *Second Treatise*, are "not to be varied in particular cases, but to have one rule for rich and poor, for the favorite at Court, and the countrymen at plough."[36]

Finally, the ultimate locus or source of authority in a rational enterprise is the informed and noncorrupt opinion of its participants. Authority in scientific inquiry ultimately lies in the conscience of all individual scientists, taken as a group. And so it is with any rational practice. This is not to say that some individuals may not be more knowledgeable and hence more "authoritative" than others. It is only to say that even where special weight is given to the views of some, it is only because their exceptional capabilities and knowledge are recognized and appreciated by the informed scientific *demos*. As Gadamer has written, "the authority of persons is based, ultimately, not on the subjection and abdication of reason, but on recognition and knowledge—knowledge, namely, that the other is superior to oneself in judgment and insight and that for this reason his judgment takes precedence."[37] Whether this is true generally, of course, is debatable. But it is true of rational authority.

To assert that authority in a rational enterprise is vested democratically in the conscience of all participants is not necessarily to deny the supposition of the natural law tradition that there is an objective order of good and bad that should be authoritative for human beings. It is only to recognize that, in practice, any putative *jus naturale* must be validated by a form of *jus gentium*. Authority in a rational society must be distributed as widely as reason itself. And although all human beings are only imperfectly rational, it is a delusion to suppose that a privileged few are privy to reason while all others are merely creatures of impulse. It may be a debatable conclusion based upon empirical judgments about the actual distribution of rationality among various classes and categories of people, but the best view is that reason is widely disseminated and that a rational society is a "priesthood of all believers."

Condorcet was, then, in a sense correct to say that public opinion is the ultimate authority in a rational society—"a tribunal independent of human coercion . . . whose scrutiny is difficult to elude, and whose verdict it is impossible to evade."[38] But the logic of rational practice suggests that this vesting of authority in public opinion should not be confused with a simplistic doctrine of "vox populi, vox Dei." For in the context of a rational enterprise, "opinion" does not mean what the Greeks called "doxa"—blind subjective belief. Instead it means rational *judgment*—subjective in the sense that it is autonomous in the individual but objective in the sense that it is subject to standards and is directed to the ascertainment of a transsubjective good. To cite Alasdair MacIntyre once again, "in the realm of practices the authority of both goods and standards operates in such a way as to rule out all subjectivist and emotivist analyses of judgment. De gustibus *est* disputandum."[39]

The claim that the aspiration to make politics a rational enterprise was—at the intuitive level—essential to early liberalism receives additional support from observing the parallels between this account of authority in a rational society and Locke's account of "the extent of the legislative power." Locke argues in the chapter of the *Second Treatise* bearing that title that the legislative power has certain bounds. And these bounds, as Locke spells them out, bear close resemblance to the authority structure of a rational enterprise. The criterion of rational authority is the force of the better argument about the common good. And Locke stipulates that "the law also ought to be designed for no other end ultimately but the good of the people." The mode of rational authority is through the rule of law. And Locke insists that legislatures "are to govern by promulgated established laws, not to be varied in particular cases." The ultimate locus of authority in a rational enterprise is in the free consciences of its participants. And Locke argues that exactions on the people require "the consent of the people given by themselves or their deputies."[40]

It is interesting to note, moreover, that Locke claims universal application for these guidelines. They bear, he argues, not simply on seventeenth-century England. They are applicable not only to bourgeois regimes. Instead, he sees these guidelines as defining the extent of legitimate government power "of every commonwealth, in all forms of government."[41] In a sense, our argument gives some support for Locke's universalistic claim. In his account, these bounds are universally applicable because they are set by the terms of popular trust and by "the law of God and nature." What our account suggests is that the pattern of authority that Locke sketches is intrinsic to rational enterprises. If not universally valid, then, it is a pattern that at least is valid wherever people aspire to run their common affairs in a rational manner.

Civic Virtue

Political philosophies that impute extraordinary potency to institutions may be able to do without a conception of civic virtue. If, for example, it is true—as Kant speculates—that a race of devils may be well governed if its institutions are deftly contrived, or if an invisible hand can transform private vice into public good, then citizens may need have no virtues. Let them be nefarious or negligent, the force of the institutional devices will yet guarantee a happy outcome.

All other political philosophies, however—those less sanguine about the ability of clever format to triumph over problematic human material—have some kind of theory of civic virtue. In some cases, the theory may be relatively underdeveloped, whereas in other cases it is a clearly articulated feature of the philosophy. In either case, a theory of civic virtue is a conception of the capabilities and dispositions that would characterize an ideal citizen of a good society. Assuming that the institutions cannot achieve the good society automatically, then at least some citizens must be able and willing to behave in certain ways to make the system work. Sometimes, it is a few heroes that are desired: Plato's philosophers, Hegel's world-historical individuals, Machiavelli's prince. In other cases, the necessary civic virtues are depicted as more widely dispersed among the citizenry: Marxism's vision of "socialist man," the public-spirited citizens of civic republicanism, and so on.

In some respects, the institutional dynamics of a rational society can mitigate the consequences of human imperfection. As we observed in the previous chapter, once the democratic dialogue is established as authoritative it exerts a constraining influence on political conflict even if selfish individuals accommodate the demands of reason only under duress. Nevertheless, it is clear that a rational society makes substantial demands upon its citizens. Political society can be conducted as a rational enterprise only if—as the early liberal rationalists realized—a substantial portion of its citizens are "enlightened." The nature of that enlightenment is more complex and attaining it more difficult than these early liberals appreciated, however. People do not become rational and enlightened merely by the expedient of disposing of traditional authority figures such as princes and prelates. Instead, people become rational only through a complex and difficult process of education and acculturation.

The good citizen of a rational republic, first of all, is one who is devoted to the common good as the appropriate goal of political life. He or she does not conceive of politics as an arena for sublimated warfare—a zero-sum game among individuals seeking simply to gratify their appetites at others' expense. Whatever the uneliminable element of conflict in all political life, the good citizen of a rational society is oriented toward achieving more than his or her own private satisfaction. Above and beyond that individual concern, the good citizen is one who recognizes that the polity must be directed toward attaining the best possible life for all of its citizens.

Civic virtue in a rational society also consists in the acceptance of the discipline of reason. A good citizen is one who understands that the ultimate authority should be the force of the better argument, and not superior force *simpliciter*. He or she may bargain with other members of the society, but good citizens will not merely bargain with each other but also will engage in mutual discussion about their common goals and about prudent policy. Good citizens, in short, are willing to reason together and they know how that is done.

It follows, also, that civic virtue in a rational society requires a willingness both to speak and to listen. A good citizen recognizes an obligation to give his or her fellow citizens reasons for his or her political views and goals. Bruce Ackerman is too lenient on his liberal citizens when he says: "once having asserted his right to pursue his conception of the good, no citizen is under any obligation to defend the merits of his ideals in any forum not of his own choosing."[42] Of course, no one is under an obligation to explain himself or herself whenever and wherever someone else demands it. But good citizens owe their fellows at some time and in some appropriate forum a serious accounting of the considerations that sustain their actions. That much is required by, in the words of the Declaration of Independence, a "decent respect to the opinions of mankind" in conjunction with a decent respect for the competence and authority of practical reason.

Equally important is the obligation to listen seriously to the ideas and arguments of other citizens. The heart of a rational enterprise is mutual dialogue. That requires interaction and exchange, not merely serial monologues. The good citizen of a rational society, therefore, owes his or her fellow citizens not only an accounting for his or her own view, but also a careful hearing of their views. He or she might learn something. Lack of awareness of others' needs and concerns and a lack of understanding of other perspectives, indeed, will almost surely render his or her own political judgments defective.

The phrase "political judgment" is significant in this context. For one of the fundamental obligations of the good citizen in a rational republic is to develop his or her capabilities for making good political judgments. It is through reaching and expressing good political judgment that a citizen of a rational society manifests his or her dedication to the human good, his or her responsibility as a mind and as an actor, and his or her interdependence with other citizens in the pursuit of an unforced consensus—i.e., a common judgment.

The norms of rational practice also generate a set of constraints and expectations regarding the way the citizen of a rational society deals with his or her peers. A rational society requires rational beings, and rational beings have rights. Civic virtue hence requires respect for those rights. Second, recognizing the fundamental equality of all rational beings, the good citizen of a rational society treats his or her fellow citizens as equals. Race, sex, creed, and social status may be real properties that distinguish individuals from one another; but they are always of secondary significance and can never be legitimate grounds for political discrimination. Finally, because of the fallibility of our knowledge and the plurality of the human good, the good citizen of a rational society must be tolerant. He or she is tolerant not because "all values are equal" but because all intimations of a flourishing human life are partial.

These criteria for civic virtue are not especially novel, although they do go considerably beyond the very limited conceptions of civic virtue found in the pluralist or libertarian interpretations of liberalism. In effect, they amount to the norms of individual behavior that foster the "tradition of civility" that has historically informed and inspired Western politics at its best. What is notable, however, is that these enabling conditions of a tradition of civility are not philosophically adventitious. Instead, they can be derived from the necessary features of rational practice. When Walter Lippmann wrote that "rational procedure is the ark of the covenant of the public philosophy,"[43] therefore, he was correct in ways more profound than he himself realized.

The conception of civic virtue derived from the requisites of rational practice also lends credence to Mill's insistence that representative government will not be successful where the people are thoroughly corrupt. Where citizens are "incapable of calm deliberation," devoid of "concern . . . for . . . the general interest," and are "mere masses of ignorance, stupidity, and baleful prejudice, every operation of government will go wrong."[44] If a liberal polity is to be the good and free society its early advocates thought it was, it needs to recognize the republican concern with civic virtue as its own. For politics cannot be a rational enterprise where the people are not equipped to act in accordance with the necessities of reason.

Conclusion

Citizenship in a society that institutionalizes the norms of rational practice thus can be said to entail a complex pattern of privileges and obligations. Participants in the politics of a rational society are not free to be simply power seekers or possessive individualists. They are constrained in their public activities by a variety of constraints intrinsic in the life of reason. They must be tolerant of the rights of others, they must respect the legitimacy of rational authority, they must acknowledge the discipline of reason, they should strive to improve their capacity for good political judgment, and they should be oriented toward the common good. On the other hand, citizens in the republic of reason possess a corresponding panoply of rights and privileges that protect their autonomy, respect what Godwin enshrined as the "right of private judgment," encourage their participation in the life of the community, and underwrite their claims of fundamental equality.

This conjunction of rights and obligations may seem quite unsurprising, in that our moral common sense tends to take for granted that privileges and burdens must go hand in hand. In the history of political theory, however, and in the recent contention between rights-based liberals and communitarian republicans, it has not always proved easy to provide a good logical account of this correlativity. Natural law theories put the emphasis on what the citizen owed to his or her society and often had trouble specifying or protecting the citizen's rights in the face of social pressure. Natural rights theorists, in contrast, made these rights of the individual their starting point, but have had difficulty explaining the origins and warrants for political obligation and therefore seem predisposed to slide toward the problems of possessive individualism, free riders, acquisitive societies, and the like. In recent years, therefore, civic republicans have condemned rights-based liberalism for its excessive individualism and its consequent derogation of community, whereas the rights-based liberals have rejoined with expressed fears about the despotism of virtue.[45]

Small wonder, then, that Christopher Lasch can write in a footnote to a very thoughtful article that "I believe the vocabulary of rights to be fundamentally incompatible with the vocabulary of virtue."[46] A great deal of history and some logic lend weight to this assertion. The problem is that when either virtue or rights is taken as the axial norm for a regime, the other must fall into a subservient role. If the promotion of virtue is *the* orienting purpose of a society, rights can be contingent at best. And if rights are postulated as nonnegotiable side constraints circumscribing all potentially legitimate political obligations, the demands of virtue lose their force.

The capacity of norms of rational practice to lessen the gap between liberalism and republicanism, integrating some of their major concerns into a more capacious synthesis, is, then, largely a function of their ability to reconcile these often antithetical vocabularies. The conception of politics as a rational enterprise exhibits this capability, I think, because of the way it is derived. Rather than taking some moral standard—such as the greatest good for the greatest number or individual rights—as an absolute norm and then building a theory around that postulate, it begins by reflecting upon the requisites of a real world form of life. And since this form of life is a complex practice rather than a simple a priori standard, we can find in it a pattern of rights and duties that are functionally related in a way that reduces neither to simple subservience to the other. The conception of politics as a rational enterprise coalesces with our intuitive appreciation of the proper correlativity of burdens and benefits in a well-ordered polity. We need not find ourselves coerced into making an either/or choice between a liberal politics of individual rights and a republican politics of virtue. We can instead, by reflecting upon the intrinsic norms of rational endeavor, appreciate the necessity of both rights and duties—and the relationship they bear to each other.

Chapter Six **Understanding**

Liberal Democracy

In chapter 1 I traced how the long-standing quest to understand the role of reason in politics had, in large part because of the modern tendency to mathematicize rationality, eventuated in the Weberian confinement of reason to merely technical means-end calculations. In chapter 2, I reviewed how linguistic philosophy and the philosophy of science has in recent years taken a pragmatic turn; and in chapter 3 I argued that these developments have afforded us the basis for a less purely formal conception of rationality and have allowed us to recognize the practical dimension of all rational enterprises.

In chapters 4 and 5 I attempted to tease out what this conception of rational practice might mean in the context of politics. I argued that, upon this understanding of the life of reason, a rational society should be understood as a community of rational persons oriented toward achieving an open-ended common good through a process of problem solving governed by the discipline of rational dialogue and implemented through the rule of law. Citizens of such a rational republic, I argued, are characterized by their possession of certain rights and by their subjection to certain complementary obligations—both of which are intrinsic to the status and function of participants in rational enterprises.

The conception of a rational society I have sketched is, of course, based upon analogical rather than deductive inferences. In some of its particulars, therefore, it is subject to reasonable critique even by those sympathetic to the basic line of argument. The analogical judgments I have made, however, add up to a plausible answer to the question: what, given our best current understanding of what rationality entails, would it mean to organize a political society as a rational enterprise? Certainly, I would argue, the conception articulated here provides both a more plausible and a more politically and morally salutary answer to that question than those earlier answers to the same question embodied in Plato's philosopher kings, Hegel's Geist, Hobbes's Sovereign, Bentham's felicific calculators, or Weber's bureaucrats.

In the two concluding chapters, this one and the next, I pursue the implications of this conception of political rationality for the theory and practice of liberal democracy. In this chapter I consolidate the comparison between our conception of liberal democracy as a rational enterprise and other understandings of liberal democratic goals and norms. And in the final chapter I offer some suggestions about the bearing of this normative conception upon policies and practices in contemporary democratic societies.

Perhaps the best way to appreciate the distinctive theoretical implications of the ideal of a rational republic, therefore, is to juxtapose that model to other leading conceptions of liberalism and democracy— to delineate some of the more important contrasts and affinities between them and our own conception. If that is done, a number of assessments and implications of other theoretical perspectives—both traditional and contemporary—can be derived. Conceiving the liberal democratic ideal as one of rational practice, I argue: (1) rehabilitates as it transforms the Enlightenment intuition regarding the liberating and civilizing role of reason in politics; (2) recovers for contemporary practice some of the salient features of classical Greek democracy; (3) suggests the possibility and desirability of effecting a creative synthesis between competing contemporary schools of liberalism and civic republicanism; (4) provides a better foundation for some of the more salutary classical theories of democracy than they provided for themselves; (5) provides an appropriate philosophical vehicle for grounding and integrating some of the most insightful recent critiques of liberal democratic norms and practices; and (6) helps to bring into greater relief the principal inadequacies of other major conceptions of liberal democracy.

Rehabilitating "the Faith of Reason"

In *After Virtue*, Alasdair MacIntyre argued persuasively that what he calls "the Enlightenment project" was foredoomed to failure. By "the

Enlightenment project" MacIntyre refers to the pervasive seventeenth- and eighteenth-century attempt in moral philosophy to provide "an independent rational justification of morality." This project was inherently incapable of attaining a successful conclusion, according to MacIntyre, because it was "internally incoherent."[1] Given the positivistic conception of reason endemic to the Enlightenment, it is simply impossible to respect the defining limitations of that form of cognitive activity and at the same time attain normative truths. Recent moral philosophy—and to some extent the self-understanding of liberalism—can be seen as governed by the necessity of dealing with the consequences of this project's internal collapse. As MacIntyre would have it, it forces upon us a choice between Nietzsche and Aristotle.

It is important to recognize, however, that when MacIntyre says that the hope of giving morality an "independent rational justification" was incoherent, he is giving a philosophically specific meaning—one widely accepted by Enlightenment thinkers—to the term *rational*. This is a rationality that "does not comprehend essences or transitions from potentiality to act," a rationality that "is calculative [and] can assess truths of fact and mathematical relations but nothing more."[2] When the nature and scope of reason is understood in this particular manner, then it is in fact not capable of generating a moral doctrine on its own. MacIntyre is, I believe, entirely correct to render that judgment. And he is also correct in his account of how it took two centuries or more for that negative conclusion to be reached. It took that long because the moralists in question—in common with their cultures in general—tended to invest rationality tacitly and illicitly (by their own premises) with powers appropriate only to substantive conceptions of rationality that they had rejected on principle. Or they anticipated future culminations of a "moral science" that would be built piecemeal on an empirical basis. Or both. It took time for philosophical critique to reveal the logical inadequacies and for repeated frustration to reveal the empirical incompetencies of these illusory expectations. At the heart of the Enlightenment mentality, however, lies a deeper intuition that is not invalidated by the failure of a specific philosophical doctrine. That intuition centers around an appreciation of the profound similarity between the procedures that govern successful acts of inquiry and the procedures that govern humane and civilized political regimes. However misled the Enlightenment may have been by a Cartesian fixation upon quasi-mathematical analytic modes of thought, it was not mistaken in its larger devotion to the norms of rational practice as the best recourse for political development. For in ways that Enlightenment thinkers clearly recognized much better than they could conceive or articulate, the norms of the scientific achievements they venerated and the norms of the social achievements they desired exhibit genuine symmetry.

In *The Faith of Reason*, Charles Frankel made an important observation concerning the Enlightenment's conception of rationality and its relationship to politics. "There was more than one element embodied in the *philosophes'* ideas of progress, and their notions of reason and science were larger and less single-minded than their own polemics, and equally polemical criticism, have sometimes permitted them to seem." In particular, Frankel continued, "underlying the ideas of the *philosophes* on progress were two widely divergent interpretations of science."[3]

The first of these two conceptions of reason-as-embodied-in-science was a substantive conception tied to a specific metaphysic that was deemed absolutely true. "Rationality" was whatever conformed to this metaphysical framework—a framework that combined "elements drawn from Descartes with ideas drawn from empiricist sources"—and rationality in politics meant "movement toward fixed moral goals which were also established absolutely." The other conception of reason was procedural rather than substantive. For it, the essence of rationality was revealed by the self-corrective methods of science. Accordingly, the road to intellectual progress lay not in the fleshing out of a particular metaphysical conception of truth but rather in "simply the preservation and extension of the conditions and methods of inquiry." And, correlatively, on this account the key to social progress was "the extension of the habit of free inquiry."[4]

Frankel's own historical account, however, affords ample evidence that the *philosophes* themselves did not generally appreciate this distinction and its significance. In Frankel's view, it is the procedural interpretation of the faith of reason that is both more valid and more beneficial in its political consequences. But in their mixture of substantive and procedural definitions for rationality, the *philosophes* encumbered their notions of liberalism and progress with a priori beliefs "which exalted the categories of physics into the exclusive properties of nature,"[5] told them in advance what the content of scientific truth would be, and also told them what political progress would entail.

What Frankel's analysis does not point out, moreover, is that the substantive and metaphysically specific conception of rationality to which the Enlightenment was addicted not only prevented the *philosophes* from accurately understanding that it was the method instead of the specific beliefs of science that was crucial; it also prevented them from understanding what the definitive features of that method were. For the *philosophes* were not unaware that procedural considerations were crucial to science and reason. Far from it. Instead, the problem was that they tended to interpret the nature of scientific method in light of their attendant metaphysical commitments. As a consequence, "rational method" came to be conceived not so much as a generally applicable and content nonspecific mode of inquiry but rather as a *methodos* uniquely appropriate to a particular kind of world. Rational method thus became essentially what it was for Descartes in his *Discourse on Method:* namely, a set of cookbook rules an individual should follow in a world composed of simple natures transparent to the mathematicizing mind.

Thus beguiled by a belief in what Condorcet termed "simple truths and infallible methods," the *philosophes* interpreted political rationality in a manner inevitably problematic for the liberalism they advocated. Reason was destined to follow the path of Prometheus in the parable crafted by Camus in *The Rebel:* it entered the world as a rebel, but turned into a tyrant. It was originally conceived as liberating and humane, but it was dogmatic in its certainty—hence potentially illiberal—and reductive in its conception of human nature—hence potentially inhumane. By the middle of this century, then, the divorce of political rationalism from liberalism was essentially complete. At the level of explicit doctrine, at least, reason was claimed as handmaiden by some illiberal political theories, whereas the leading conceptions of liberalism were conventionalist, subjectivist, and skeptical.

The political significance of recent developments in our philosophical understanding of scientific inquiry and linguistic communication, I would argue, is that they permit contemporary liberals to make productive use of Charles Frankel's insight about the different modes of conceiving political rationality. As Frankel rightly intimated, the real connection between science and liberal ideals—intuitively perceived but misconstrued by the *philosophes*—lies in their common appropriation of procedural norms of rational practice. The philosophical developments here alluded to, moreover, permit us to understand the nature of these procedural norms in a nontrivial way. To proceed in a rational manner does not mean, *à la* Descartes, for an individual to follow a set of mechanistic *regulae* as he or she seeks to provide a clear and distinct theoretical account of reality. Instead, rational procedure refers to the pattern of institutionalized practices followed by a community of inquirers as they grapple with impediments to their understanding.

Thus conceived, the close affinity between a rational society and the traditional aspirations of the liberal tradition seems apparent. For, as George Sabine wrote in his well-known analysis of "the two democratic traditions," these two traditions shared a common core of ideals that are embodied in the conception of a rational society. "The ideal common to both traditions," he said, "was social and political organization through mutual understanding and agreement, and hence as little coercive as possible, and that liberty and equality were conditions of there being any such understanding."[6] The post-positivist conception of reason in politics thus vindicates the intuitive perception of Enlightenment liberals that liberal ideals and practices are linked in some fundamental way with the constitutive norms and practices of rationality, even as it rejects their attempt to interpret rationality as empirical-analytic *theoria*.

Liberalism and Classical Greek Democracy

Liberal conceptions of democracy are often distinguished from the classical Greek conception of democracy. And there are ample reasons for insisting upon the differences between them. The Greeks considered the polity to be a work of nature, whereas modern liberalism construes it as an artificial product of the human will. Greek democracy was oriented toward an integrated community; liberal democracy is individualistic and libertarian in emphasis. The Greeks saw civil freedom as best expressed in the right to participate in common decisions; modern liberalism tends to focus in contrast on civil liberties as private rights against public power. Underlying these differences, moreover, are some basic differences in cosmology and philosophical anthropology.

Not withstanding these divergences, the post-positivist conception of a rational society suggests that a liberalism that is fully modern philosophically both can and should assimilate some of the more vital aspects of classical Greek democracy. The centrality of the *agora* in Greek democracy is reincarnated in the institutionalized public dialogue of a rational society. Although it cherishes individual rights and accepts the importance of a protected realm of the private, a rational society cannot function without a vigorous public sphere. As the Greeks recognized, it is the encounter of citizens in public discourse that reflects and ratifies their moral equality and their moral standing. And the focus of the public sphere on the common good, likewise embodied in the rational society, creates the sense of community and obligation to larger goals that keeps a liberal society from disintegrating into a mere instrumentality of possessive individualism. The Greek derogation of anyone who was purely private, finally, is echoed by the rational society's insistence on the necessity of widespread participation.

Because post-positivist rationality is a form of *praxis* rather than *techne*, moreover, understanding liberalism as a quest for a rational society permits it to reincorporate the Greek conception of politics as a "practice" in Alasdair MacIntyre's sense of that term. A "practice" is "any coherent and complex form of socially established cooperative human activity through which goods internal to that form of activity are realized in the course of trying to achieve those standards of excellence which are appropriate to, and partially definitive of, that form of activity." By this definition, as MacIntyre observes, "politics, as Aristotle conceives it, is a practice with goods internal to itself. Politics, as James Mill conceives it, is not."[7]

The difference between Aristotle and James Mill on this point is neither adventitious nor purely a product of changed political circumstances. Instead, the contrast grows directly out of the difference between conceiving rationality as practical and conceiving it as technical. Technical rationality is by definition instrumental. It is a means to an end outside of itself that is established prerationally. Politics as *techne* cannot be a practice, then, because the goods it seeks are always goods external to its own activity. To conceive political activity as *praxis* rather than *techne* as the post-positivist conception of rational practice does in agreement with Aristotle, in contrast, makes it, properly done, a virtue rather than a skill. It has standards of excellence internal to the form of activity, standards expressed in the conception of civic virtue implicit in the idea of a rational society. Under the aegis of positivistic philosophy, "rationalizing" society came to mean Weberian bureaucratic instrumentalism or Leninist manipulation. The conception of a rational society articulated here, however, is not the "iron cage" of technical reason. It is instead the supremely human practice in which citizens flourish as they create a good life together.

Liberalism and the Communitarian Critique

One of the major ongoing battles in contemporary political theory has been waged in recent years between defenders of pluralist, rights-based liberalism and their communitarian critics. The communitarians, such as MacIntyre, Sandel, and Robert Bellah, find both liberal practices and the underlying theories behind them to be undesirable. The philosophies undergirding liberalism are depicted as incoherent or unconvincing. And liberal practices are construed as unrestrainedly individualistic in ways that verge upon anarchism or nihilism. At the very least, liberalism is seen as frustrating and detracting from the achievement of a political community that "can know a good in common that we cannot know alone."[8] Defenders of liberalism have provided spirited rejoinders to these criticisms. Rawls has simply denied that liberalism rests upon the (inadequate) metaphysical basis Sandel argues to be implicit in it. Amy Gutmann has argued that rights-based liberals "can recognize the conditional priority of justice without embracing deontological metaethics or collapsing into teleology."[9] Stephen Holmes has averred that MacIntyre's "portrait of liberalism is ludicrous," animated by "the need to believe and to belong."[10] And Don Herzog, in the context of posing a thoughtful challenge to communitarians "to explain in some more detail than they have just what sort of politics they are offering," wonders out loud "if there are deep similarities between civic humanists in the academy and the Moral Majority . . . [and] if the republican tradition has an element of hostility to individualism itself, if virtuous citizens are unpleasantly like robots."[11]

What the conception of politics as rational practice offers in the context of this debate, I would argue, is a philosophical vehicle for something of a synthesis between these positions. It is not the case, of course, that all the differences between the camps are capable of reconciliation. But in the model of a rational society some of the major concerns and most valid contentions of both viewpoints are incorporated and *aufgehoben*. As Amy Gutmann has thoughtfully suggested, "communitarianism has the potential for helping us discover a politics that combines community with a commitment to basic liberal values," because communitarian values "are properly viewed as supplementing rather than supplanting basic liberal values."[12] Conceiving the liberal ideal as a politics of rational practice helps us to understand how that may be so.

This partial reconciliation between liberalism and communitarianism proceeds at both the political and philosophical levels. At the political level, rational conduct requires the insistence upon some of the most fundamental liberal values. As we have seen, politics cannot approximate the standards of a rational enterprise unless all participants are accorded basic rights and enjoy basic liberties of thought and expression. Rationality mandates respect for the personal autonomy that liberalism cherishes. The toleration of individual viewpoints and differences that liberalism considers fundamental is also a hallmark of rational societies. Authority in rational enterprises is exercised, as liberals have insisted, only on the basis of consent. And rationality requires the generality in political prescriptions that liberals have traditionally insisted upon under the heading of rule of law.

At the same time, the requisites of rational political practice also include some of the most characteristic features of republican thought. In the first place, republicans have been properly critical of the excessive privatism that often afflicts liberalism. Republicans insist that healthy democracies need a vital public sphere. And this insistence receives validation in the ideal of a rational society; for the rational discourse so central to its practices can flourish only where the public domain is a lively *agora* rather a mere cipher or space for self-interested bargaining. Like republicanism, moreover, politics as a rational enterprise mandates a basic equality of status and empowerment among its citizenry. These citizens are, in addition, answerable to certain standards of civic virtue—standards intrinsic to meaningful participation in a rational society. And finally, as we have seen, the democratic dialogue of a rational society is constitutive of the kind of human community to which republicans seem to aspire.

Our model of a rational society also, I would argue, offers a defensible middle ground on the question that in recent years has seemed to stimulate some of the sharpest controversy between liberals and communitarians. The basic problematic for most recent rights-based liberal theorists has been provided by their insistence that the members of a modern pluralistic society are incapable of agreement about the good life. This insistence can be based upon both philosophical and empirical grounds. The philosophical argument is an epistemological skepticism that finds the grounds of belief about the good shrouded in metaphysical assumptions that lie beyond the competence of reason. Beliefs about the human good are, on this account, both conflicting and incommensurable; hence they are inadjudicable; hence they provide no consensual moral basis for a liberal society. Historical experience, say these skeptics, confirms the impossibility of achieving public agreement about the human good. Hence the liberal state must, as one of its essential trademarks, be neutral among the miscellany of competing conceptions of the good; and some other basis for social unity in a liberal society—whether simple self-interest or a public conception of neutral justice—must be found.

Communitarians retort that no political regime can possibly be entirely neutral *vis à vis* conceptions of the good life. The very structure, organization, constitution, and procedural norms that any regime must have embodies a mobilization of bias that privileges some conception of the human good—however broad and general it may be—against other possible conceptions. Moreover, even were such neutrality possible, it would not be desirable. Any decent society must be concerned about achieving the human good; and a society that utterly disregards this obligation invites a gradual disintegration into at best a society of strangers and at worst an anarchic war of each against all.[13]

The conception of politics as rational practice incorporates elements from both sides of this argument. It shares the communitarian conviction that a democratic society should be dedicated to attainment of the common good; but it would require decisive abandonment of the premodern claim that a single substantive conception of the good can be ascertained and made politically definitive. Conversely, it accepts the rights-based liberals' argument that a full and univocal discernment of the human good is beyond the competence of human cognitive capacities and that the belief in such a univocal standard is probably misleading and morally hegemonic in any case; but it considers the neutralist argument in its strong form to be unnecessarily pyrhonnic and also arguably incompatible with the aspiration to develop a consensus about principles of justice.

Stated more positively, the assumptions about the human good, its cognizability, and its role in felicitous politics that inform our conception of rational political practice are as follows. The human good is the rationally desirable flourishing of human life. Because we can effectively deploy our cognitive powers both to illuminate the nature of human wants and needs and to understand the circumstances within which these wants and needs must be pursued, it makes sense to say that the human good is at least to some degree knowable. Moreover, since we are—whether by necessity or inclination—animals destined to live in association with our fellows, there will be elements of commonality in what is rationally desirable for the individual members of any given society. The good for particular individuals will not likely be exhausted by ends shared with others, but it is nonetheless reasonable to suppose with Michael Sandel and with a long tradition of political theorizing that we can in fact at times "know a good in common that we cannot know alone."[14]

Because of the nature of human cognition and the circumstances of life, however, it is also true that our knowledge of the human good is always partial and imperfect. In the real world—as contrasted with the *ex post facto* abstract reconstructions of philosophers—we come to apprehend the good only through the concrete and piecemeal process of running into and contending with impediments to a flourishing existence. People differ. The world changes. Our experiences and our horizons are always limited. Hence our apprehension of the human good is made in fits and starts and is perceived only through a glass darkly.

Thus the rational political society orients itself toward the human good as a scientific community orients itself toward the truth; with a conviction that the attainment of the human good is its proper end, with a commitment to procedures and institutions that seem best designed for its recognition and pursuit, with humility about the actual likelihood of its attainment, and with a dedication to safeguarding the individual rights dictated by the open-endedness and systematic elusiveness of the *telos* of the enterprise. This understanding of the human good and its political functions will not, of course, be acceptable to all liberals or to all republicans. It is too robust for the resolutely antinomian and the devoutly relativist members of the liberal camp. And it is too indeterminate for republicans such as Benjamin Rush, to cite one historical example,[15] who consider themselves more privy than most mortals to a univocal and universally valid substantive conception of the human good. But it provides an appropriate meeting ground for those more moderate liberals whose skeptical claims are advanced against dogmatism and oppression rather than on behalf of moral pyrrhonism and those republicans who claim that a democratic society must pursue the common good and not that they have found it.

This potential partial synthesis of liberal and republican concerns indicated and facilitated by the conception of rational practice at the political level parallels and to some extent is grounded in a similar convergence at the philosophical level. Liberalism has traditionally been associated with modern empiricism. And republicanism, in the hands of some of its contemporary exponents, is associated with a fundamentally Aristotelian account of public good and individual virtues. Both empiricism and Aristotelianism, however, stand in need of fundamental repair if either of them is to be a viable contemporary philosophy. And the repairs that seem called for in each case, it can be argued, push the two perspectives in convergent directions.

The relationship between liberalism and empiricism has been grounded in their common attraction to the procedures and achievements of modern science. Both liberals and empiricists have been animated by the conviction that they embody and articulate the scientific ideal—the one in social practice and the other in the realm of philosophical theory. As I have argued in the preceding chapters, however, following Wittgenstein, Toulmin, Lakatos, and others, empiricism must renounce its positivistic aspects if it wishes to maintain its linkage with our current understanding of scientific inquiry. It cannot hold on to its original aspirations to be the philosophical account of modern objectivist *theoria*, but it must adapt to our understanding of science by taking a pragmatic turn. When that is done, we have seen, the empiricist project of providing a reflective account of scientific rationality turns toward a philosophy of rational practice. It leads us toward the identification and recognition of the procedures and institutions constitutive of the republic of reason.

But Aristotelian philosophy can hardly be untouched by the need to remain compatible with our best current understanding of the world and our knowledge of it. Some have even argued, of course, as did many Enlightenment reformers, that Aristotelian conceptions are simply incapable of being reconciled with the findings and epistemological assumptions of modern science. That indictment goes too far, sinking all Aristotelian insights beneath the weight of that tradition's undeniable failures and incapacities in physical theory. Nevertheless, as almost all of its contemporary adherents have willingly affirmed, a persuasive neo-Aristotelianism has no choice but to jettison certain features of Aristotle's own philosophy.

MacIntyre affirms, for example, that Aristotle's account of the virtues can be compelling to us today only if it can be disengaged from his metaphysical biology, the sociological particularity of the Greek city-state, and his Platonic conviction that genuine goods cannot be in opposition and that political conflict should be eliminable from a well-ordered state.[16] For these necessary philosophical amendments to be possible, a fundamentally Aristotelian account of knowledge and virtue must be provided that is not corruscated by Aristotle's own bewitch-ment by a metaphysics of finitude. Aristotelian insights into the natural sociability of human beings, into the dynamics of human excellence, and into the role of our cognitive abilities in politics must be placed into an amended philosophical framework that recognizes and validates both historicity and pluralism.

If that is done, however, what would seem to emerge as the heart of a revised neo-Aristotelian moral philosophy is an account of communal prudence in an open-ended world. What remains potentially viable and illuminating in the original Aristotelian outlook is the account of natu-rally political animals bound together in a quest for their common good through the joint deployment of their rational faculties. Such an ac-count of communal prudence, now unencumbered by Aristotle's own metaphysical and historical limitations, however, would seem to be largely reconcilable with a depositivized pragmatic empiricism. For both of these philosophical traditions, after repair, move in the direc-tion of a philosophy of rational *praxis*.

To the extent that is so, then, the claim with which I began achieves plausibility: namely, that the normative account of rational political practice provides an appropriate vehicle for a partial but significant reconciliation and synthesis between the liberal and republican tradi-tions—at both the political and philosophical levels. And the reason for this possibility, I would argue, is that both traditions possess an intui-tive apprehension of the beneficial and potentially powerful role of practical reason in political life—even if in each case this intuitive appreciation has been somewhat obscured and distorted by its embed-dedness in a dogmatic metaphysic that is no longer tenable.

Rational Practice, Locke, and Mill

To the extent this is so—that is, to the extent that leading liberal democratic theorists within the empiricist tradition have had their intuitive insights into the political role of reason weakened by their explicit philosophical commitments—the possibility suggests itself that a post-positivist conception of rational practice would actually provide a more appropriate foundation for their political theory than they provided themselves. And in fact, I believe that a persuasive argument can be made to that effect. Such claims are inherently somewhat presumptuous and hypothetical, of course. But a good case can be made that the political theories of Locke and Mill gain in both clarity and consistency when they are interpreted in light of the conception of rationality in politics provided here.

This argument parallels Habermas's critical interpretation of Marx. Habermas has persuasively contended that Marx's political insights were in important ways constrained and distorted by the positivistic limitations of his fundamental philosophy. Marxist theory can in his view come into its own—can avoid reification and corrupt manipulative consequences—only when it abandons Marx's own determination to positivize the human sciences and instead preserves Marx's intuitive insights by revivifying the reflective and critical dimension of social theory his own metaphysical failures undermined. The same general claim can be made *vis à vis* both Locke and Mill. For each of them explicitly adhered to positivistic-empiricist assumptions that provided a highly problematic base for their political and moral theories. As a consequence, they are rightly subject to criticism for philosophical incoherence—for having a lack of fit between their philosophical starting points and their political conclusions. And they also receive criticism for what appear to be inconsistencies among various strands of their political theories. If we take the liberty of substituting the post-positivist conception of rational process for the empiricist and utilitarian assumptions that Locke and Mill adopted, however, some of these problems become considerably less vexing.

Take Locke first. It is a commonplace of critiques of Locke to observe the apparent mismatch between the empiricist and hedonist doctrines of his *Essay* and the insistence on rights, natural law, and common good in his *Second Treatise*. This gap has led to a variety of hermeneutic strategies, including the suggestion of Leo Strauss that the real Locke was the subversive hedonist/empiricist while the seemingly divergent moral conceptions were a conventionalist smokescreen to appease the uninitiated.[17] If post-positivist practical reason is put in place of the positivistic theoretical reason that Locke could neither live with nor live without, however, his difficulties at this point lessen greatly. For the moral conceptions Locke included in his political doctrines are sustainable in terms of practical reason in ways they are not in terms of empiricist rationality.

Astute observers have also found in Locke serious tensions among his acceptance of natural law, his focus upon natural right, and his derivation of legitimate power from consent. The result, once again, is that interpreters and critics have often felt forced to choose among those apparent incompatibles. One strand of Locke's theory is taken as primary, the others subordinated or abandoned. And thus we are given Locke the pure majoritarian, Locke the fideist, or Locke the proto-Nozickean defender of absolute property rights. This impulse to interpret Locke in such a univocal fashion is thoroughly understandable, for it seems almost necessitated by the demands of logical consistency. As Patrick Riley rightly suggests, however, the impulse needs to be resisted and some means of integrating the several strands found; for each strand is important to Locke even if he never adequately reconciles them. "The problem," as Riley puts it, "is that all three characterizations (i.e., Locke as natural law theorist, Locke as natural right advocate, and Locke as contractarian) are correct; the difficulty is to find an equilibrium between them so that none is discarded in the effort to define Locke's complete concept of right."[18]

The prospect of finding a logically acceptable equilibrium among the three major elements in Locke's political theory would have been greatly enhanced had he had available to him the conception of the "politics in reason." For on that conception, the different strands of Locke's theory can relate to each other as parts of a larger whole rather than as contestants for exclusive supremacy. Locke's natural law strand finds embodiment in the rational society's orientation toward the human good and in the moral competency attributed to practical dialogue. The natural right strand finds expression in the rights accorded to rational agents and hence to citizens of the republic of reason. And the contractualist strand of Locke's theory is incorporated in the initial freedom and equality of citizens in the rational society and in that society's derivation of authority from a process of discursive will formation.

The situation with respect to John Stuart Mill is quite similar. It has always been problematic to see exactly how Mill's utilitarianism and his empiricist conception of nomological human sciences squared with the concrete values he espoused and with the importance he ascribed to a form of rationality in politics that was more prudential than scientific.

Had he been able to appropriate the post-positivist account of rational procedure, he might have been able to spare himself some of these difficulties. His concern for qualitative rather than merely quantitative pleasures would have made more sense in terms of the norms intrinsic to the life of reason. And he might have been spared his unhappy surprise at the Comtean political consequences of deploying the positive human sciences had his account of the human understanding incorporated the discursive, participatory, and libertarian features intrinsic to an adequate account of practical rationality.

Likewise, Mill might have been able to deflect from the outset the common complaints about his ideological incoherence. At times, it is said, he sounds like a classical liberal with his emphasis on individual freedom and rights. But he can also sound like a conservative when he insists upon the necessity of wisdom, virtue, and authority. And then he apparently muddies the waters still further by flirting with socialism in his political economy and by insisting on widespread participation. What may seem erratic and inconsistent when viewed through the grid of standard ideological categories, however, may seem considerably more coherent when viewed *sub specie* rational *praxis* in a post-positivist mode. Instead of representing a kind of idiosyncratic electicism, the different strands of Mill's political theory appear as components of a more complex but nonetheless coherent model. For the conception of a rational society, like "conservative" Mill, requires its citizens to embody civic virtue. Like the "liberal" Mill, it confers on its citizens extensive rights and liberties that are so essential to the enterprise as to be unassailable—especially in the area of freedom of thought and discussion. And in line with a "socialist" Mill, a rational society cannot function properly without the widespread participation of citizens who stand on an equal footing. In short, the model of a rational political enterprise is capable of conferring upon the various elements of Mill's diverse political writings considerably more structural integrity than he himself was able to give them.

Rational Practice and Contemporary Liberal Theory

Finally, the conception of political rationality developed here performs two functions within the context of recent discussions of liberalism. First, it helps bring into sharper relief the inadequacies of several recent claimants to the mantle of liberalism. And second, it provides a coherent philosophical framework for validating and integrating some of the most thoughtful critiques of contemporary liberal practice.

By contrast with the complex multiplicity of human values incorporated within a post-positivist conception of liberal rationalism, for example, laissez-faire and libertarian versions of liberalism appear simplistic and narrow. Too monocular in their vision of both reality and the good society, they extract the single norm of liberty from its proper situatedness in a human community of moral equals and give it total hegemony over all other aspects of the good life. Such a truncated conception of a liberal society is not only morally simplistic, but it would seem to permit the dissolution of the elements of moral community essential to a successful democracy. On its terms, citizens could be merely strangers and competitors, possibly grossly unequal ones at that. And in such a society, liberty itself becomes neither secure, nor justified, nor satisfying.

Liberal pluralism, on the other hand, may capture in its conception of liberalism the tolerance and moderation that are crucial to liberal society. However, its moral subjectivism leads it to misconstrue what a healthy democratic decision-making process entails. The pluralist scheme dissolves rational discourse into instrumental bargaining among self-interested groups. In the process, it subverts the rule of law and drains the liberal state of its legitimacy. Like Hume, the pluralists offer a conservative utilitarian version of liberalism that gives too much moral weight to the status quo. And like the libertarians, they depend upon political friendships and habits of civility taken for granted by their theory to place some bounds on the pursuit of self-interest.

Deontological liberals, on the other hand, seem both too pessimistic and too optimistic, extolling the virtues of a liberal polity while simultaneously deprecating some of its most important resources and processes. Because they are so skeptical about the possibilities of rational discourse concerning the human good, deontological liberals dismiss the public dialogue that both helps to generate some elements of common purpose in a liberal society and at the same time helps create friendship and moral respect among the citizens who participate in it. In light of this diminution in the practices and relationships of liberal citizens, the deontological liberals then seem unduly confident that abstract agreement on principles of justice will in fact come about and will in the process create "social union."[19]

If some of the most familiar contemporary general accounts of liberalism come to appear simplistic, misconceived, and potentially destructive by juxtaposition with the ideal of a rational society, other more partial arguments and critiques of contemporary liberal practice find a natural home within the same philosophical model. For them, the conception of rational political practice offered here can perform the same function that Rawls claims for his principles of justice *vis à vis* the familiar ideas and principles of modern liberal democratic culture. As Rawls notes, "a political conception need not be an original creation but may only articulate familiar intuitive ideas and principles so that they can be recognized as fitting together in a somewhat different way than before. Such a conception may, however, go further than this: it may organize these familiar ideas and principles by means of a more fundamental intuitive idea within the complex structure of which the other familiar intuitive ideas are then systematically connected and related."[20] In just this fashion, I would suggest, the conception of a society governed by the norms of a rational process provides a complex and more fundamental philosophical idea within which these recent more specific critical insights concerning liberal practice can be "systematically connected and related."

Rawls was rather vague and general regarding exactly which "familiar intuitive ideas" he had in mind that his conception of fairness embraces and ties together. One could charitably assume that he is vague at this point because the ideas he has in mind are themselves rather vague and general strands of a "public political culture"—something not easy to pin down. Or one could less charitably conjecture that an attempt at greater concreteness might render his basic claim somewhat suspect. In any case, because I have in mind strands of academic arguments rather than strands of a diffuse political culture, I can be more specific. I went to claim that the conception of liberal politics as rational practice both confirms and integrates more focused critiques of liberal practice recently offered by William Galston, James Fishkin, Benjamin Barber, Charles Anderson, Theodore Lowi, and Jane Mansbridge. This is not to say that these commentators on contemporary liberalism would necessarily agree with all I have said or even with my central thesis. Nor is it to say that my argument necessarily conforms to all aspects of their viewpoints. Instead, my contention is simply that some of the most central and astute observations of each of these theorists can be given philosophical warrant and can be systematically related to each other when they are seen as particular constituent elements of the larger normative conception of rational political practice.

For example, the logic informing the ideal of a rational society confirms William Galston's contention that assumptions about the human good are fundamental to the liberal project. It is not that a liberal society adopts and enforces a single homogeneous conception of the good life. That policy would in fact conflict, as we have noted and as Galston writes, with the liberal acknowledgment of "the diversity of human types and the inherent incapacity of the public sphere to encompass more than a portion of human activity or to fulfill more than a part of human aspirations."[21] Instead, liberalism *sub specie* the rational society incorporates the idea of the human good in two fundamental ways. In the first place, it is assumed that attainment of the good is the animating purpose of human life and that the common good—however conceived—is the orienting *telos* of a well-ordered society. Second, and equally important, it is clear that the constitutive values and practices of a rational society depend upon and are compatible only with a certain set of assumptions about features of the good life, for individuals and for human collectivities. Specifically, the normative conception of rational practice rests upon the assumption that an individual good life must be the purposive self-determination of a rational agent. In the context of group life, therefore, it involves the assumption that extensive liberty, toleration, respect for rights, and moral equality are essential elements of the human good.

The conception of rational political practice also provides grounds for sustaining James Fishkin's insistence that the heart of a legitimate liberal polity is what he calls a "self-reflective political culture." A self-reflective political culture, he writes, is "one that is significantly self-undermining when its regulative institutions (and their supporting rationales) are subjected to widespread and conscientious criticism from any of the diverse moral and political perspectives in the population." By "conscientious criticism" Fishkin means "verbal arguments offering reasons sincerely held by some members of the community." Such a self-reflective political culture, he notes, "will be continually engaged in a serious effort to purge itself of bias . . . [and] provides the conditions necessary for its own rational self-evaluation."[22]

This formulation clearly converges with the model of a rational society at several points. The notion of a political culture that is "self-undermining" conforms closely to Charles Frankel's characterization of rational processes as "cumulative and self-corrective," a characterization given philosophical embodiment in the notion of the "politics in reason." The necessary conditions of this self-undermining culture, in turn, centering in Fishkin's view around the conditions of "unmanipulated dialogue" echo the centrality of what I have termed the "conversation of democracy." And Fishkin's stipulation that the "conscientious criticism" fundamental to this dialogue involves "arguments offering reasons" represents an attempt to capitalize on the beneficent consequences of what I have called the "discipline of reason."

For similar reasons, the assumptions behind the ideal of a rational society lend support to some of the principal contentions of Benjamin Barber's *Strong Democracy*. The focus of the rational society upon democratic dialogue parallels Barber's insistence that "at the heart of strong democracy is talk." As Barber insists, moreover, not just any talk will do. "Strong talk" involves not merely the articulation of interests familiar to interest-group liberalism; it also requires the expression of "public judgment" directed toward apprehending and creating public interests and common goods. And both "strong democracy" and the rational society are characterized by the same dialectic of participation, citizenship, and community.[23]

The norms and institutions of the rational society also provide a home for Charles Anderson's contentions about the structure of a healthy policy process. As Anderson has observed, a positivistic understanding of evaluation and an associated instrumental conception of rationality have led to a narrow and distorted view of policy evaluation and decision making. Policy analysis, on this account, begins by accepting policy "preferences" as stipulated givens that are then "weighed," "compared," and maximized in utilitarian fashion by the "rational" policymakers.[24] Although such an account may conform to some technical policy analyses in a context of obligatory neutrality among competing interests, it does not, as Anderson correctly insists, provide an adequate account of rational decision making, either empirically or normatively. In an ideal sense, and at least sometimes in the real world of politics, rational policy evaluation involves not merely weighing and calculation, but also deliberation and judgment. "Good reasons" must be offered as warrants for desired alternatives, and among these good reasons are principles such as justice, authority, and efficiency.

Anderson's enlarged conception of deliberative and principled policy analysis squares nicely with the rational society's emphasis upon deliberative discourse concerning the common good. For both require argumentation that offers warrants—"good reasons"—for desired policy alternatives. Both insist that legitimate decisions are not the product of a simple aggregation of preferences, but instead arise from the force of principled argument. And both place discourse about communally desirable outcomes rather than utilitarian calculations of net aggregate benefits at the center of democratic decision making.

The argument for rationality in politics, next, lends added weight to Theodore Lowi's contention that a legitimate liberal polity must be a "juridical democracy."[25] The norms and practices of the liberal regime have been deranged in this country, Lowi argues, by the ascendancy of procedures and standards derived from the pluralist transformation of capitalist ideology. This new public philosophy of interest-group liberalism not only acquiesces in but encourages the devolution of public authority into a system of delegated power, administrative discretion, and the mutual accommodation of powerful interest groups. As a consequence, the resultant "Second Republic of the United States," as he calls this system of governance, finds it difficult both to plan effectively and to achieve justice. Even as the government's power and activity increase, then, its effectiveness and legitimacy suffer a decline.

Where Lowi's analysis converges with the logic of rationality in politics is the common insistence upon the exercise of authority via the rule of law. Political rules and regulations that are devised and justified in accordance with rational procedures and criteria can only be implemented in the form of law-like, generalized mandates. Governmental mandates that do not embody general rules but rather ratify an adventitious equilibrium among self-interested bargainers do not pass muster by these standards. They cannot qualify as genuinely authoritative rules of a rationally conducted enterprise. As Lowi observes in an apt "homely parable," the informal bargaining norms of interest-group liberalism are tantamount to eliminating the abuse of ticket fixing by universalizing it.[26] Such a stratagem is egalitarian, at least in principle. But it is an ultimately self-defeating way to effectuate a return to legitimacy. Whatever the merits of Lowi's specific recommendations, then, the advocate of a rational society can only concur with Lowi's basic claim that governance in a legitimate democracy must be exercised through an institutionalized rule of law. For that is the definitive and characteristic mode of authority in a rational enterprise; and anything less can therefore not be expected to elicit the moral support of a rational citizenry.

Finally, the conception of a rational society lends credence to Daniel Bell's view that a "reaffirmation of liberalism" requires attaining some recognition of what he terms the "public household" and a reacquisition of a "sense of *civitas*."[27] And it likewise sustains Jane Mansbridge's contention that "to maintain its legitimacy, a democracy must have both a unitary and an adversary face."[28]

In calling for the role of the "public household" in a healthy liberal society, Bell invokes themes that play an integral role in the model of a rational society. "The centrality of the public household . . . is, to go back to Aristotle, a concern more with the good condition of human beings than with the good condition of property. . . . It is the centrality of conscious decisions, publicly debated and philosophically justified, in the shaping of directions for the society." It is, in short, the moral community of rational beings who conduct their affairs through rational dialogue, even as they respect "their diversity as individuals and as groups." And the sense of *civitas* that Bell deems important is the attitudinal expression of the civic virtue of a citizen in the rational republic. It is "the spontaneous willingness to obey the law, to respect the rights of others, to forego the temptations of private enrichment at the expense of the public weal."[29]

In a similar vein, Jane Mansbridge has argued that the norms and practices of "adversary democracy" alone are not adequate for a good liberal society. Adversary democracy assumes that conflict among self-interested individuals is the starting point of all societies, that no grounds exist to establish some interests as better than others, and that the essence of democratic government is thus the equal protection of the interests of competing citizens. Because conflicts of interest are in fact inevitable and legitimate, and because no large-scale pluralistic society is likely to exhibit moral unanimity, the practices and institutions of adversary democracy—such as bargaining, voting, and majority rule—will always be necessary in contemporary liberal democracies.

Adversary practices, however, have their serious limitations, Mansbridge notes, when they are relied upon exclusively. By sanctioning selfish desire, by assuming that people behave like Hobbes's domineering egoists rather than like Aristotle's social animals, the idea of adversary democracy "verges on moral bankruptcy."[30] By offering protection against the depredations of potentially tyrannical competitors, the institutions of adversary democracy help prevent the worst. But they hardly encourage, or create, or even recognize the best; and they can warrant appreciation but not inspire enthusiasm.

Where possible, then, the ideals and practices of "unitary democracy" should be looked for rather than perennial conflict expected, the common good pursued, citizens considered friends rather than competitors, and equality expressed more through equal respect than through equal protection. Mansbridge thus appeals to key elements of a rational society: to consensus, to the quest for the common good, to what I have termed liberal *homonoia*. And she insists that not only at the local level but "even on the national level, some unitary, or almost unitary, moments can be preserved," and that wherever possible they should be made "available to . . . citizens."[31]

These recent critiques of liberal democratic theory and practice, then, can be summarily recapitulated in the following way: Liberal polities are not and cannot be utterly and totally "neutral," but instead aim at the good life and incorporate beliefs about what that entails (Galston); the heart of liberal practice is a "self-reflective" culture that opens itself to continual correction via conscientious criticism (Fishkin); strong talk and participation are essential to healthy democratic practice (Barber); healthy policy formation depends upon rational argumentation involving general principles (Anderson); liberal polities cannot be effective or legitimate if they abandon the rule of law (Lowi); a reaffirmation of liberalism requires a sense of *civitas* and a conception of the public household (Bell); and liberal democracy needs to incorporate features of "unitary democracy," involving political friendship and common interest, where it can do so (Mansbridge).

Each of these critics, I suggest, should be seen as intellectual archaeologists digging in the sands of what until fairly recently had been the prevailing account of liberal society as a concatenation of possessive individualists who muddle through by logrolling in a moral desert. Each of them has uncovered an important feature of liberal democracy that was obscured by that account. If we dig further, however, we can perhaps see each of these discoveries as a component part of a considerably larger philosophical whole—the once grand but now faded and neglected ideal of liberal society as the most noble rational enterprise of them all.

By applying restorative materials borrowed from post-Wittgensteinian philosophy of science and of language, moreover, this philosophical relic can be restored to something of its original splendor. Although its outlines are no longer so "clear and simple" as its early adherents believed, it can be exhumed and transformed into a viable structure for our contemporary political imagination. It is high time, in short, that this refashioned and revitalized ideal take its place alongside the pluralist, libertarian, utilitarian, and deontological conceptions of what liberal politics is all about. Indeed, for reasons adduced throughout this study, the conception of liberalism as the attempt to approximate the standards of rational practice in political life represents a more compelling account than any of its more recent and more popular competitors.

Chapter Seven **Approximating**

a Rational Society

I at first resisted the suggestion that I spell out some of the policy implications of the normative conception articulated and defended here. My reluctance had two principal sources.

In the first place, philosophers who enter too directly into the arena of practical politics rarely present an edifying spectacle. In retrospect, Plato appears naive in his futile missions to Syracuse. Hobbes's role in the royal court was neither elevated nor significant. Habermas seems to me far more impressive in his philosophical analyses than in his sociological prescriptions. And so on. Examples could be multiplied. The difficulty is that political "casuistry"—the movement from general principles to specific applications—involves a host of empirical and tactical judgments that do not derive from philosophical ideas alone. However discerning in their own intellectual bailiwick, philosophers are not necessarily the most knowledgeable or adept at rendering these judgments. Comte may have been right about very little; but his insistence on a functional distinction between the roles of *savant* and *industriel* was based on an accurate perception of the different competencies involved.

Second, too much of a focus upon the potential practical implications of conceiving liberalism as a philosophy of rational practice could easily create a misimpression I have labored to avoid. The idea of a rational society, I have taken pains to emphasize, is a valid ideal, but not, for any number of reasons, a fully realizable possibility. Still less is it a finished and finite political blueprint. Enlightenment enthusiasts of reason in politics undermined and discredited their ideas and their efforts by making this mistake, partly because they misconceived rationality as simple and partly because they misjudged the human will as less problematical than it is. I want to be as certain as I can that no careless or unwary reader will misunderstand my intentions or assertions as in any way replicating that error of judgment. And offering "how to" suggestions about creating a more rational society could encourage this serious misinterpretation.

Nevertheless, ideas do have consequences. The conception of liberal democracy as an aspiration to embody in politics the standards of rational enterprises is not a pure abstraction devoid of implications for conduct. For the sake of illustration and for purposes of discussion, then, some practical applications of rational practice norms can be ventured here. It only needs to be remembered that these are tentative proposals in the service of approximating a systematically elusive ideal.[1]

Thinking and Acting

In the first place, how we think about ourselves and our political world from the outset exerts a pervasive influence over our political behavior. In this respect, attachment to the ideal of a rationally governed society is no exception. The acceptance of the basic norms of the model carry implications for the ideologies that shape the way we see our world and for the conceptions that govern our individual modes of political activity.

In ideological terms, the ideal of a rational society has distinctive but not entirely determinate implications. It clearly disqualifies some ideological conceptions. It tends to crosscut certain other conventional ideological cleavages. And it leaves some ideological space open as an area in which reasonable people may differ.

Some ideologies seem clearly unable to qualify by the norms of rational practice. In these cases, it is either/or: one either must renounce the intrinsic norms of rationality or forfeit the ideological orientation. The overt antirationalism of fascist ideologies, for example, would seem to disqualify them immediately. One cannot deprecate the power or validity of rational discourse, argue for forms of political authority grounded in purely emotional appeal and manipulation rather than rational consent, and convert natural differences of race or ability into political hierarchies without decisively abandoning key standards of rational practice.

Likewise, explicitly theocratic conceptions of politics fall beyond the pale. Because it incorporates restrictions based upon a recognition of the limitations of our cognitive powers, a rational society could never preclude or discourage expressions of religious faith. A dogmatically atheistic regime claims knowledge it cannot legitimately possess. But for the same fallibilistic reasons, no society can claim to incarnate God's will. Here the conception of rational humility provides secular confirmation for the religious humility that knows idolatry when it sees it.

Similarly, technocratic, totalitarian, and bureaucratic authoritarian ideologies represent departures from our understanding of rational norms. All technocratic justifications of political power are based on a misconception of what can be known, how it can be known, and who can/cannot know it. Specifically, technocratic ideals embody a positivistic misassimilation of political and technical knowledge, overstate the certainty with which political norms can be ascertained, and accredit a subset of political leaders with an expertise they cannot really possess. In their most potent form, modern totalitarian ideologies make use of these technocratic delusions. But in any form, totalitarian conceptions are flatly incompatible with a rational society's dedication to toleration, consent, participation, and citizen autonomy. The pretensions of all authoritarian regimes, in parallel, must be seen as unjustified by rational standards—whether these are justified in technocratic terms or in traditionalist ones.

The determination to conduct politics as a rational enterprise, therefore, is not ideologically neutral or impotent. The practices it dictates are inconsistent with a number of important ideologies. When it comes to adjudicating among the major contending ideologies in the West, however, things become more difficult. Contemporary liberals, conservatives, and democratic socialists could all conceivably interpret their ideologies in a way that would make them reasonably consistent with the ideal of rational politics. It is simply that each of these ideologies would find different aspects of the conception of a rational society most congenial and other aspects somewhat problematic.

The ideal of a rational society crosscuts liberalism, conservatism, and democratic socialism—each of these being a part of the larger tradition of Western liberalism in the broadest sense. It incorporates some of the leading values and goals of each of them. The liberal, for instance, would consider the rational society's insistence upon individual rights and civil liberties the most important part of the model. The socialist would emphasize the elements of equality and community. And the conservative would find the role of the human good and the norms of civility quite consistent with his or her dominant political concerns. The bearing of the conception of a rational society on these ideologies, then, is not so much to single one of them out as superior to the others. Instead, it would suggest that each represents a somewhat narrow and parochial conception of the good society—one in which some aspects of the good society are given undue ascendancy while others are unnecessarily subordinated or forgotten.

If the norms of rational practice carry ideological implications at the general level, they also bear directly upon the self-conceptions that govern our individual behavior. The question "what ought I to do as a political actor?" is to an important degree a function of the answer to a prior question of political identity: "who am I as a political animal?" Hence, anyone who ascribes to the norms of rational practice will translate the "what is to be done" question into "how should I conduct myself as a citizen of a rational republic?" And although the answer to the latter question cannot be made absolutely determinative regarding all specific actions, it nonetheless has a powerful bearing upon one's political orientation, sense of responsibilities, and sense of rights and privileges.

Those who see themselves as participants in a rational political enterprise will, for example, orient themselves toward the common good. They will be dedicated to the process of what Habermas calls "discursive will formation." They will seek to discern through investigation and discussion where the general interest lies, considering it obligatory to work on its behalf. In their everyday social conduct, those who see themselves subject to reason's discipline will consider themselves obliged to be tolerant of their fellow citizens, to respect their rights, to be willing to listen to their ideas and expressions of interest, and to offer "good reasons" for their policy preferences when asked. They will, at the same time, not be bashful about claiming the rights and status due them as rational beings, about exercising their freedoms of speech and action, about participating in public affairs, and about insisting upon their right to be "treated as an equal."

This kind of rational process orientation to the political world can be contrasted with the orientations that would be logically appropriate for utilitarian democrats, for pluralists, and for rights-based liberals. A utilitarian democrat would—to the extent he or she internalized the norms of this theoretical conception—see himself or herself in considerably more passive terms. For citizens of enterprises governed by utilitarian norms are essentially equal-status component recipients of the proceeds of a welfare-maximizing project. Pluralist democrats would logically see themselves as political bargainers or gamesmen, essentially concerned to maximize their own self-interest through tactics of coalition and compromise. Libertarians would similarly be oriented to the market-wise maximization of individual welfare, with the additional concern of minimizing the public domain wherever possible. Adherents of Rawlsian principles of justice, on the other hand, would be more public spirited. But they would seem to have, as befits adherents of deontological norms, a somewhat abstract and formal orientation toward their fellow citizens and to the public weal. Rather like Kantian moral actors—and the analogy is obviously not accidental—they would be creatures of duty who carefully obeyed neutral rules that regulated their mutual interaction. They would be concerned to do what is just and right in public life, but they would likely be relatively privatistic in their conception and pursuit of the good life. And in the long run, whether they could sustain the possible self-sacrifices demanded by the principles of justice in the absence of a more robust sense of community and general good might be questionable.

In sum, acceptance of the rational process conception of liberal democracy exercises a broad influence over political practice by constraining ideological affiliations and shaping political self-images. Many possible orientations to the world of politics are precluded, obligations are mandated, rights and privileges validated—all in ways that exert a pervasive control over what can be seen as acceptable political behavior. As we turn now to examine some more specific institutional patterns and policies suggested by the norms of rational practice, it is worth remembering that these more subliminal influences on our actions may be the most important of them all.

Strengthening Democratic Discourse

The heart of a rational society is democratic discourse about the common good. A society committed to the norms of rational process will therefore give continual and careful attention to measures that can sustain and strengthen this central social institution.

The presence of significant and vital public practical discourse in a society represents a very difficult and complex cultural achievement. Even if Mill's historicist and somewhat ethnocentric argument in *Considerations on Representative Government* is not entirely satisfactory to a cosmopolitan twentieth-century readership, that account nevertheless incorporates two valid and important observations. First, the possibility of grounding stable government upon the consent of a free people is contingent upon certain virtues and abilities provided by the prevailing political culture. Second, the presence of these virtues and abilities cannot be mechanically contrived by formal institutions or simple public policies. Societies gain an understanding of and allegiance to the disciplines of practical discourse only through a long process of sociological and educational habituation. Political reformers wishing to approximate the ideal of a rational society can only take advantage of these cultural achievements where present; when they are absent, they cannot be artificially manufactured, and they cannot be substituted. The best we can do is to nurture those cultural attainments and to build upon them.

Beyond nurturing those aspects of the educational process that contribute most to practical discourse, social policy can bolster the viability of the democratic forum in a number of ways. It is fundamental, of course, that access to the *agora* be unrestricted. The standard liberal civil liberties—of speech, association, thought, and communication— must be defended against assaults from whatever quarter. And more positively, social policy can promote and facilitate public discourse in a variety of technical and economic ways. As Benjamin Barber points out, for example, some of our policies seem perversely to impede rather than to promote the crucial exchange of ideas while favoring less consequential forms of communication. "It is something of a scandal", he writes, "if a fit tribute to the privatized priorities of our society, that the government subsidizes junk mail offering trivial information about consumer options and choices by delivering such mail at a second-class bulk rate, while it penalizes newspapers and journals offering significant information about political and social options and choices by saddling them with higher third-class rates."[2] Barber goes on to make a number of other suggestions regarding possible innovative uses of telecommunications technology to promote what he calls "strong talk." But whatever the logistical pros and cons of suggestions like these, the crucial general point is that it should be a priority of public policy to permit and promote reasoned discussion of social ideas and policies whenever feasible.

A democratic society that wishes to govern itself in accord with the norms of rational practice also needs to give serious attention to the quality of political journalism. Technical advances in the communications media have made the role of the journalist increasingly central to the dynamics of democratic decision making. Communications between leaders and citizens, between the government and the larger society, and between contending political groups are conveyed and filtered through a media screen. The abilities and predispositions of those who report, interpret, and comment upon political happenings are thus increasingly important. If their reports are unilluminating, their interpretations misleading, and their commentaries obtuse, the quality of public deliberation and discourse is seriously impeded. Conversely, skilled and thoughtful journalism can vastly enhance the ability of political leaders and ordinary citizens alike to make sense of their common world and to reach sound judgments about it.

Accordingly, a rational society should foster serious and responsible political journalism in any way it can. Philanthropic institutions can offer funds to support and improve journals of political analysis and social commentary. And they could establish "think-tank" centers where journalists could—like academics on sabbatical—share ideas and deepen their knowledge. Universities can, as Harvard and Duke among others have done, create programs that allow journalists to explore academic resources useful to them. Awards can be made to those who achieve distinction in political journalism. And so on. These are social efforts, not specifically governmental ones—for obvious reasons. And their goal is a simple one: to help journalism make a vital contribution to the quality of democratic discourse. No rational society could survive the absence of publications such as *The Public Interest*, *The New Republic*, and *The Louisville Courier-Journal* or subsist on an exclusive diet of tabloids and *The National Enquirer*.

Another expedient to strengthen democratic discourse would be the promotion of what might be called "cross-paradigm" forums. Especially within large contemporary pluralist societies, it is easy for cultural and ethnic groups to turn into enclaves that speak to each other only in stylized rhetorical broadsides hurled over the barricades. And when that occurs, the always difficult effort to discern and work toward a common good is made nearly impossible. At best, the distinctive groups engage in a politics of bickering and compromise; and less happily their relationship may turn into a zero-sum war of attrition.

Unless the old notion of a cultural "melting-pot" were to become a reality—probably not a desirable one—differences and conflicts among these groups will be a constant in a free society. But when occasions and institutions are available wherein leaders of the different segments of society can speak directly to each other about their beliefs, their interests, and their concerns, the prospects of rational cooperation among them are generally improved.

When Sen. Edward Kennedy went to speak at Jerry Falwell's Liberty College, for example, he did not convert to the Moral Majority or turn his listeners into devotees of Massachusetts liberalism. But he gained an appreciation that they were not mere bigots and they saw that he was not a "secular humanist" with horns and a tail. The differences remained, but the prospects of mutual understanding and the possibilities of making common cause in some areas were promoted. In like fashion, the systematic sponsorship by civic associations of opportunities for candid and direct discussions among representatives of different class, racial, religious, and cultural groups can fortify democratic dialogue. The norms of rational process do not presuppose the absence of conflict nor do they promise its disappearance; they assume only that people of good will who communicate subject to the discipline of reason are considerably more likely to identify common problems and achieve a common good than those who spurn the opportunities for discourse.

Encouraging *Homonoia*

Homonoia is created in part by common allegiance to the same beliefs and values. Because contemporary pluralist societies encompass variant ethical and religious perspectives, they will never attain the kind of extensive *homonoia* engendered by moral unanimity. But that degree of sociological "compactness" is necessary neither for social stability nor for the successful resort to rational practices in governance.

For one thing, a common dedication to rational procedure is itself the holding of a common value that can transcend other credal divergences. Mutual participation in the conduct of practical discourse creates bonds among the participants. By submitting to the enabling conditions of discourse, they achieve a common identity of a thin sort as rational beings; and they implicitly join in a quest for common goals, such as the attainment of mutual understanding and the solution of common problems. Democratic dialogue, in short, both presupposes and creates a limited form of *homonoia*.

This limited *homonoia* generated by practical discourse by itself, however, is probably insufficient to sustain the working relationships of a rational society. Citizens require some elements of common identity and mutual respect to be impelled toward dialogue in the first instance; and if that does not occur, then the reciprocal reinforcement of dialogic interaction and like-mindedness may never get off the ground. It would seem entirely appropriate, therefore, for those who want to push their society toward the ideal of a rational enterprise to seek supplementary ways of promoting *homonoia* among their fellow citizens. And although *homonoia* may be in its full achievement a complex cultural feat, some contrivances can be effectual in its promotion—because like-mindedness is created not only by holding common beliefs per se but also by having common experiences directed toward mutual purposes. And these latter forms of experience can either be fostered or discouraged by public policy.

In the first place, for example, it would seem almost mandatory for a rational society to include a vibrant public sphere. However flawed may have been Plato's argument for common property among the guardians, the basic starting point behind that argument is pertinent here. Namely, having some parts of our landscape and some experiences that all can call "mine" helps promote a common identity. Adherents of the rational society need therefore to combat the denigration of the public sphere that some forms of liberalism have encouraged. A wholly privatized society of fragmented particular wills is not an adequate sociological matrix for a politics of rational practice. A society of strangers ultimately does not possess sufficient grounds for reasoning together. The wherewithal for vital democratic dialogue withers where "public" comes to be a residual category for charity cases.

It is especially important that a society dedicated to rational practices have a strong system of public education. The abilities and awareness good education provides are so essential to effective citizenship and to a successful life in general that no one can be denied access to it. One of the unfortunate by-products of political trends in the sixties and seventies in this country was the weakening of public education. The public schools were damaged by the subordination of their educational mission to a social agenda, were starved at times by tax revolts, and were abandoned by many of the wealthier and more conservative elements of society. It is a welcome development, then, that public education and its problems have received more attention, more sympathy, and more resources in recent years.

Public buildings, public parks, public rituals, and public celebrations also play an important part in constituting sufficient *homonoia* to fuel a rational society. Most citizens of a free democratic society, I think, instinctively appreciate this need. But they do not always possess the language or concepts to articulate their instinctive awareness. For example, the college students I teach are generally somewhat surprised and dismayed when they encounter Milton Friedman's argument that most public parks, including Yellowstone and the Grand Canyon, should be turned over to private enterprise. But they find it almost impossible to say exactly why the prospect of auctioning off Old Faithful for private merchandizing seems to them so undesirable.

Despite the serious logistical problems that make it a difficult idea to implement, moreover, the basic concept of universal citizen service would seem highly compatible with the needs and norms of a rational society. The basic reason for this compatibility is that participating in such an enterprise would be exactly the kind of common experience directed toward mutual purposes that creates a sense of community. Tocqueville taught us long ago the dangers of professional armies in a democracy, and purely "volunteer" armies share some of the same defects. Not only are they essentially mercenary forces who can become a separate enclave within society, but they tend de facto to produce a situation in which the children of the poor are sent to die in defense of the privileges of the better-off. A universal citizen service, encompassing but not limited to the military, would prevent these problems while at the same time providing broader opportunities for a sense of common purpose across class, racial, and geographic boundaries.[3]

Finally, the need for *homonoia* and the importance of a universal medium for public discourse suggests the practical importance of a single common language in a society. Sharing a language means, in part, to share a common mind—in a limited but nonetheless powerful way. And it is very difficult to conduct a satisfactory democratic dialogue through translators. Those in this country who champion making English the "official language" of this country tend to be paranoid and parochial. Formal declarations to that effect are neither necessary nor appropriate. But the goal of a common linguistic culture rather than a

Babel of linguistic enclaves is a worthy one. In this instance, I fear, the compassion of those concerned for the welfare of citizens for whom English is not a first language may be misplaced. In the long run, protecting these citizens from the rigors of gaining fluency in the dominant language in the name of preserving their cultural autonomy does them no favor. Not only are they likely to be handicapped by alienation from the principal medium of national public dialogue, but the country as a whole suffers both from this exclusion and from the *heteronia* thereby perpetuated.

Promoting Participation

A society aspiring to be a rational enterprise cannot rest content with the pluralist acceptance of political apathy. The pluralist argument should not be caricatured into a straw man, of course. Even as they insisted, for example, that "high participation is not required for successful democracy," pluralists recognized that "it is essential that a sizable percentage of citizens participate in choosing their public officials."[4] The brunt of the pluralist argument was simply that democracy could function rather well with relatively low levels of participation and that high levels of political mobilization could be destabilizing. Nevertheless, the sanguine acceptance of political passivity induced by the pluralist account of "the functional system" is not entirely healthy by the norms of rational practice. A rational society tries to encourage a high level of interest and participation in political affairs; and it emphasizes the disciplining power of reason over the passions rather than apathetic indifference as the principal force for stability in the political system.

Various strategies can be employed to enhance participation levels to a point reasonably attuned to the demands of rational process. Such strategies should be assessed and employed, however, with the recognition that it is the quality and not the quantity alone of participation that is important. For some purposes, such as the function of "interest articulation" for example, shouting slogans and waving placards may be useful. But from the standpoint of a rational enterprise, the truly important forms of participation are those that incorporate citizens into the democratic dialogue.

Voting still has to rank as one of the most salient acts of democratic participation. It is true, of course, that votes can be cast in ways that diminish their significance as contributions to rational process. A "good" vote, from the perspective of the rational society, is one that conforms generally to the hopeful expectations of Rousseau and Mill. That is, it is a conscientious expression of reasoned judgment about the general welfare and not simply a mindless registration of unreflective and uncaring individual will. All votes, of course, are at least partly expressions of will and not pure acts of dispassionate judgment. That is both natural and inevitable. It is only when voting is wholly corrupt that it does not serve as a crucial act of democratic participation in the context of a rational society.

Public policy therefore should be concerned about improving both the quantity and the quality of participation via the ballot. The mechanisms of voter registration should be constraining only to the extent necessary to minimize fraud. Other than that, all eligible voters should be given every encouragement to register and to exercise the franchise. Thoughtful application of emerging computer technology should make it possible, one could surmise, to minimize procedural obstacles to voter registration and at the same time make fraud exceedingly difficult. Calculations of partisan political advantage should not stand in the way of efforts aimed in this direction.

Attention should also be given to improving the delivery of relevant information that bears on voters' judgment making. Newspapers disseminate some information about candidates and their views. Television and radio contributes in this regard, as well. But considerable improvements could be made by the media in this area. And it may be that some more official medium of communication regarding candidates and issues needs to be developed. Voters need to have access to data necessary for a reasoned judgment, and they need to be reminded by the very ubiquity of information made available to them that in fact they are being called upon to be knowledgeable participants. In a recent runoff election for judgeships in the state I inhabit, voter turnout was infinitesimal. People predictably decried the voter apathy allegedly on display here, but the fact was that information about the candidates was so unavailable that staying away from the polls was actually the most rational thing most voters could do. It is crucial, then, that public policy develop modes of communication with the voter that are essential in keeping elections from approaching this particular *reductio ad absurdum*.

In some instances, moreover, it would be extremely useful to present the voter with more nuanced and multiple choices than the yes/no, either/or format provides. Voters could be allowed to rank candidates in multicandidate primaries, for example. And they could be permitted a range of responses on referendum issues. Once again, the possibilities of microelectronics technology could and should be harnessed in ways designed to provide a more subtle and accurate registration of popular views. Moreover, as Benjamin Barber has astutely observed, the presentation to voters of multiple and nuanced alternatives helps convey an important message about the act of voting that comports with the norms of a rational society. As Barber writes, a multichoice format "discourages purely private choices and encourages voters to have public reasons for what are after all public acts." Such a format "is thus a form of civic education even as it is a form of balloting, and it strengthens democracy not simply by allowing citizens to choose alternative futures but by compelling them to think like public beings."[5]

Adherents of rationality in politics should also be concerned about the strength and the quality of political parties—or their functional equivalent. When they are strong and healthy, political parties are peculiarly apt vehicles for the infusion of norms of rational process into a democratic polity. They provide an important forum for discussions of policies and principles, whether in local caucuses, on platform committees, or on convention floors. They provide opportunities for citizen involvement that turn around more general concerns than those pursued by interest groups. They require, at a minimum, negotiation and compromise among special interests; and they provide at a maximum a framework in which these special interests can be modified, transcended, and integrated into a broader conception of the public good. They can bring people together across boundaries of race, class, and culture and can foster—even amid and through the wrangling for advantage—strands of *homonoia* and mutual respect.

To perform these functions, it is not necessary that parties meet the somewhat intellectualistic and unrealistic standards of the Burkean model. Democratic parties will never be simply institutions of public-spirited people animated by common principles. They will always be political coalitions among various factions making common cause for mutual advantage as well as for general principles. It is essential, however, that parties not be merely passive vessels dominated entirely by highly organized and particularized special interests. Parties need to provide some leavening of more general concerns to the struggle of interest groups, or else they begin to forfeit their distinctive function *vis à vis* norms of rational process. It has been distressing in recent years to see in this country, therefore, the trend toward increasing interest-group power within and at the expense of the parties. Delegates to national conventions seem often to behave like emissaries from acronymic principalities such as NOW, NEA, and others like them. The consensus-building quest for common interests is thereby frustrated, and party deliberations have difficulty escaping the cycle of threat, bluff, and pork-barrel promise.

Expanding the role of primary elections exerts some countervailing restraint on the role of interest groups in parties. But this is not an altogether satisfactory palliative. Parties instead wind up being torn between interest-group aggrandizement on the one hand and plebiscitary pressures and distortions on the other. Some critics of our current parties have rather wistfully wished for the good old days of smoke-filled rooms, when professional politicians ran the parties. But this surely is a vain hope for a return to a somewhat romanticized past. There is much merit to E. E. Schattschneider's insistence that democracy lies *between* parties and not within them. Now that they have been democratized, however, there is probably no turning back. The real question now is not so much whether the parties shall be open to popular participation and control but what form that participation will assume.

From the standpoint of a rational society, the best alternative would seem to be a strong caucus system of party organization. Some states have a healthy tradition of active and meaningful local party caucuses that could be further strengthened. Iowa is one example. It is true, of course, that in "low-interest" political years, these caucuses would likely be controlled by a somewhat unrepresentative segment of activists; but some self-selection in political life is inevitable and not entirely undesirable. And in "high-interest" years, the party caucuses could approximate a pyramid of town meetings. Many of the Kentucky county caucuses in 1968, when the Vietnam War was at issue, drew large turnouts of citizens eager to participate in the process of selecting leaders and determining policy. In the state I now live in, however, parties are considerably more assiduous at soliciting contributions from their members than they are at telling them when precinct meetings or county conventions are going to be held. Most interested but non-professional party members wind up excluded simply because they are not timely informed. The interest of some adherents of participatory politics in Jeffersonian "neighborhood assemblies," I would argue, could productively be focused on local party caucuses that would serve some of the same functions but incorporate them into an existing decision-making structure. The arguments on behalf of the virtues of such neighborhood assemblies are appealing.[6] But unless they are part of a meaningful decision structure, they would die of neglect. Political parties, however, could utilize the basic idea to become more fully democratic in a rational mode.

Participation in a rational society, moreover, is not limited to the political domain narrowly conceived. Practical reason is a cognitive activity that emerges and deploys itself in response to problems, deficiencies, frustrated needs. These problems arise at all levels of human interaction, and it would be neither efficient nor proper for a society to address all of its problems through specifically governmental channels. In a rational society, therefore, institutions develop spontaneously around problem clusters that themselves bubble up out of our common life. This phenomenon parallels the way that new scientific fields and specialties periodically emerge or decline as anomalies or gaps in our knowledge appear and are resolved. The creation and dissolution of human rights commissions, arts councils, chambers of commerce, and school-reform task forces thus institutionally mimic the continual reorganization of academic disciplines, subdisciplines, and cross-disciplinary programs. These social institutions are part of a rational response to practical problems as the academic institutions are a rational response to theoretical problems.

In any rational society, therefore, participation in these spontaneous social structures should be encouraged. This area of volunteerism is often ignored in political and ideological analysis, because it is neither a market phenomenon nor a governmental one. But it is an important mechanism in which the dynamics of a rational enterprise are productively manifest. Advocates of *laissez-faire* properly recognize the virtues of private enterprises generated by a response to demand; but they improperly confine and conceive the dynamic they praise within a narrowly individualistic and economic dimension. Rousseau, on the other hand, would have these rationally functional intermediary associations discouraged, because he simplistically sees them as factions and presumes that all genuinely public-spirited activity must be channeled through the state. From the perspective of a rational society as here understood, both of these polarized accounts are wrong. A rational society needs to recognize these spontaneous, participatory, quasi-governmental associations for what they are and to encourage their operation. Fortunately, the combination of a healthy political culture and extensive political freedom is usually enough to accomplish this task.

Finally, the norms of rational procedure suggest the presence of some valuable truths in the drive toward "workplace democracy." This is a term, of course, that can have many meanings. In the hands of some advocates it is an unworkable utopian ideal that is essentially based in fantasizing about escape from the socially beneficent discipline of a competitive economy—a hope, as it were, to eat our cake without baking it. But the insistence upon the necessity of more participatory and egalitarian modes of workplace organization in its more sensible form is based upon a recognition of the irrationality of purely command-oriented organization structures. Not only within an economy as a whole but also within large economic enterprises themselves, necessary information of both a technical and a human sort cannot be adequately processed by a rigidly hierarchic structure in which decisions are always made at the top.

Economic enterprises that are more participatory and collaborative in their decision structure are not only more efficient in the long run (compare the flexibility and innovativeness of a participatory company such as Hewlett-Packard with the stagnation of the rigidly hierarchic American auto industry, for example), but such enterprises also help to foster the kinds of skills and attitudes appropriate to good citizenship in a rational political order. Employees who are not treated as mere cogs in a machine but who instead take an active responsibility for the results of the overall effort partake in a school of public spirit similar to that which Mill saw provided by exercise of the franchise. Rationally organized political systems should therefore encourage creative efforts aimed at workplace democracy for their indirect benefits as well as for their direct contribution to the welfare of employees and their businesses.

Protecting Human Rights

For much recent liberal theory, rights are the axis around which all else turns. From the perspective of a society dedicated to norms of rational procedure, rights are equally fundamental; but they are not axial in the same way. Rights are not merely positive, but they do not have the status of wholly prior, independent, and transcendent claims that individuals possess *ab initio* against and prior to any acts of legitimate social power. Instead, rights are seen as an essential constitutive element of a larger and more comprehensive process that is—taken as a whole—the definitive normative base for political legitimacy. Rights are—for reasons discussed earlier in this book—a *conditio sine qua non* of rational procedure. Only where individuals have rights to freedom of thought, expression, and action can a society defensibly contend that it is a rational enterprise directed at achieving the human good. But rights do not stand in abstract and splendid isolation as *the* standard of political rectitude.

Put into traditionalist terms, the rational society's doctrine of rights is neither one of natural rights nor one of positive rights but one of civic rights. They occupy the status that Hume was groping to express when he characterized the norms of justice as "artificial but not arbitrary." They are "artificial" in the sense that they do not originate or subsist meaningfully apart from the conventions that distinguish a human society from a state of nature. But they are not arbitrary, because they turn out to be intrinsic and essential elements in any adequately configured pattern of social conventions. Tocqueville puts the emphasis in the proper place and states it well when he says that without the idea of rights "there can be no society, for what is a combination of rational and intelligent beings held together by force alone?"[7] Since "adequately" here means adequate by reference to the nature of an association of rational and intelligent beings, one could by a pardonable ellipsis speak of natural rights. The only problem with this designation is that it might induce one to forget the truly crucial middle term. And when that is done, the way is open—especially once "nature" loses the teleological connotations it possessed in classical thought—for the idea of rights to translate into liens held by anomic individuals against society instead of into a standing that society must grant its citizens to operate rationally.[8]

In practical terms, the essential role of rights in a rational society puts its adherents in agreement with rights-based liberals concerning the dangers of the utilitarian calculus as a norm for public policy. As Rawls correctly insists, a straightforward standard of maximizing average or aggregate utility does not take due regard of the separateness and moral integrity of persons. A rational society is predicated upon the autonomy and integrity of its citizens, and it cannot countenance the sacrifice of these *conditiones sine quibus non* for merely contingent advantage. Alternatively, of course, a utilitarian might bring the imperatives of a rational society *vis à vis* individual rights under his or her conceptual umbrella by interpreting these imperatives as embodying a consequentialist judgment that is accorded such weight as to render it overwhelming whenever it figures into a welfare calculus. No matter. At this point the issue is purely conceptual, with the practical conclusion that rights are essential remaining intact in either case.

The distinctive status and justification given rights by norms of rational process, on the other hand, leads its adherents to diverge from the libertarian implications some have considered—whether to applaud or condemn—to be characteristic of liberalism. The conception of rights as fundamentally civic in their origin and justification, for example, suggests that libertarians strike the wrong balance between property rights and civil rights. The former are made too sacrosanct and the latter are left too contingent. This misconception occurs in part because the libertarian account tends to conceive society as nothing more than an amalgam of private contracts, and it has little conception of an autonomous public space. Hence individuals are granted almost total control over whatever property they can amass and they can ignore others' civic rights except in the exceedingly limited public domain that they recognize only grudgingly.

In our conception, in contrast, it is civic rights that are fundamental and property rights that are derivative. A rational society need not timidly worry whether it has any business intruding obligations of civic respect and equality into what is seen as almost exclusively private terrain. Instead, one of its first and most central obligations is to ensure that its members possess the full rights and liberties necessary to their participation as autonomous citizens of a rational enterprise. The realm of genuinely private action must be respected, of course. But no allegedly private actions that infringe upon the full civic rights of other citizens need be tolerated.

A rational society should therefore have strong civil rights laws at its core. Anyone can be as bigoted as he or she likes in his or her own home, but no one can be allowed to impose those prejudices on the public world in a way that demeans other citizens who also must inhabit that world. The dignity of citizenship is not something that should be left to private caprice, but it must be publicly recognized and publicly defended. From the perspective of a rational society, then, the public accommodations section (Title 2) of the 1964 Civil Rights Act was not only justified but mandatory. Its enactment was an important step toward protecting the citizen rights necessary for rational process. And it would have been better as a matter of principle had the constitutional justification for the act been, as Justice Douglas argued in his concurring opinion in *Heart of Atlanta*, the Fourteenth Amendment rather than the commerce clause. As Justice Douglas wrote, the right of people to be free of discrimination on the basis of race "occupies a more protected position in our constitutional system than does the movement of cattle, fruit, steel, and coal across state lines."[9]

What is interesting about Justice Douglas's plaintive words is how closely they echo Burke's complaint about what he saw as the liberal tendency to dissolve society into a set of "subordinate contracts" made at the pleasure of individuals: "the state ought not to be considered as nothing better than a partnership agreement in a trade of pepper and coffee, calico, or tobacco . . . to be taken up for a little temporary interest, and to be dissolved by the fancy of the parties." A rational society may not be "a partnership in every virtue and in all perfection,"[10] as Burke would have it. But since it is a community of rational beings oriented toward their common good, it has a moral status and a *raison d'être* that go beyond merely private whim. Individuals thus have civic rights that private actions cannot be permitted to abridge, and the status of these rights—whatever the legal avenue necessary to enforce them—should be seen as more fundamental than a merely prudential regulation of commerce.

The greater centrality of civil rights than property rights to the logic of a rational society does not mean that the latter need be disenfranchised completely. An argument on behalf of property rights can be made in a more contingent form. Although a rational society need not recognize property claims held as trump over the scope of collective action, it has to recognize the role of property rights in enabling people to be genuinely autonomous and hence rational. Because we are material beings, we require some control over our immediate environment to be free. Individuals who had no license whatever over the material possessions in their immediate bodily vicinity would be reduced to a state of utter dependency and servitude. Whether one is the wholly exploited wage slave of a private entrepreneur or the wholly dependent ward of the state, the alienating and debilitating consequences are essentially the same. A rational society follows the logic of Jefferson more than that of either Friedman or Marx. It is crucial that individuals be truly free and autonomous. That is what rights are all about. And that translates into a private space for "freeholders" rather than into either *laissez-faire* or egalitarian statism.

Beyond a strong bias toward granting all individuals sufficient property rights to sustain their autonomy, the norms of rationality in politics do not offer a hard and fast blueprint for how extensive property rights should be. In detail, then, property rights in a rational society fall under the heading of positive rights rather than having the status of natural rights. Neither the right-wing claim that individuals possess an inviolable right to control those economic resources they have accumulated without force or fraud nor the left-wing claim that individuals have an inalienable right to food, shelter, and health care can find support within the more limited political conception of rights that befits a rational enterprise. Instead, the various moral and prudential arguments on behalf of market distributions and welfare redistributions are properly to be heard and adjudicated within the normal decision-making institutions of a rational society. Economic rights and obligations are a policy product of this society, not a part of its constitution.

In the Lockean conception of democratic society, the individual enters the society fully vested with rights to all he or she has accumulated in the state of nature. In Rousseau's account, individuals agree wholly to alienate their property to society as part of the social contract. The enabling conditions for conducting politics as a rational enterprise suggest a norm that falls somewhere between these extremes. A rational society is in practical terms under an obligation to grant its citizens rights to privacy and property sufficiently extensive to sustain their genuine autonomy. Actions and decisions can be rational only when they result from the choices and judgments of independent participants; and no person deprived of personal sovereignty over some limited space can function as an independent agent. Beyond the imperative to recognize these rights, however, a rational society may determine through its policy process what norms of economic justice and what mix of justice, prudence, and compassion shall govern the allocation of resources. If the political culture is not corrupt and if the mode of authority is not corrupt—i.e., if there is civic virtue and rule of law— no genuine property rights of individuals are likely to be abrogated by this process.[11]

Rights in a rational society, in sum, have both a public and a private face. They are derived from the requisites of citizen roles rather than from abstract principles of justice. The public rights that guarantee the dignity of all citizens, their freedom of thought and expression, and their ability to participate as moral equals in the public world are the paramount rights for a society dedicated to rational norms. But private space and power must also be respected as a condition of genuine citizen autonomy. It is simply that these private property rights to control an individual's space and things are not absolute and socially anomic. They must complement and sustain the individual's role as a citizen and not be allowed to expropriate the public realm altogether.

Preserving Equality

The same logic that governs rights in a rational society governs equality as well. The central concern of a rational society *vis à vis* the nature and extent of permissible inequalities among its participants relates to their capabilities and relationships as citizens. For reasons discussed previously, participants in a rational enterprise must stand on roughly an equal footing. Differences in rank, status, and authority are based on consent and grow out of the mutual purposes of the enterprise rather than being foisted upon it from the outside. This requirement suggests that political and legal equality be essentially an absolute norm, that moral inequalities be limited to those distinctions legitimately earned and freely conferred by one's peers, and that economic inequalities not be so great as to undermine civic equality.

It is appropriate, therefore, for a rational society to manifest and celebrate the civic equality fundamental to its operation. "Rites" of equal citizenship should be performed on regular occasions. One of the great latent functions of voting, for example, is the profound symbolic reaffirmation of civic equality embodied in the experience. At the polls the local bank president and the fast-food worker, the minister and the liquor-store proprietor all stand in the same line and have an equal say. However sobering it may be at times to contemplate the weaknesses of the voting public whose judgment is sovereign in democracy, it is always exhilarating to sense the equal dignity conferred upon them as individuals by the electoral process. Meetings of the public school PTA have something of the same effect and for the same reason: whatever the differences among the participants in other realms of life, here they stand as equals in a common project. Public parks, public museums, public beaches, and public universities also play an important role in this respect. They are places where the necessary civic equality of a rational society is concretely embodied. It is important, therefore, that such institutions be prominent in a society that wishes to approximate a rational enterprise. And it is equally important that these public facilities not be clearly second-rate, merely leftovers from the private domain. Where "public" connotes the status of table scraps from private plates a message is also conveyed, and the message is not one of civic equality.

It should also go almost without saying that a rational society must take pains to ensure equal access to public forums and equal standing before public institutions. Opportunities for "ordinary citizens" to be heard by city councils, school boards, and the like are extraordinarily important. Equal access to the courts of law and guarantees of adequate legal counsel are also crucial requisites. In these respects, actually, current practices in this country measure up rather well—probably because equal access is a norm shared by almost all theoretical accounts of liberal democracy. As Robert Dahl puts it: "A central guiding thread of American constitutional development has been the evolution of a political system in which all the active and legitimate groups in the population can make themselves heard at some crucial stage in the process of decision."[12]

A rational society must also be always on guard to preserve its constitutive civic equality by astute practice of what Michael Walzer calls "the art of separation."[13] What exactly the art of separation requires in terms of specific institutional and legal walls is properly a subject for debate in a rational society. But what is clear in principle is that civic equality is meaningful only so long as the political domain remains essentially autonomous from the other spheres of social life. In particular, emphasis has to be given to preventing the political sphere from succumbing to the potentially hegemonic sway of economic power. To the extent that votes—and senators—can simply be bought, civic equality is reduced to a myth.

It has been a prime tenet of Marxism and other leftist ideologies, of course, that such separation is simply impossible—that economic power radiates unchecked and uncheckably throughout society. And it seems indisputably true that liberal apologists have given this problem insufficient concern or even glossed over it altogether. Marxist skepticism on this point is no doubt justified at least to some extent, in that it seems highly doubtful that any free society could ever entirely insulate its political sphere from the incursions of economic power. Whether that incapacity justifies trading partial subjection to economic-based hegemony for straightforward political domination, of course, is another question.

Despite the inherent difficulties of the task and despite traditional liberal blindness to its necessity, some reasonably effectual measures can be taken to provide considerable insulation for the integrity of the public sphere—and hence to protect the civic equality associated with it. For a rational society, such measures are fundamental: if what ultimately talks is money rather than citizens, political outcomes become covert private purchases rather than reasoned public judgments.

Guaranteeing equal access to public forums—regardless of economic status—already goes a long way toward demarcating and defending the political sphere of civic equality. Additionally, some restrictions on campaign financing may be necessary. The right of free speech does not include the right to buy elections by controlling the forum through wealth. Even better would be full public financing of campaigns. The critical interest at stake is not the private interest of the contending parties, but the public interest in a full and fair hearing of all candidates. Public subsidy is therefore entirely justified in this instance. Moreover, the necessary funding level need not be tremendously high. At the present, the principal cost of campaigns is the high price of television spots. But all television franchises hold their place on the airwaves by public leave and license—very profitably, one might add. There is no excuse for the public to pay the private franchisees twice over, once by giving them a valuable license and then by paying for the use of the very airspace it has signed over to them. A condition of holding a television franchise should be the setting aside of an appropriate amount of time for the use of candidates for public office. All stations could use the same time slot for this public service portion of their broadcasting, so that no competitive disadvantage be suffered. The time allotted should be in blocs sufficient to allow—even effectively require—candidates to give a reasoned presentation of their views rather than going for the quick strike at the emotions that the thirty second or fifteen second advertisement favors. Candidates who wished to do so could purchase additional segments of time; but money no longer could effectively monopolize the voters' awareness and hence distort the public sphere.

Other specific reforms may be usefully considered as well. In any case, the central purpose is the same: candidates for public office and holders of public office cannot be left to beg at the door of moneyed interests simply to perform their public role. Unless public officials possess that degree of financial autonomy, the wall between the *polis* and the market will be porous indeed. And when that is the case, civic equality is truly at peril. Financially autonomous representatives may still listen to what captains of industry have to say more closely than they do to the average voter. But at least they can be free to evaluate what they hear against the demands of the general welfare instead of being practically obligated to curry the favor of those who sign the checks they need to survive politically.

The demands of rational procedure also suggest that a rational society cannot be entirely indifferent to the nature and extent of income inequality among its citizens. It is not that a single abstract definitive standard of economic justice can somehow be logically inferred from the norms of rational practice. That is not possible. Indeed, it seems highly doubtful that any such standard can be derived in a neutral and universally persuasive way. Nonetheless, the parameters of economic distribution are a legitimate and even necessary concern for a rational society—for two reasons. First, some economic deprivations seem clearly inconsistent with the demands of citizenship in a rational enterprise. And second, vast disparities in financial resources clearly threaten the civic equality that makes rational policy deliberations and determinations a real possibility.

The concern of a rational society with economic equality and inequality, therefore, is neither narrowly economizing nor purely moral. It is not specifically focused upon either efficiency or equity or upon finding some balance between these two norms. Instead, the concern is fundamentally a political and prudential one—of a piece with the concern expressed by Aristotle in his discussion of the best practicable constitution and carried on by the civic republican tradition. For its own reasons, relating to the requisites of rational dialogue, a rational society can concur with Aristotle's view that "it is therefore the greatest of blessings for a state that its members should possess a moderate and adequate property."[14]

In middle-class societies, citizens stand on the roughly level ground necessary to address each other as do rational beings—as equals. It may also be generally true, as Aristotle also claims, that people in an economic middle condition "are the most ready to listen to reason."[15]

People at both the upper and lower extremes are more likely to exalt force over reason, the former because they have the capacity to exert force and the latter because they have nothing else on which to rely. The former are rapacious by opportunity, the latter by necessity.

Because the case for a market economy is so strong on grounds of economic efficiency—useful to all societies—and personal liberty—a value of particular importance to rational societies—a rational society will most likely leave much of its economic activity to be organized by the invisible hand. It will, however, insist upon intervening in the marketplace whenever market outcomes threaten to undermine the society's capacity for remaining a rational enterprise. It will, at the top, try to prevent concentrations of private economic power strong enough to tilt the public arena. And it will, at the bottom, try to keep its members from falling beneath the economic threshold of participation in the *polis*. These limits—of "tilt" and "threshold"—are impossible to specify precisely. Where they should be drawn is a matter for the polity to decide rather than something to be determined by a formula imposed by philosophers from the outside. But some ceiling and some floor seem clearly required by the basic architecture of rational enterprises.

In its justified fear of excessive concentrations of wealth, a rational society will, for example, seek to limit the political and social power of large corporations—and for that matter of large trade unions as well. Each of these economic giants must be legally restricted in the control it can exercise over its employees or members. Antitrust legislation may also be useful in preventing economic power from expanding and feeding upon itself. And so on. Measures of this sort need to be an ongoing effort for a rational society. Individual fortunes, on the other hand, may rarely be so great as to cause the same level of concern. Even here, however, some restrictions are probably necessary on the political deployment of these fortunes—as, for example, in setting restrictions on the number of newspapers and radio stations an individual can control.

Despite libertarian insistence to the contrary, moreover, a rational society need not be indifferent or wholly permissive regarding the transfer of wealth between generations. Whatever the moral and prudential considerations on behalf of permitting people to retain control of economic resources they have legally obtained, these are not compelling when it comes to policies governing estates and inheritance. At this point, the concern of a rational society with concentrations of wealth and power can be fairly invoked to prohibit the perpetuation of vast inequalities over time. Whatever the moral claims of one who justly acquires wealth, these cannot be similarly asserted by the heirs; and the right to control what one has earned need not extend beyond the grave into a right to skew the economic circumstances of a succeeding generation. Even if the society chooses to refrain from limiting estates, allowing individuals substantial freedom to designate the disposition of their worldly goods, it need not refrain from setting limits upon what a recipient individual may inherit.

At the other end of the economic spectrum, a rational society would seem to require some kind of income maintenance program to keep its poorest members from falling beneath the threshold of citizenship. The proper level of this income floor has, for good cause, been irremediably controversial in most societies; and the norms of a rational society cannot by themselves provide an answer to this complex question. What the logic behind the ideal of a rational society does imply, however, are certain grounds for such policies. And these grounds, in turn, carry implications for the proper mode and focus of any income redistribution that is undertaken.

The ground for welfare policy in a rational society is not compassion but collective prudence. A rational society engages in income maintenance not so much out of natural pity for suffering animals as out of prudent concern for the common good and for citizen competency. It provides a hardheaded rather than a softhearted rationale for welfare. There is nothing wrong with natural pity per se. But the objects of pity are, by definition, the pitiable rather than those with the dignity of citizens. And uses of the public purse should have a public purpose.

If this be so, several consequences seem to follow vis à vis the implementation of an incomes policy. In the first place, wherever possible the redistributed funds should be conveyed in ways that are directly tied to public roles and citizen competency. Free access to good public education, to Head Start programs, to literacy training for those in need of it, and to other such programs are a significant mode of economic redistribution. But they carry no particular stigma and they foster those skills that are necessary for active citizenship. The point of the visually muffled redistribution is also clear and proper in this case: we the society convey resources to you the needy individuals in order to assure ourselves that you can fulfill your responsibilities as participants in the common enterprise. On the other hand, purely private needs such as those for food and clothing should be a lesser priority for public intervention. Obviously, in the case of the most destitute or incompetent these needs will have to be addressed. But in the more marginal cases it is appropriate to convey the message that public assistance is in support of public purposes and that wherever possible private needs and wants should be individually pursued. By these standards, the recent decline of public schools and expansion of the food stamp program represents movement in the wrong direction. It seems clear that a federal food stamp program is the only realistic option in our large-scale, bureaucratized, and fragmented society, wherein too many needy people might fall between the cracks if private assistance were the only recourse. But in general the receipt of public welfare funds should be linked as much as possible to public needs rather than to private ones.

It also seems perfectly appropriate for a rational society to expect some public service in return for public assistance. When welfare funds are presented as charitable disbursements made out of compassion, placing demands upon its recipients may seem grudging and possibly even demeaning to some and as appropriate groveling by others. On the other hand, where they are conceived as merely granting what people deserve as a private right, then demanding anything in return is seen as an improper imposition. The debate between left and right ideologies over "workfare" in this country has generally reflected these distorted conceptions, partly because it tends to be conducted in a narrowly economizing and privatizing frame of reference. If the receipt of welfare funds is conceived neither as private charity nor as private right, however, but as a civic right, then it is neither demeaning nor improper for the recipient to render some public service in return. The funds are received by right as a citizen, but citizens are those who shoulder responsibilities on behalf of the common good. The benefit of receiving welfare funds and the burden of contributing a public service (possibly through job training that prepares one for later productive employment) are not in this view parts of an economic *quid pro quo* so much as an embodiment of one coherent pattern of the privileges and obligations of citizenship.

Fostering the Rule of Law

At least superficially, the ideal of rule of law seems to command almost universal respect in this country. But appearances can be deceiving. For most people, rule of law seems merely to mean governance through legislative promulgation on the part of the state and obedience to law on the part of the populace. Its opposite, then, is arbitrary will and reliance upon force. That account is, of course, acceptable as far as it goes; but it is quite incomplete. The ideal of rule of law requires not simply governance through legislative pronouncements. It also places important constraints upon the nature and form these pronouncements must take to be legitimate.

The crucial feature of these constraints is the requirement of generality and universality. A legislative dictate, to be a genuine law, must apply universally to everyone and must have a general object. Rule of law means, as Locke puts it, "to have one rule for rich and poor, for the favorite as Court, and the countryman at plough."[16] It means, in the words of Rousseau, that "law considers subjects *en masse* and actions in the abstract, and never a particular person or action." He continues: "Thus the law may indeed decree that there shall be privileges, but cannot confer them on anybody by name. It may set up several classes of citizens, and even lay down the qualification for membership of these classes, but it cannot nominate such and such persons as belonging to them. . . . In a word, no function which has a particular object belongs to the legislative power."[17]

By this standard, it seems clear that prevailing practices in this country come up substantially short. It is not only that, as Theodore Lowi has demonstrated, decision-making power is often parcelled out by Congress to be appropriated in the "cozy triangles" of bureaucratic agency, interested congressmen, and special-interest groups. It is that the statutes enacted by Congress often themselves do not live up to the standards of universality and generality. Congressional actions, in other words, violate the spirit of rule of law not only by omission but by commission as well.

Congress violates the universality principle, for example, whenever it exempts either its members or the institution as a whole from requirements it imposes on the rest of the population. Whatever affirmative action requirements are imposed on employers throughout the nation pursuant to civil rights laws, for example, should certainly apply as well to congressional hiring practices. It is equally improper for Congress to exempt federal employees from statutory mandates that others must obey. Not long ago, for example, a leader of Social Security Administration employees was quoted as saying that the one thing most likely to cause his people to strike would be if they were placed under the social security system. In cases such as these, it seems that those who enact and enforce the laws consider them binding only on the peons in the provinces and not on themselves.

Congress violates the generality requirement of the rule of law, moreover, whenever it singles out particular individuals or firms for special treatment. The whole institution of "private bills" seems to be questionable in this respect, for example. I am a tennis fan myself, but Ivan Lendl can stand in line like everyone else to wait his proper turn to become an American citizen. He should not be given special preferment by congressional enactment. Even more reprehensible are those pseudo-classes embedded by influential congressmen in statutory enactments in order to shelter particular constituents from their provisions. Whenever exceptions are written into statutes to provide privileges or exemptions for a precarious savings and loan company in the home district of the Speaker of the House, to take a recent example, a mockery is made of the whole legislative process. Democratic legitimacy erodes because rule of law principles are not respected.

Part of the problem concerning rule of law in this country is an intellectual one. It stems from a defective public philosophy. The dominance of the group theory of politics and the pluralist ideology it generates has led to a conception of the legislative process as fundamentally one of bargaining among specific interests. The rational and general components of legislation are essentially ignored or derogated in favor of a focus upon the clash of interests. Thus what is really a corruption of the legislative process comes to seem its essence. We should not be so naive, of course, to think that the intrusion of special interests can ever be screened from the legislative process. Nor can human bias ever be eliminated. Hence bargaining, logrolling, and compromise will always be a constant of democratic legislative decision making. But it is important that this phenomenon be seen as a necessary concession to human frailty of the sort appropriate to "second-best" theory rather than be seen as the democratic ideal.

Practical remedies for the decay of rule of law are very hard to designate. The ideal remedy, perhaps, would simply be a political culture that would not tolerate political leaders who spurned its principles or violated its spirit. Apart from that somewhat utopian hope, the best remedy would be a constitutional provision that would serve as the basis for invalidating the more egregious discriminatory and pork-barrel pieces of legislation that come along. Since almost everybody these days seems to have a pet proposed constitutional amendment, from the ERA to school prayer to a balanced budget requirement, let me add my own contender to the list. Call this the rule of law amendment, whose provisions would read something like the following:

Except for general classifications relevant to a law's purposes, all laws passed by Congress shall be universal in application.

Congress shall pass no law that takes a particular object.

Congress shall not exempt itself, any governmental agency, or governmental employees from the provisions of any law.

No member of Congress shall contact an executive agency on behalf of any of his or her constituents, any particular citizen, or any group.

The last section of this proposed amendment would, of course, change the life of congressmen and the structure of their offices quite dramatically. The several members of congressional staffs who devote themselves to constituent "case work," pursuing veterans' benefits, social security cases, and the like, would no longer be needed. And congressmen would no longer be able to—or be under a political obligation to—push the cause of home district firms or interests on the folks "downtown." These tasks, which consume an excessive amount of congressional time and attention, are partly instances of illegitimate special pleading and partly instances of acceptable ombudsmanship. The special pleading pressures on the bureaucracy should as far as possible be eliminated. The ombudsman function on the other hand is a valuable one that should not get lost; but it should be transferred. Each state should be given an appropriate staff—possibly with a gubernatorially selected director—in a new Ombudsmen Office whose job would be to serve as representatives for individuals needing some intercession with the federal bureaucracy. This is an important role that should be both highly visible and well institutionalized. It is not, however, a legislative role. And the way that it has fallen by default to members of Congress has had numerous deleterious consequences. It has distracted legislators unnecessarily from their true legislative role and responsibilities; it has distorted their perception of their role and orientation in a particularistic direction; and it has encouraged voters to perceive and evaluate their representatives in a similarly particularistic manner. In short, the inappropriate blending of the legislative and the ombudsman function in the congressional office has altered both the appearance and the reality of that office in a manner highly adverse to legislative universality and generality. Creating separate offices for the two distinct functions, conversely, would help greatly to restore the legislative office to its proper functions and thereby to renew our understanding and appreciation of the rule of law.

Nurturing Civic Virtue

In Book 3 of his *Politics*, Aristotle pointed out that to be a good person and to be a good citizen are not exactly the same thing. A good person is one who embodies the excellences of a human being as such, whereas a good citizen only embodies those excellences appropriate to the functioning of a particular form of political order. In Aristotle's account, shaped by his metaphysics of finitude, this meant that the excellence of a human being *qua* human being was absolute and invariant, but the criteria of citizen excellence were quite variable.

A rational society can appropriate Aristotle's basic insight about the difference between human excellence and citizen excellence and use it to somewhat different effect. And by doing so, it can provide itself with an appropriate general solution to one of the persistent conundrums of liberal politics. When it comes to the question of virtue and its political role, liberal theory has been torn between two apparently unacceptable extremes. Either it embraces and promulgates a specific conception of human virtue, which seems inconsistent with its fallibilist understanding of reason and its commitment to toleration. Or it avoids that unattractive option by lapsing into a total moral agnosticism and complete neutrality, which threatens to undermine its own moral standing and humane aspirations. By giving an epistemological twist to Aristotle's distinction between the good person and good citizen, however, and by placing it into the context of its own philosophical principles, a liberal society *sub specie* a rational enterprise can escape this apparent difficulty.

A rational society should say to its citizens: "We cannot tell you what human virtue is. We do not possess the capability of knowing the answer to that encompassing moral question, because rational minds differ on this issue. You must face up to that question as a matter of conscience, as both the privilege and the burden of an autonomous rational being. We can, however, tell you something about the demands of good citizenship in our society, for these are inherent in the requisites of participation in a rational enterprise. As Alasdair MacIntyre has observed, Plato noted long ago in the *Gorgias* that 'successful engagement in dialectic requires certain initial virtues of character.'[18] In like fashion, and for very much the same reasons, our own society requires certain virtues of character. Specifically, a good citizen must be dedicated to truth and oriented toward the human good as he or she conscientiously understands it, must be candid and tolerant, must have a capacity to give and to listen to rational justifications for policies and actions, and must respect both legitimate authority and the rights of others. If we cannot pretend to know or presume to enforce a conception of human virtue, therefore, we nevertheless have a conception of civic virtue that we can officially recognize and encourage. This conception is not part of a 'civil religion' of the sort Rousseau espoused, for it makes no specifically religious claims. But it performs some of the unifying and guiding functions Rousseau was thereby trying to achieve. Nor is this conception of civic virtue in any way irreligious or antireligious, some kind of surreptitious 'secular humanist' creed. Instead, it is simply an account of those particular citizen excellences necessary for the successful conduct of our political order."

John Stuart Mill's trenchant rhetorical questions, piled one on another, make this vital point through counterexamples: "of what efficacy are rules of procedure in securing the ends of justice, if the moral condition of the people is such that the witnesses generally lie, and the judges and their subordinates take bribes? . . . Of what avail is the most broadly popular representative system, if the electors do not care to choose the best member of parliament, but choose him who will spend most money to be elected? How can a representative assembly work for good, if its members can be bought, or if their excitability of temperament, uncorrected by public discipline or private self-control, makes them incapable of calm deliberation, and they resort to manual violence on the floor of the house, or shoot at one another with rifles? How, again, can government, or any joint concern, be carried on in a tolerable manner by a people so envious, that if one among them seems likely to succeed in anything, those who ought to cooperate with him form a tacit combination to make him fail?"[19] The fact is that a self-governing free society depends upon the presence of some specific virtues of character more than any other kind of society does.[20] A liberal democracy need not exceed the bounds of rationality, therefore, to acknowledge these virtues as constitutive of its own unique civic morality. Nor need it be bashful about trying to nurture those virtues in its citizens.

Exactly how that can be done is not easy to say. At a minimum, however, no public official or public institution should feel inhibited by norms of state neutrality in a way that would prevent them from explicitly acknowledging these civic virtues, according honor to those who exemplify them, and attempting to foster them in the populace. These norms of state neutrality should, of course, prevent official proselytizing or institutionalizing of complete systems of morality or religious creeds. But in promoting the elements of civic virtue as we have characterized them, a rational society is simply affirming its own implicit morality in a perfectly acceptable way.

Many of our most common civic rituals and political practices actually give formal backing to various aspects of the morality of a rational society. When courts of law swear in witnesses and jurors, the importance of citizen dedication to the truth is expressly avowed and imposed as an obligation. When judges publish their opinions and legislatures their deliberative proceedings, they exemplify the need to give reasons for political actions and the need to give a hearing to those who dissent from our views. When members of Congress refer to each other as "the honorable and esteemed representative from X" in the midst of heated debate, they illustrate the civility and respect for the rights of others necessary for rational procedure. When presidents bow to judicial decisions or to the writ of special prosecutors, they acknowledge the rule of law and the importance of respect for it. We may take these rituals for granted, but in many places they can hardly be seen as routine. And we should appreciate them as de facto official acknowledgment of the various tenets of a legitimate civic credo.

This account also carries implications for the whole issue of moral education in the schools. Amy Gutmann has helpfully identified a spectrum of viewpoints on this issue,[21] which she denominates as including: "amoralism," which insists that the schools have no business teaching morality and should stick to technically cognitive skills and factual knowledge; "liberal neutrality," which advocates a noncommittal exploration of whatever values students bring with them ("values clarification") on the grounds "that none of us has the 'right' set of values to pass on to other people's children";[22] "conservative moralism," which advocates the inculcation of the traditional values of Western civilization; and "liberal moralism," which *pace* Kohlberg seeks to lead students toward moral autonomy and an ethics of principle.

If our account of rational fallibility *vis à vis* comprehensive ethical beliefs and our account of the implicit norms of civic virtue in a rational liberal regime are basically sound, then none of these conventional theories is compelling—in large part because none of them gives sufficient notice to the logical and epistemological differences between civic morality and morality *simpliciter*, between our knowledge of what it takes to be a good citizen of a rational liberal regime and what it takes to be a good person in a complete sense. "Amoralist" and "liberal neutralist" pedagogies are unnecessarily fastidious and self-abnegating, because they do not appreciate that we can as a society speak with more authority about our civic creed than we can about what makes people good in a more complete sense. On the other hand, what Gutmann terms the "liberal moralist" and "conservative moralist" positions seek to inculcate a general ethical doctrine, because they do not seem to appreciate that these doctrines exceed the scope of the rationally warranted and hence the democratically authoritative. The latter two models go too far with their moral education, whereas the former two do not go far enough.

Instead of these models, all of which elide the distinction between civic virtue and human virtue per se, we should approach moral education in public schools along two tracks. Considerations of human virtue per se need not be banned from the schools, but they should be confined to the academic study of religious creeds and ethical systems. Students can in this context obtain objective accounts of major belief systems, and they can presumably "clarify" their own "values" as they come to understand them in relation to these alternative viewpoints. The demands of our civic morality, on the other hand, should be examined in the context of civics courses or some functional equivalent. The various elements of civic virtue in a liberal society governed by norms of rational practice can be identified and explained. It is not that students should be catechized or browbeaten into accepting these standards. Such attempts would likely be unavailing in any case. Rather the various elements of our civic morality should be presented as the logically derivable criteria of good citizenship implicit in the constitution of our particular political system. Students would be free, of course, to challenge the standards of their derivation, but they would be (intellectually) forced to defend the compatibility of their own account of civic virtue with the structure and goals of the liberal democratic system. A student who came with the idea that bigotry was acceptable, for example, could not rest with a mere "clarification"—i.e., reflective illumination—of this "value" position. He or she would have to explain how a rationale for bigotry could be squared with the egalitarian and rights-respecting pronouncements and practices of our political system. And when that presumably would prove a logical impossibility, the student would then be confronted with the tension between his or her inherited behavioral norms and the norms that are generally and properly seen in a liberal democracy as those appropriate for a "good citizen." This would be the recognition of a demonstrable fact—and hence well within the purview of liberal education. But it is a recognition that should also have salutary effects upon popular civic values and political practices.

Moreover, as Gutmann observes, "even if schools avoid all courses that deal explicitly with morality or civic education, they still engage in moral education by virtue of their 'hidden curriculum,' noncurricular practices that serve to develop moral attitudes and character in students."[23] By their "noncurricular practices," then, primary and secondary schools can educate their students in the most fundamental moral habits of a rational society: that is, students can learn that the first recourse in group decision making is to "reason together." Students can learn quite early in life what discursive will formation is all about. They can learn that decisions about what is to be done begin rationally with canvassing the ideas and interests of all concerned parties. They can learn to give good reasons for their choices, to listen to their peers with tolerance and respect, to look for solutions that best advance the general interest, to distinguish rational authority from the imposition of arbitrary will. They can also learn the proper role of voting as a mechanism for adjudicating disagreements democratically once the limits of rational consensus have been determined.

The contribution of higher education to the nurturance of civic virtue also seems to me to be very important in an advanced society. We have recently seen a spate of discussions regarding the teaching of ethics in universities—discussions that recur whenever we have to confront revelations about corrupt or ethically insensitive behavior among professionals or officeholders. The academic study of ethics and metaethics is an important subject—one that more students should encounter in their curricula. But most discussions of the teaching of ethics in universities misconceive what the academic study of ethics properly involves and likewise misconceive the way that the university experience best serves civic virtue.

It is not the proper role of courses in ethics, or of any other courses for that matter, to indoctrinate students with a particular moral creed or to engage in moral uplift sessions. Nor is it either appropriate or likely that universities—other than sectarian ones—seek to inculcate moral virtue in the student body by having compulsory chapel or a secular equivalent. Instead, good universities make their principal contribution to civic virtue in more subtle but more powerful ways. They do so by exposing their students to courses that explore the finest expressions of the human spirit, by examining human history and society as in part a record of human choices, excellences, and weaknesses, by encouraging students to be sensitive to the very real ethical issues implicit in subject matters ranging from literature to biomedical engineering, and by honing the capacity of students to render responsible critical judgments.

Above all, colleges and universities nurture some of the most central elements of liberal democratic civic virtue by the procedures they follow and the commitments they exhibit. Unless they are somehow corrupt or incompetent, institutions of higher learning are dedicated to the discovery and dissemination of the truth, accept and enforce the discipline of reason, practice an egalitarianism of merit, protect conscientious dissent, and demonstrate respect for intellectual authority. In these respects, colleges and universities provide a laboratory for the exercise of rational practices. Even the densest student cannot go through four years of socialization into these practices without becoming at least partially habituated to them.

There are many reasons for the relative success of the American experiment in self-governance, among them the astute institutional craftsmanship of the Founding Fathers and the benefits of a large and fertile land. But surely one significant factor has been the access by a large proportion of society to our thriving and diverse system of higher education. It is very hard to imagine that this vast and pluralistic nation could have survived the rough and tumble of democratic politics without the leaven of rationality brought to it by those who have absorbed the discipline of reason and who have experienced the liberating and civilizing power of rational practices. And our colleges and universities have done much to produce citizens who meet that description.

In policy terms, it follows that a liberal society should do its best to guarantee access to higher education for those able and inclined to undertake it. Federal grant and loan programs and the generosity of private philanthropists have been important in this regard, and public policy should be careful to maintain and expand the opportunities thereby provided for students of whatever means to attend college. And the colleges and universities themselves need to remain cognizant that they best serve the liberal societies that nurture them not merely by improving the technical skills of their students but by acculturating them into their own values. For at bottom it is the faith of reason that animates both the good university and the good society.

Conclusion

This survey of the potential policy implications of conceiving liberal democracy as an attempt to live by the norms governing rational enterprises is both cryptic and somewhat tentative. Our discussions only touch the surface of the policy questions, and the recommendations are offered more for the sake of argument than as hard and fast conclusions. It is in the nature of these policy applications that they can be only contestable casuistic judgments rather than demonstrable theorems. Even those who are persuaded by the central thesis about the relevance of rational practices to democratic politics may easily dissent from some of these more concrete and specific analogically derived prescriptions.

These suggestions, however tentative, nonetheless indicate that the practical implications of the ideal of rational political practice are both extensive and—considered as a whole—rather distinctive. They add up to a form of communal prudence that overlaps in many respects with other theories of liberal democracy. But there are some notable contrasts as well.

The contrasts with the libertarian view of liberalism are perhaps the most obvious. Libertarianism seeks to reduce the public sphere to an absolute minimum, whereas a vital and substantive public sphere is central to the politics of a rational society. Libertarians accept market distributions of income and power as definitive, but a rational society limits the permissible extent of economic inequality and envisions significant redistributive consequences in the operations of the public sphere. The libertarian account has no place for a common good beyond a summation of individual self-interested goods, whereas politics as a rational enterprise takes the common good as its goal. And rational political practices both require and value a sense of community, whereas a libertarian society will settle for mutual forbearance among its membership.

The communal prudence of a rational society is also clearly quite different from the collective prudential calculus of utilitarian democracy. In the first place, a rational society is not committed to the dogmatic supposition that the general welfare is an aggregation of personal pleasures. The rational society also places great emphasis upon participation, rather than seeing its members as passive recipients of benefits. The rational society asks its citizens to render judgments rather than merely register wants. And a rational society insists upon a citizen autonomy that Bentham considered inessential, as it militantly protects rights that he considered apocryphal.

The norms of political rational enterprises contrast with those of pluralist liberalism most clearly in the great importance they assign to the rule of law, rather than settling for the outcome of interest-group bargaining. A rational society also demands reason-giving of its citizens instead of allowing them merely to articulate their preferences. Participation is not as important to pluralism, which has in some contexts been content with citizen apathy. The standards of rational political practice generate explicit criteria of civic virtue, something that pluralism may in fact require but something it essentially ignores and in some respects tends to undermine. And a rational society is more sensitive than pluralism has usually been to the need to maintain buffers between the economic and political spheres in a democratic society.

Although it insists upon the fundamental equality of all citizens and does not sanction any ascriptive distinctions among its members, a rational society is also not equivalent to simple egalitarianism. It considers liberty, autonomy, and toleration to be crucial elements of a good political order. It does not require complete economic equality among citizens. It appreciates the value of diversity in society; and it has room for some meritocratic hierarchial elements in its operation, so long as these are rationally grounded and consensually generated.

On a conventional ideological spectrum, the conception of politics as rational practice may seem fairly close to the middle-ground welfare liberal position occupied by John Rawls. Here too, however, there are significant differences. The bonds of social union in Rawls's good society are provided by consensus on formal principles of justice. The norms of a rational society, in contrast, do not contain within themselves the capacity to discern and prescribe such distributive principles a priori; in any case a rational society would leave such crucial determination to the outcome of principled public dialogue. Moreover, for a rational society this greater indeterminacy regarding its distributive rules is not as crippling as it would be for Rawls, since it presupposes a community centered around mutual pursuit of a common good that is broader and more concrete than anything Rawls could hope for. And the emphasis on citizen autonomy in a rational society is not compatible with the incipient moral fatalism in Rawls that breaks surface when he dismisses all claims of moral desert as untenable.[24]

Finally, our conception of the politics of reason may come closest, among the widely circulated extant theories, to the civic republican account of a good democratic society. Like civic republicanism, the ideal of a rational society turns around a dialectic of citizen equality, community, public good, participation, civic virtue, and prudential reason. That is why it was suggested earlier in this study that a post-positivist conception of rational practice might provide republicanism with the philosophical underpinnings it has not really had. Having said that, however, it is also important to observe that the norms of rational political practice are much clearer than republicanism has often been about the crucial role of individual rights and toleration in the good society. The emphasis in our account upon the open-endedness of the human good also stands as a salutary amber light to republican enthusiasm. There is certainly no place in a rational society for moral dogmatism or for a tyranny of virtue.

The norms and policies of a society that aspires to be a rational enterprise, therefore, overlap in many respects with the norms and policies of its various liberal and republican siblings. But the implications of our model do not coincide exactly with those of any other conception. Instead, the prescriptive lessons derived from understanding the good society as a rational enterprise assume their own distinctive shape. They point toward a complex form of social practice that protects rights but does not enshrine them in a vacuum, that protects and promotes equality but is not mindlessly egalitarian, that seeks justice but does not abstract it from the common good, and that promotes community and civic virtue but does not forget the demands of tolerance or the value of diversity.

Conclusion

To recapitulate, the aspiration to infuse politics with the virtues of rational practice received early paradigmatic form in Aristotle's account of prudence and in Plato's account of the rational intuition of moral order. When modern philosophers tried to adapt these models to a philosophical universe dominated by the calculative ideal, their accounts became increasingly thin morally and increasingly problematic philosophically. The penultimate stages of this modern project were best and most influentially embodied in John Stuart Mill's *Logic of the Moral Sciences* and in Kant's second *Critique*. Both of these accounts, however, proved to be but anterooms to the Weberian conception of purely instrumental rationality directed toward purely subjective and arbitrary purposes.

Recent developments in the philosophy of language and the philosophy of science have afforded us an avenue of escape from the Weberian impasse, however, by directing attention to the constitutive pragmatics of rational speech and rational inquiry. Reflection upon the pragmatic dimension of language and science converges upon a common pattern of organizing human activity that can justifiably be conceived as the constitution of rational enterprises.

Although applying this pattern to other domains is possible only by analogy and only with appropriate qualifications, it is possible to ask what a political society would look like if it were organized in accord with these norms of rational practice. Pursuing this thought experiment leads us toward a complex account of political praxis that incorporates the most fundamental norms of both the liberal and republican traditions. Citizens of "rational" political enterprises participate in the common pursuit of an open-ended public good. They relate as equals, possess extensive rights and liberties, and find themselves subject to standards of civic virtue that reflect the requirements of participation in a rational association.

The normative pattern derived from the analogy with rational inquiry and rational communication, I have argued, is more capacious and attractive than the pluralist, deontological, or libertarian versions of liberalism. It is, moreover, true to the profound intuition of Enlightenment philosophers and liberals such as Locke and Mill that some basic symmetry exists between the means of intellectual progress and those of humane politics. And it is a normative pattern that both integrates and sustains some of the most astute critical and constructive insights into the theory and practice of contemporary liberal democracy.

As a guide to current policies and institutions, I have also argued that the norms of rational practice point us toward a form of liberal democracy that incorporates important aspirations of both rights-oriented liberalism and community-oriented republicanism. This perspective would encourage us to emphasize civic education, to promote both equality and public responsibility among citizens, to bolster the institutions that foster public dialogue, to insist upon the rule of law in its deep sense rather than merely in its superficial meaning, to emphasize the search for common ground transcending the pluralism of interests, to facilitate participation, and to protect and emphasize civic rights rather than merely positive or abstractly individualized "natural" rights. In policy terms, therefore, it would be fair to see the politics of rational practice not as radically innovative but as nonetheless distinctive in its emphases and in its complex balance among norms often considered irreconcilable.

In order to forestall misunderstanding, two disclaimers need to be entered before I conclude. First, I have no illusions that what appears in these pages qualifies as a philosophically definitive account of reason in politics. And second, I do not intend to suggest that the account of politics as a rational enterprise provides us with a complete and comprehensive theory of liberal democracy.

Regarding the first of these disclaimers, I think it is clear that I have not made the case for the viability of reason in politics in any philosophically definitive manner. Instead, I have only done what seemed necessary to make that task appear viable and significant: analyzed the demise of the classical conceptions of political rationality under the aegis of modern philosophy, identified philosophical resources and promising strategies for revitalizing the valid intuitions behind the rationalist project, sketched a normative model based on this transformed version of practical reason, and suggested some of the theoretical and policy implications of taking such an approach.

To flesh out the argument and make it more philosophically compelling—rather than merely suggestive and, I hope, appealing—would require more work. For one thing, we need to develop a much better understanding of the logic and dynamics of practical discourse, especially as conducted in the political arena. Logic in this context means, of course, not mere formal logic—for the standards of purely deductive inference are only imperfectly capable of capturing what goes on in practical reasoning. It is not that practical reasoning is illogical, but that some of its key aspects transcend deductive inference. Practical reasoning is by nature not "objective" in the sense of detached, devoid of passion, unanimated by interest. To the contrary, as a problem-oriented cognitive enterprise it always has its roots, its purposes, and its reference points in the concrete desires and aspirations of human beings. Consequently, it possesses an uneliminable rhetorical dimension that is not—as Platonist and scientistic prejudice would have it—epistemologically disqualifying but rather necessary and valid.

Since none of this practical discourse takes place in the abstract, a "logic" of practical reason relevant to politics would require a better phenomenology of political dialogue than is currently available. For the same reasons that recent philosophy of science has evolved toward reflection upon case studies of the dynamics of specific scientific discoveries/innovations, a more adequate understanding of political rationality needs to be grounded in an appreciation of how expanded political conceptions develop out of social dialogue about specific problems and institutional failures. Such accounts would be harder to produce than the correlative accounts in the context of natural science because the relevant discussions are so much more diffuse and therefore more complicated, less refined, and less accessible. But they should not be impossible to produce, even though they would be somewhat impressionistic.[1]

An adequate philosophical defense of the role of reason in politics also needs to engage recent arguments that might appear—at least on their face—to be incompatible with the accreditation of reason as a meaningful and significant political norm. Doing these arguments justice would require an additional volume. Some brief remarks, however, might be useful in order to indicate that I am not oblivious to the challenge of these arguments and to suggest what I consider to be the appropriate line of response to them. The specific arguments I have in mind here are: the epistemological/sociological relativism that depicts a commitment to reason as a form of Western ethnocentrism; the view of various postmodern deconstructionists and genealogists that "reason" is a mythological construct designed to privilege a particular constellation of interests in society; and Alasdair MacIntyre's argument in *Whose Justice? Which Rationality?* that conceptions of practical reason are plural and specific to particular moral traditions.

The relativist objection to the notion that rationality is a meaningful and valid norm for human behavior has recently received considerable discussion in two contexts. The first of these contexts is reflection by anthropologists, sociologists, and philosophers about the proper role of interpretive and critical reliance on norms of rationality in characterizing different cultures—some of which do not subscribe to Western or scientific modes of thought.[2] The other context is the attempt to assess Habermas's claims about universal pragmatics and his Kohlberg-and-Piaget-derived norms of rational conduct.[3]

Epistemological/sociological relativists contend that what we are pleased to call rationality is in fact simply a culturally specific and ethnocentric construction without universal standing or validity. On this view, it is accordingly inaccurate to hold that these putative norms of rational thought are genuine universals and it is improper to deploy them in describing (and implicitly criticizing as primitive or irrational) societies that do not embrace them. This position is grounded either in anticritical hermeneutics or, what amounts to pretty much the same thing, in a relativist construction of Wittgenstein's injunctions about "leaving everything as it is." The epistemological/sociological relativist follows the lead of Peter Winch, who uses as his epigram for *The Idea of A Social Science* Lessing's admonition that "it is unjust to give any action a different name from that which it used to bear in its own times and amongst its own people."[4] That admonition, informed by a relativistic understanding of the integrity and mutual irreducibility of different language-games and forms of life, is then taken to mean that it is unjustified and misleading, for example, to speak of the Zande people as "primitive," "superstitious," or "irrational" because they see the world in magical terms. Stylizing and thereby stigmatizing them in that way is, according to the relativist, simply a specious and arrogant piece of ethnocentric prejudice. All that can be said fairly is that they inhabit the world one way and we another; and when we interpret their culture we must do so in their own terms. They are just as "rational" by their own premises as we are by ours.

The principled humility of the relativist critique has the genuine merit of alerting us to the perils of bad anthropology and smug ethno-centrism—intellectual and moral sins that often appear in tandem. For it is indeed bad anthropology to fail to understand another culture in its own terms, and it is ethnocentric to assume unreflectively the universal validity or the superiority of our own cultural habits. These valid caution flags, however, need not prevent us from reaching the critical and reflective judgment that the norms of rational practice exhibited in scientific inquiry and in truth-oriented communication have merit and utility extending beyond the confines of a single culture.

The implicit (and sometimes explicitly cited) bogeyman of the rela-tivists is Sir James Frazer. In his famous *Golden Bough*, which ridiculed the customs and beliefs of premodern peoples, Frazer in fact exhibited the narrow-minded incomprehension and parochial smugness the prin-cipled relativist fears and seeks to avoid. Frazer erred, however, not because he was reflectively critical concerning the cultural practices and beliefs he surveyed. He erred by failing in his hermeneutic task, on the one hand, and by uncritically accepting the norms of one particular culture on the other. The relativist strategy of avoiding Frazer's igno-rant *hubris*, therefore, is unnecessarily extreme and inappropriate. In-deed, in the sense of being utterly uncritical, it mirrors one aspect of Frazer's failure: it merely substitutes an uncritical acceptance of all cultures for Frazer's uncritical acceptance of one culture. The appropri-ate remedy is not to avoid thoughtful critique altogether, but instead to essay normative reflections and assessments first with due tentativeness and humility and second only after having succeeded in the essential prerequisite hermeneutic task of understanding each culture in its own terms.

It is perhaps pertinent to note in this context that Wittgenstein's own critical commentary on Frazer is not itself relativistic. His argument is not that primitive religious practices are just as good for those cultures as Victorian Christianity is for Frazer and his ilk and that Frazer erred by not recognizing this parity of value among culturally relative forms of life. Instead, Wittgenstein argued that Frazer's sensibility was in certain respects inferior to that of his primitive subjects. "What narrowness of spiritual life we find in Frazer," he writes. "Frazer cannot imagine a priest who is not basically an English parson of our time with all his stupidity and feebleness. . . . Frazer is much more savage than most of his savages, for they are not as far removed from an understanding of spiritual matters as an Englishman of the twentieth century."[5]

We should, then, I would argue, emulate Wittgenstein's own willingness to make what might be termed post-hermeneutic critical judgments rather than adhering to the wholly uncritical relativism for which he is sometimes cited as authority. We need not choose between the equally unattractive and equally uncritical alternatives of naive parochialism and utter relativism. Instead, even after understanding other cultures in their own terms, we can venture the critical judgment that social practices—both cognitive and political—governed by the procedural norms of rational enterprises tend to be more productive than practices that ignore or violate those norms.

It is not the case, moreover, that the norms of rational practice are wholly and specifically confined to a single culture. Arguably, all cultures that employ truth-oriented communication tacitly invoke the norms of rational practice in this aspect of their own form of life. Moreover, one can find good examples of rational political practice in a whole variety of cultures, certainly not alone—or perhaps even best— in Western cultures. Western philosophers may have produced a disproportionate share of the world's analysis of rationality, but it in no way follows that Western culture is essentially rational or that rationality is peculiarly Western. Any attempt to assess the rationality of different cultures by the standards set forth here would, I suspect, produce very mixed results. The councils of most Indian tribes, for example, are obviously better approximations of rational political practice than are, say, typical meetings of the Chicago City Council.

Relativist objections to the notion of a universal pragmatics also seem to me to miss their target. Typical of these complaints is Raymond Geuss's denial that the ideal of an unforced consensus among competent minds is implicit in truth-oriented speech. It is not so, he writes, "that to be a human agent one must hold Habermas's consensus theory of truth. . . . I find it quite hard to burden pre-dynastic Egyptians, ninth-century French serfs and early twentieth-century Yanomamo tribesmen with the view that they are acting correctly if their action is based on a norm on which there would be universal consensus in an ideal speech situation."[6]

The descriptive assertion here is no doubt accurate, but it is beside the point. Habermas's claim about the "universality" of the norms of unforced consensus in an ideal speech situation is a logical claim, not an empirical one. He is making an argument about the implicit logic of a practice—namely, the practice of truth-oriented speech—not a factual claim about the explicit values and understanding of all speakers. Whether speakers recognize it or not, he claims, the constitutive logic of the game of human communication about the truth embodies the norms of unforced consensus. It is in this sense, and this sense alone, that the norms of rationality could be said to be "universal."

Recalling MacIntyre's conception of a "practice," Habermas's communicative ethics can aptly be seen as his attempt to elicit and articulate the intrinsic "standards of excellence"[7] of a particular practice—the practice of using speech to ascertain truth. As in all similar cases, these standards may be understood very well, somewhat imperfectly, or even quite poorly by individual participants. And these standards may be well or poorly manifest in their individual performances—whether the performance in question is communicating about the truth, playing chess, dancing the polka, or whatever. But these variations in comprehension and competency do not themselves represent or justify per se a challenge to the presence or the content of the standards of excellence themselves. They would represent such a challenge only if they could coherently be claimed to embody an alternative and competing conception of the practice in question and hence to adhere to alternative and competing standards of excellence. Put concretely, my weak grasp of the intricacies of chess and my stumbles on the dance floor do not amount to a reproach to the intrinsic standards of excellence we can see alive in the performances of a Kasparov or an Astaire. They would amount to such a challenge only if I could coherently claim to be adhering to a better way of performing the activity in question. It may be, then, that such a challenge could be mounted to the alleged standards of excellence of chess, or dancing, or communicative speech. But it would need to be done in that way and at that level—not simply by citing examples of behavior or understandings that do not embody or affirm the standards in question.

The assumptions and arguments of post-Nietzschean deconstructionists and genealogists, exemplified in and inspired by Derrida and

Foucault,[8] represent a somewhat similar relativistic critique of any aspirations to conduct politics in a rational manner. In essence, this critique is a philosophically sophisticated and epistemologically extreme form of the sociology of knowledge. Its practitioners analyze, often revealingly, the manner in which ostensively "objective" justifications of political policies and institutions—legal systems, penal strategies, and so on—develop from and then serve to privilege a particular set of interests within society. The clear challenge to any form of political rationalism here is the implication that all political uses of reason are merely, or at least essentially, "rationalizations"—i.e., tendentious *ex post facto* pseudo-cognitive means of exercising power over others.

The proper rejoinder to the deconstructionist/genealogical project depends upon the interpretation one gives to the varied, sometimes ambiguous, and sometimes tacit formulations of its proponents. For as William Connolly aptly notes, the precise depth of skepticism about reason and morality embodied in these critiques is not entirely clear or consistent: "Some forms of deconstruction/genealogy seem to be in the service of nihilism, while others, by bringing out the constructed character of our most basic categories, aim at opening up new possibilities of reflection, evaluation, and action."[9]

The most radical view of the deconstructionist project is to see it as denying the meaningfulness and validity of rational argumentation in its entirety. All claims to be speaking, discussing, or behaving in a rational manner are, on this account, either fraudulent or self-delusionary. What may appear to be or be presented as rational discourse is in fact only a "play of forces." And as such, these covert power-plays are not to be debated—which would imply that they contain the cognitive content and the possibility of vindication which they do not possess—but only parried, exposed, and subverted. This derogation of the powers of reason is hard to maintain in a coherent fashion when pushed to this extreme, however. It is susceptible to the charge of self-contradiction. For anyone who, in effect, tries to provide a convincing argument that rational argumentation is a fraud turns into an ambulatory version of the Paradox of the Liar.

Deconstructionist criticisms of the legitimacy of reason can be given a slightly less radical interpretation, however, that is not so easily refuted and is still sufficiently skeptical to be incompatible with any advocacy of reason in politics. The premise underlying these criticisms can be construed as the claim that theoretical or descriptive reason is valid but that practical or prescriptive reason is fraudulent. Thus it is possible for us to use our powers of (theoretical) rational cognition to recognize the unflattering truth about ourselves and our deployments of (practical) reason on behalf of politically prescriptive goals. This truth is realistic to the point of cynicism. It, in effect, replicates Thrasymachus's argument about justice *vis à vis* rationality. The proper response, on this account, to the question "what is (practical) reason?" becomes: "reason" is a symbol misleadingly deployed for the tactical purpose of legitimating the exercise of power.

Assessing this critique requires complex judgments that yield no definitive conclusions. One can only try to assess one's own experience, both immediate and secondhand, and try to assess how successful particular deconstructionist/genealogical critiques are at establishing the "nothing but" hypothesis—that is, that the cases they examine in fact reveal reason as nothing but the cloak of power and interest. My own assessment is that this reductive theory does not adequately account for my own experience and does not fully and convincingly explain, say, the legal conceptions or penal practices to which it has been applied. It would obviously take me far afield to try to make that case here. I only register my own serious doubts about the empirical plausibility of this reductive account of reason and leave the reader to make his or her own assessments. (I also might add that I have the sense that the cynical dismissal of rationality may in part stem from an insensitivity to the difference between practical reasoning in its generic procedural form and "practical reason" in its technocratic and positivist deformations. These are hardly the same thing, but one gets the sense that Foucault, for example, tends to move from critiques of specific instances of the latter—such as Benthamite projects of social control— to more sweeping implied conclusions about rationality in general.)

Potentially more instructive and unsettling than what I would regard as the falsity of this Thrasymachan rendition of deconstruction/genealogy is the possibility of its becoming true. For even if this reductive account of politics does not convincingly describe social life as we know it, it certainly describes a possible form of social life—and one that would be increasingly approximated the more widespread the reductive view of things. Deconstructionist cynicism has the capacity to be a self-fulfilling prophecy. For the conventions of rational practice are exactly that: conventions. They are not givens of nature that exist apart from the values and convictions that give them life, and they could not reasonably be expected to survive the demise of these values and convictions. If people believe that reasoning together is an impossibility and a fraud, that form of life will surely become extinct—even if the impossibility thesis is itself mistaken. The "faith of reason" is precisely that, and as such it possesses a fragility unsuspected by its Enlightenment adherents. It is in this context that the sweepingly Thrasymachan conception and practice of the deconstructionist/genealogical project seems to me potentially dangerous and destructive.

Given a more moderate and discriminating embodiment, however, the critical tools and insights of deconstruction/genealogy are not necessarily incompatible with the norms and institutions of rational practice. Indeed, these tools and insights may serve constructive purposes in the context of public dialogue, providing ways, to recall Connolly's words cited earlier, of "opening up new possibilities of reflection, evaluation, and action."

In the first place, the insistence of deconstruction/genealogy that all moral and political argument is ineluctably rhetorical and grounded in human interests is not problematic for the conception of rational practice defended here. For the procedures and institutions of practical dialogue do not depend for their power or viability on the Platonic/Cartesian conception of "objectivity" that these critics attack. Instead, I have explicitly acknowledged the rhetorical dimension of all practical discourse. What provides practical reasoning with its disciplinary force—with its objectivity—is not some putative transcendence of all historically contingent human desires, interests, and limited perceptions. Its disciplinary power inheres instead in the way it compels its participants toward the general and away from the particular. Practical reasoning, in short, does not require the attainment of an Archimedean perspective or the achievement of total disinterestedness. It is sufficient that it forces us toward the attainment of a common point of view and toward the understanding and appreciation of the general interest. And this more modest, but significant, achievement requires only that our rhetoric be systematically constrained, not that it be abjured altogether.

The felicitous conduct of public dialogue does not depend upon the triumph of some alleged normative science over interest-based rhetoric. No such science exists. What is needed in response to the challenge of deconstruction/genealogy is not some reprise of the epistemological battle between Plato and the sophists, with the adherents of rational practice being forced into defending Plato's untenable position. Instead, the adherents of reason in politics need to shoulder only the more modest burden of distinguishing healthy from corrupt forms of political rhetoric and indicating how the dynamics of practical discourse work on behalf of the former. Morally defensible and politically salutary rhetoric is consensual; corrupt rhetoric is manipulative. Healthy rhetoric appeals to general interests; corrupt rhetoric seeks to cloak particular interest in deceptive encomium. Good rhetoric seeks sustenance in morally defensible or praiseworthy emotions, such as courage, compassion, and the desire to flourish; bad rhetoric appeals to darker passions such as greed, hatred, envy, and the will to dominate. Healthy rhetoric is forthright and open to correction; corrupt rhetoric is mendacious and dogmatic. Taken together, these contrasts distinguish the Periclean oration from the McCarthyite diatribe, the carefully reasoned and public-spirited editorial from racist or jingoistic journalistic garbage, sensitive and thoughtful policy analysis from the self-serving rationalizations of a power elite. Within the context of the deconstructionist insistence upon the rhetorical aspect of all practical argument, therefore, necessary and appropriate distinctions can be made that render this insistence not so much an undermining critique of reason in politics as the background for understanding how it works. The problem is not, then, with the methods and premises of deconstruction/genealogy per se but only with an extreme, simplistic interpretation and application of these methods and premises—with an interpretation that insists a priori that the activities of Pericles and Sen. Joseph McCarthy are epistemologically indistinguishable.

If the deconstructionist insistence on the rhetorical aspect of all practical reasoning is not—apart from faulty and extreme application—a stumbling block to our understanding of reason in politics, the concrete unmasking and debunking arguments fostered by deconstructionist methods can actually contribute constructively to public disputation. It is a perfectly legitimate form of argument in public practical discourse to identify the individual, group, or class interests/biases behind competing positions and to demonstrate how these interests/biases arguably distort the normative claims they influence. Such analyses only perform in a critical and sophisticated way what British parliamentarians acknowledge as necessary and appropriate when they declare themselves "interested M.P.s." That is, these analyses simply get onto the table the particularistic factors that may bias someone's argument, so that their influence may be seen and appropriate discounts made by other participants. The tools of deconstruction/genealogy have in their inception been for the most part a weapon in the intellectual arsenal of the Nietzschean left. The potential utility of these modes of analysis, however, is not confined to one ideological persuasion. The same techniques can be applied to the arguments of all disputants, including those of their originators. And once that stage of general facility with these argumentative techniques is attained, the public dialogue can continue on level ground once again and at a new level of reflective awareness.

A third recent argument that seems on its face incompatible with the invocation of norms of rational practice as, in a loose sense, universally valid is that of Alasdair MacIntyre in *Whose Justice? Which Rationality?* MacIntyre there argues that "rationality itself, whether theoretical or practical, is a concept with a history; indeed, since there are a diversity of traditions of inquiry, with histories, there are, so it will turn out, rationalities rather than rationality, just as it will also turn out that there are justices rather than justice."[10] If all conceptions of practical reason are tradition-constituted, if there are only rationalities rather than rationality, if each of these diverse rationalities establishes its own argumentative norms and standards, then it would seem that our enterprise here fails as one more episode in the delusionary Enlightenment quest for a single, non-tradition-specific rational ideal.

Closer examination suggests, however, that MacIntyre's account is not necessarily at odds with the argument made here. What MacIntyre wants to deny is that there is a neutral, substantive standard for moral and political behavior that is rationally discernible by all people of sound mind however situated and that can therefore be invoked to adjudicate conflicts between competing traditions. MacIntyre's target is the Cartesianism or moral Newtonianism of the Enlightenment—the belief that once the mists of superstition were dispelled the moral version of "clear and distinct ideas" would become apprehended and serve as the deciding algorithm for political disputes.

I would concur with this critique and can do so without inconsistency. The norms of rational practice argued for here—embodied in the constitution of rational enterprises—are not substantive but procedural. They do not purport to provide either an objective standard or a decisive means for adjudicating competing moral claims derived from divergent traditions. Hence MacIntyre's critique is not directly pertinent to or subversive of my claims concerning the virtues of rational practice. MacIntyre's characterization of the liberal tradition may be too monochromatic an account of a varied and colorful history. But his complex account of what reason can and cannot do is not incompatible with the account of political rationality offered here.

In fact, the two accounts are in some respects potentially complementary. MacIntyre believes that rationality outside of or apart from a tradition is a chimera. But he clearly accepts the idea of rationality within traditions, and indeed could be said to conceive of a genuine tradition as requiring rationality. Tradition-constituted rationalities may differ in the substantive standards they invoke. But in formal terms these rational traditions share the same features; and it is in virtue of these common formal features that the traditions can be said to be rational. As MacIntyre writes, "insofar as a tradition of rational enquiry is such, it will tend to recognize what it shares as such with other traditions, and in the development of such traditions common characteristic, if not universal, patterns will appear.[11]

These "common characteristic patterns," in turn, are conceived by MacIntyre in a way that renders them quite compatible with—indeed, quite similar to—our account of the dynamics of rational enterprises. The "rationality of traditions," in his rather brief treatment, is characterized as dialectical and historical. It is a pattern of rationality that is anti-Cartesian (in that it does not begin from indubitable and self-evident first principles) and anti-Hegelian (in that it does not move toward an absolute final truth). Rationality within traditions begins with beliefs and values that are not beyond dispute but that are nonetheless taken as paradigmatic. These paradigms provide a framework for identifying concrete problems of both theory and practice that require resolution. These problems are addressed through a process of dialectical questioning and framing of objections. And the paradigmatic beliefs are ultimately vindicated, revised, or abandoned on the basis of how well they perform in giving theoretical sense and practical coherence to the lives of the tradition's adherents. In short, in order to be rational, a tradition must conduct itself in accord with the norms of practical rationality described in earlier chapters of this book.

Because traditions are rational, on MacIntyre's account, and not merely habitual or dogmatic, they can develop what MacIntyre terms "epistemological crises." And in seeking to deal with these crises—or perhaps in confronting less dramatic anomalies—a tradition's adherents may rationally assess the claims of a competing tradition. They must do so by reference to their own standards rather than from a neutral standpoint, but MacIntyre seems to think that the dependence of all inquiries upon tradition-specific standards does not incapacitate them from understanding competing traditions—and even in extreme cases from concluding that another tradition is superior to their own.[12] MacIntyre provides little detail about this process, but presumably the situation is very similar to the assessment by scientists of competing research programs. No scientist can operate from outside of the assumptions of one research program or another, but each scientist can— with imagination and effort—assess the relative merits of competing programs in resolving the problems and anomalies generated by his or her own commitments. Because the adherents of traditions, according to MacIntyre's conception, share a commitment to the truth and because they share an involvement in the "common characteristic patterns" of rational enterprises in general, they can engage in rational confrontation rather than being doomed to blind conflict; and they can, it would appear, engage in discussions and mutual assessments of their common problems and their competing beliefs—even if they are constrained in these efforts by their divergent paradigmatic commitments. In short, MacIntyre believes in the presence and power of rationality both within traditions and across traditions. And in each case, a pattern of practices and commitments that corresponds to what I have called the constitution of rational enterprises seems to be crucial. Despite MacIntyre's emphasis on the tradition-specificity and the plurality of rationalities and my emphasis on the common features of all rational enterprises, the two accounts are not contradictory. Instead, they overlap and coincide at the point where MacIntyre provides answers to the questions: why is it that traditions can be characterized as rational? and how is it that competing traditions can "enter into argumentative dialogue"[13] with each other?

I turn now to the second disclaimer that I entered at the beginning of this concluding chapter: the caveat that the normative account of politics as a rational enterprise—however illuminative of many liberal democratic ideals, institutions, and policies—does not by itself provide us with a complete and comprehensive theory of liberal democracy. Both historically and philosophically, liberal democracy is a complex tapestry woven from a variety of materials. Neither rational practice nor any other single normative conception could possibly claim to provide *the* exclusive rationale or explanation for such a complex form of political life.

The central story line of this study, it is worth emphasizing, has not been "what is liberal democracy?" Instead, our animating question has been "what meaning and utility, if any, do the norms of human rationality possess in the context of politics?" The answer given to this central question led, in turn, to the claim that these norms of rationality provide an important framework for understanding and evaluating the liberal democratic enterprise. But it would be inaccurate and misleading to suppose that the ideal of a rational enterprise provides either a normatively complete or a practically sufficient theory of liberal democracy.

Normatively, other valid moral conceptions may be invoked in order to supplement those of rational practice. Rationality, as here understood, is an important human virtue. By some accounts—e.g., the tradition of conceiving human beings as "rational animals"—it is the defining feature of a human existence. But it is certainly not the only— and arguably not the highest—human virtue. Acceptance of the norms of rational practice, therefore, in no way precludes allegiance to other political norms grounded in other human virtues or moral values.

Two concrete examples may serve best to illustrate this point. Rational enterprises, we saw earlier, require a significant degree of liberty for their participants; and these participants also must be treated as equals in certain important respects. But civil libertarians can certainly argue on varied grounds that a good society should grant its members even more extensive freedom of action than is requisite to sustain rational practices. The value of human autonomy and the instrumental role of free self-expression for individual happiness may constitute good reasons to be as expansive as possible. Adherence to the norms of rational practice in no way bars such contentions; it requires only that no lesser degree of liberty would be acceptable and that the case for more extensive liberties be validated in accordance with the standards and practices of the rational republic. Likewise, egalitarians may invoke considerations of fraternity, compassion, or fairness on behalf of constraining social inequalities to an even greater extent than rational practice requires. Again, nothing said here prohibits or contradicts such claims; but they must be defended and pursued subject to the demands of rational procedure rather than dogmatically asserted and imposed.

The ideal of a rational society, therefore, does not by its acceptance provide a theoretical resolution for the perennial question of the proper extent and balance of liberty and equality in a good society. It does provide minimal standards for liberty and equality that are mandatory and compatible; and it provides a framework within which the remaining questions about liberty and equality have to be resolved practically. The same pattern applies to other standard normative social questions, such as detailed standards of retributive and distributive justice, the best economic system to adopt, and so on. Acceptable answers to these practical questions must not abrogate the fundamental norms of the rational society; but within those limits the floor is open—and always remains open—for proposals that can be incorporated into the shared understandings (to borrow Walzer's phrase) of the society, or failing that to be settled by the society's means of resolving rationally inadjudicable disagreements.

Because they are not normatively comprehensive, and for other reasons as well, the norms of rational practice are also not practically sufficient. They provide overarching guidelines and institutional standards for the conduct of society's business, but they do not provide all of these guidelines and standards. The conception of a rational political enterprise is not utopian in the sense of being impossible because dependent upon illusory assumptions, but it is an ideal theory, not what Bruce Ackerman calls "second-best" or even "third-best" theory. And it has within itself no definitive grounds for generating standards for the second-best institutions required to supplement rational practices in the real world.

The ideal of a rational society, therefore, should not be conceived as a direct competitor with theories of justice or with theories of democratic conflict resolution such as bargaining or voting schemes. The ideal of a rational society is at odds with these accounts only to the extent that they themselves are claimed to be sufficient and comprehensive accounts of liberal democracy. The point is not to replace or abrogate these theories and the adjudicatory practices they recommend. The point is rather to insist that they alone can never by themselves provide an adequate account of either the ideals or the institutions of a healthy liberal democratic society.

A well-ordered liberal democracy has several layers. The top layer is the "Aristotelian" layer of friendship, *phronesis*, and the common good. The middle layer is the "Kantian" layer of neutral justice. The third layer is the "Hobbesian" layer of institutionally regulated self-interested contention. Most recent theories of liberal democracy have been partial and misleading because they have focused exclusively on one—or possibly both—of the last two of these. The value of the normative conception of a rational political enterprise is that it provides a good account of the top layer along with some guidelines and constraints for the other two layers. A comprehensive and sufficient account of liberal democratic theory and practice would have to provide determinate norms and specific strategies for all three levels.

The relative significance of the top layer in the day-to-day political life of a given society is a function of many circumstances: the extent of the society's commitment to and understanding of the norms of rational practice, literacy levels, the extent and nature of the political cleavages in the society, the extent of systematic impediments to rational dialogue, the nature of the prevalent issues, and so on. One implication of our theory is that the more of a society's political business that can be conducted at this level, the better. No intelligent critic would suggest, of course, that fallible and contentious beings such as we are could ever dispense entirely with the other layers of social interaction under the best of circumstances. But any account of liberal democracy that neglects or denies the reality and normative priority of the top layer will be both theoretically inadequate and practically harmful.

Even without foolishly falling into indefensibly hegemonic claims for the comprehensiveness or sufficiency of norms of rational practice, then, it remains possible to make strong claims on their behalf. Theoretically, the strong claim is this: if we had to choose a single normative standard for the understanding and evaluation of liberal democratic political systems, the one that would get us the farthest would be neither liberty, nor fairness, nor neutrality, nor utility, nor pluralist bargaining, but instead would be the ideal of rational practice. The norms of rational practice get us closer to the heart of the liberal democratic ideal in all its complexity than any other single theory. And practically, the strong claim is this: the habits and institutions of rational practice may not be sufficient for the conduct of the political business of any real-world society, but they are indispensable to the satisfactory conduct of the business of all liberal democratic societies. For in the absence of the liberal friendship that is contingent on these habits and institutions, liberal justice becomes a highly precarious treaty among political strangers who have only the most abstract of motives for respecting it; and liberal bargaining becomes a highly volatile set of negotiations among political foes who have only the most contingent of motives to bargain in good faith.[14] Citizens who are strangers or enemies and not friends, who compete and calculate but do not cooperate, who bargain but do not reason together about their common good, are not likely to create a good or stable society.

Ultimately, we have three reasons for commitment to the ideals of a rational society. First is what might be termed the argument from human essence—a common form of argument in epic political theories. That is, we are in our human fruition—in our most complete and fulfilled form of life—rational beings. To the extent that we desire to be fully human, therefore, we must accept and abide by the canons of behavior intrinsic to rationality. No one can have the status and embody the form of life of a rational being and at the same time claim exemption from the constitutive imperatives of reason. No cosmic free riding is permissible or even logically coherent. As Kant put it, "I, as an intelligence, must recognize myself as subject to the law of the world of intellect."[15]

The second reason is pragmatic. Rational practices "work." Rational enterprises, both cognitively and politically, are more successful in accomplishing their purposes than other forms of human organization are. Whenever political societies depart from the norms of rational practice, they encounter difficulties and distortions of their own making. Societies that suppress the liberties of conscience, action, and inquiry inevitably become stagnant. Governments that rule by decree rather than by enforcing a rationally achieved consensus inevitably become oppressive and create a dialectic of rebellion and repression. Societies devoid of institutions fostering the rational discussion and pursuit of common goals become anomic. Rational enterprises, to be sure, are not infallible. They may fail for any number of reasons, not the least of which is the imperfection of human reason itself. But their odds of success are always better than those facing enterprises that clearly violate norms of rational practice. Sooner or later, systematic irrationality incubates self-destructive behavior.

A final line of argument on behalf of the rational society is that it passes Rawls's test of "reflective equilibrium." Essentially, this test is an appeal to the coherence of a normative model with the accepted moral beliefs of the audience. Because this appeal accepts the basic trustworthiness of prevalent moral intuitions, it is subjective and conventional. Nonetheless, one would properly be suspicious of any normative political conception that departed sharply from what is usually accepted as the "better judgment" of our moral and religious tradition. It speaks well for the conception of a rational society, therefore, that it does exhibit substantial overlap with what is arguably best in our moral tradition. A rational society incorporates the idea of human rights and fundamental human dignity. It sustains the belief that freedom of thought and self-determination are important to the good life. It insists upon the basic equality of all citizens. It both requires and fosters civic kinship. It counsels toleration for others. It requires and embodies a respect for the truth. The conception of the rational society thus embraces the most basic moral precepts of the great religious traditions; it embodies the Enlightenment values of liberty, equality, and fraternity; and it acquiesces in the civic republican concern for the common weal and for civic virtue.

There is no such thing as demonstrative "proof" of a political theory. The best that can be offered on behalf of the rational society as a political ideal is—as for any such theory—a set of good reasons that can recommend themselves to people of good will. In the case of a rational society, these good reasons are, as noted above, that: participation in a rational society is the mode of political behavior incumbent upon all who aspire to live as rational beings; rational practices are conducive to successful and stable regimes; and the norms of rational society cohere with our deepest moral convictions. Beyond that, not a great deal can be said. A rational society is not the same thing as the ideal society, but it is hard to imagine a truly good society that is not also a rational society. Every deviation from rational practice exacts its price and makes attainment of the human good more difficult.

With the advantage of hindsight, we can easily see that the political hopes of the Age of Reason were unrealistic and the beliefs that sustained them flawed. Enlightenment liberals believed that reason was simple and its methods infallible. They thought that reason could apprehend moral and political truths with the same certainty they attributed to scientific findings. As a consequence, they thought the advance of reason inexorable not only in theory but also in political practice. They anticipated a future "when the sun will shine only on free men who know no other master but their reason," a future "when at last the nations come to agree on the principles of politics and morality . . . and nothing will remain to encourage or even to arouse the fury of war."[16]

The twentieth century has seen these hopes confuted empirically and the beliefs that sustained them undermined logically. After a century of relative peace, general democratization, and economic advance, the years since 1914 have seemed to mock Enlightenment dreams. The "fury of war" seems greater than ever; and the tyrants, fools, and fanatics whom Condorcet expected to disappear from the pages of history seem instead to multiply. Moreover, the powers of reason have fared as poorly in theory as in practice. No one thinks that reason is simple or infallible anymore. In itself, that awareness of the complexity and fallibility of the human understanding would not be so bad, but much twentieth-century epistemology has gone on to deny the moral and political competency of reason altogether. In a reversal that would have depressed Enlightenment liberals as much as it would have dumbfounded them, those who claim to be apostles of reason in politics are usually themselves modern replicas of the oppressors those liberals detested. And their liberal heirs speak not of a reason they now deem politically impotent, but of utility or convenience or moderation or stability or equilibrium or entitlement.

If my argument is correct, however, contemporary liberals would find it worth their while to reconsider the faith of reason that sustained their Enlightenment predecessors—not to resurrect it but to refashion it in the light of contemporary philosophy. The reaffirmation of a humane and capacious liberalism should go hand in hand with the reaffirmation of a complex and chastened form of rationalism. The conception of rational practice that I have argued is implicit in the recent philosophy of science and language permits us both to recognize the illusions of Enlightenment liberal rationalism and at the same time to appreciate its intuitive grasp of important truths about the civilizing power of reason in politics.

The life of reason is not simple, but complex. Its advance is not unilinear and inexorable, but fitful and reversible. Its reign in human affairs is not impregnable, but all too fragile. It does not function automatically, but only when enfranchised and empowered by human commitments, obligations, and habits that represent a difficult social achievement. Nevertheless, as Enlightenment liberals knew better than they could explain, it is possible to conduct political affairs in a rational manner and desirable to do so wherever conditions permit. The leaven of reason makes politics something more than war by other means. Where a society conducts its political affairs in conformity with the norms of rational practice, it answers to the deepest concerns of humane liberalism. Its citizens are free and equal. They have rights. They participate. They are tolerant. They speak and listen to each other as members of a moral community united by a continuing quest to identify and attain the common good. As a consequence, reason in politics, as Voltaire says, "is mild, it is humane; it teaches us forbearance and dispels discord; it fosters virtue and makes obedience to the laws agreeable rather than compulsory."[17]

Notes

___

Introduction

1 Thomas A. Spragens, Jr., *The Irony of Liberal Reason* (Chicago: Univ. of Chicago Press, 1981).

2 Aristotle, *Nicomachean Ethics*, trans. J. A. K. Thomson (Baltimore, Md.: Penguin Books, 1955), 4, 5.

3 John Dunn, *Rethinking Modern Political Theory* (Cambridge: Cambridge Univ. Press, 1985), p. 10.

4 See, for example, the articles in part 3 of Henry Kariel, ed., *Frontiers of Democratic Theory* (New York: Random House, 1970).

5 Benjamin Barber, *Strong Democracy: Participatory Politics for a New Age* (Berkeley: Univ. of California Press, 1984); Theodore Lowi, *The End of Liberalism*, 2d ed. (New York: W. W. Norton, 1979); Jane Mansbridge, *Beyond Adversary Democracy* (Chicago: Univ. of Chicago Press, 1983).

6 John Rawls, "Justice as Fairness: Political not Metaphysical," *Philosophy and Public Affairs* 14 (1985): 229. In the Conclusion, I note several other constructive critiques of liberal theory and practice that can also be incorporated within the communal rational practice framework.

7 For a concise account, see Michael J. Sandel, "Introduction," in *Liberalism and Its Critics* (New York: New York Univ. Press, 1984).

8 John Rawls, *A Theory of Justice* (Cambridge, Mass.: Harvard Univ. Press, 1971).

9 Sandel, *Liberalism and Its Critics*, p. 5.

10 Robert N. Bellah, Richard Madsen, William M. Sullivan, Ann Swidler, and Steven M. Tipton, *Habits of the Heart: Individualism and Commitment in American Life* (New York: Harper and Row, 1985).

11 This is a very capsulized account of Sandel's argument in *Liberalism and the Limits of Justice* (Cambridge: Cambridge Univ. Press, 1982).

12 Sandel, *Liberalism and Its Critics*, p. 10.

13 Ibid.

14 John Rawls, "Justice as Fairness," pp. 225–26.

15 Richard Rorty, in the context of trying to pull Rawls onto his own turf of a pragmatism benignly neglectful of fundamental philosophical issues when it comes

to politics, quite aptly observes that: "on the relativity of justice to historical situations, Rawls is closer to Walzer than to Dworkin" (in *The Virginia Statute of Religious Freedom: Two Hundred Years After*, ed. Robert Vaughan (Madison: Univ. of Wisconsin Press, 1988). For Walzer's views, see his *Spheres of Justice* (New York: Basic Books, 1983).

16 Rawls, "Justice as Fairness," pp. 228–29.

17 Ibid., p. 229.

18 Ibid., p. 230–31.

19 Ibid., p. 227.

20 Ibid., p. 240fn.22.

21 William M. Sullivan, *Reconstructing Public Philosophy* (Berkeley: Univ. of California Press, 1986), p. 21.

22 Reinhold Niebuhr, *Moral Man and Immoral Society* (New York: Charles Scribner's Sons, 1932), p. xxv.

23 Ibid., pp. 30–31.

24 For similar reflections from a contemporary Niebuhrian, see "On Moral Crusades and Also on a Really Realistic Realism," in William Lee Miller, *Of Thee, Nevertheless, I Sing* (New York: Harcourt, Brace, Jovanovich, 1975). Miller writes, "It is important to be realistic, but it is even more important to know what purposes one's realism serves. . . . I think we overdid it. We did not make clear enough the subordinate place of this realism" (pp. 43–44).

One. Reason, Rational Practice, and Political Theory: The Making of a Problem

1 Thomas Hobbes, *Leviathan* 4, 46.

2 Plato, *The Republic* 7, 521–24.

3 Ibid., 7, 525.

4 Ibid., 7, 534 and 532.

5 Aristotle, *Nicomachean Ethics* 4, 5.

6 Aristotle, *Posterior Analytics*, trans. Jonathan Barnes (Oxford: Clarendon Press, 1975), p. xi.

7 See Aram Vartanian, *Diderot and Descartes* (Princeton, N.J.: Princeton Univ. Press, 1953), for an excellent account of how philosophical and ideological appropriations of Descartes in ways repugnant to them forced the *philosophes* to renounce "Cartesianism" even as they became more Cartesian in fundamental respects than Descartes himself.

8 René Descartes, "Meditations on First Philosophy," in *Descartes: Philosophical Writings*, trans. Norman Kemp Smith (New York: Random House, 1958), p. 229.

9 For an analysis of this problem, see Alexander Koyre, *From the Closed World to the Infinite Universe* (Baltimore, Md.: Johns Hopkins Univ. Press, 1957).

10 Hobbes, *Leviathan*, 1, 5.

11 Plato, *The Republic* 7, 521.

12 Ibid., 6, 500.

13 Aristotle, *Nicomachean Ethics* 6, 5.

14 Ibid.

15 For a useful recent commentary on this and other aspects of Aristotle's moral theory, see John M. Cooper, *Reason and Human Good in Aristotle* (Cambridge, Mass.: Harvard Univ. Press, 1975).

16 Aristotle, *Nicomachean Ethics* 6, 8.

17 Regarding the need for experience, see Aristotle, *Nicomachean Ethics* 6, 8; and regarding the need for virtue, see Ibid., 6, 13.

18 See Cooper, *Reason and Human Good in Aristotle*, pp. 19–22.

19 Aristotle, *Nicomachean Ethics* 3, 3.

20 Ibid., 6, 5.

21 Ibid.

22 Niccolò Machiavelli, *Discourses*, trans. Christian Detmold (New York: Random House, 1950), p. 103.

23 Ibid.

24 Ibid., p. 105.

25 Niccolò Machiavelli, *The Prince*, trans. Luigi Ricci and rev. E.R.P. Vincent (New York: Random House, 1950), p. 56.

26 Ibid., p. 55.

27 Machiavelli, *Discourses*, p. 263.

28 Hobbes, *Leviathan* 1, 5.

29 Ibid., 1, 3.

30 Ibid., 2, 20.

31 Ibid., 2, 18.

32 Ibid., 1, 5.

33 Ibid., 1, 11.

34 Thomas Hobbes, *English Works*, ed. William Molesworth (London: John Bohn, 1839), vol. 4, p. 33.

35 Georg Wilhelm Friedrich Hegel, *Reason in History*, trans. Robert S. Hartman (Indianapolis: Bobbs-Merrill, 1953), pp. 41, 44.

36 Jeremy Bentham, "An Introduction to the Principles of Morals and Legislation," in John Stuart Mill and Jeremy Bentham, *Utilitarianism and Other Essays*, ed. Alan Ryan (Harmondsworth, England: Penguin Books, 1987), p. 65.

37 Bentham, "Principles of Morals and Legislation," p. 111.

38 John Stuart Mill, "Bentham," in Mill and Bentham, *Utilitarianism and Other Essays*, pp. 135, 150.

39 John Stuart Mill, *On The Logic of the Moral Sciences* (Indianapolis: Bobbs-Merrill, 1965), pp. 22, 47, 88.

40 Ibid., pp. 116–17.

41 John Stuart Mill, *On Liberty* (1859; Indianapolis: Bobbs-Merrill, 1956), p. 53.

42 Mill, *Logic of the Moral Sciences*, p. 138.

43 John Stuart Mill, *Utilitarianism* (Indianapolis: Bobbs-Merrill, 1957), pp. 45, 41, 40.

44 Sigmund Freud, *Civilization and Its Discontents*, trans. John Strachey (New York: W. W. Norton, 1961), p. 69.

45 Mill, *Logic of the Moral Sciences*, p. 148.

46 Ibid., pp. 145–46.

47 Mill, *Utilitarianism*, p. 37.

48 Max Weber, "Objectivity in Social Science and Social Policy," in Max Weber, *The*

Methodology of the Social Sciences, trans. Edward A. Shils and Henry A. Finch (New York: The Free Press, 1949), p. 111.

49 Weber, "The Meaning of Ethical Neutrality," in Weber, *Methodology of the Social Sciences*, p. 18.

50 Jean-Paul Sartre, "The Flies," in Jean-Paul Sartre, *No Exit and Three Other Plays*, trans. S. Gilbert (New York: Random House, 1949), pp. 121–22.

51 Weber, "Ethical Neutrality," p. 26.

52 Nathanael Culverwel, "A Discourse of the Light of Nature," in *The Cambridge Platonists*, ed. E. T. Campagnac (Oxford: Clarendon Press, 1901), pp. 219–20.

53 For example, Ernest Cassirer opines that the Cambridge School's influence on Locke was "limited and indirect, and for the most part purely negative" (*The Platonic Renaissance in England*, trans. James Pettegrove [Austin: Univ. of Texas Press, 1953], p. 159).

54 Maurice Cranston, *John Locke* (London: Longman's Green, 1957), p. 215.

55 Benjamin Whichcote, "Aphorisms," in Campagnac, *Cambridge Platonists*, p. 72.

56 John Locke, *Essay concerning Human Understanding*, introduction, sec. 7.

57 Nathanael Culverwel, "Discourse of the Light of Nature," in Campagnac, *Cambridge Platonists*, p. 221.

58 John Smith, "Attaining to Divine Knowledge," in Campagnac, *Cambridge Platonists*, pp. 90–91.

59 Locke, *Essay concerning Human Understanding*, 4.3.18.

60 Whichcote, "Aphorisms," p. 67.

61 Plotinus, "Against the Gnostics," quoted by Cassirer, *The Platonic Renaissance in England*, p. 100.

62 Colin Maclaurin, *An Account of Sir Isaac Newton's Philosophical Discoveries*, quoted in Carl Becker, *The Declaration of Independence* (New York: Random House, 1922), pp. 50–51.

63 Marquis de Condorcet, *Sketch for a Historical Picture of the Progress of the Human Mind*, trans. June Barraclough (London: Weidenfeld and Nicolson, 1955), p. 151.

64 Locke, *Essays on the Law of Nature*, pp. 133, 153.

65 Jean-Jacques Rousseau, "Discourse on the Origin of Inequality," in *The Social Contract and Discourses*, trans. G.D.H. Cole (New York: E. P. Dutton, 1950), p. 189.

66 Ibid., p. 208.

67 Immanuel Kant, "Metaphysical Foundations of Morals," in *The Philosophy of Kant*, ed. Carl J. Friedrich (New York: Random House, 1949), pp. 198–200.

68 Ibid., p. 202.

69 Ibid., p. 170.

70 "The pure concept of duty," writes Kant, "unmixed with any foreign element of experienced attractions, in a word, the pure concept of moral law in general, exercises an influence on the human heart through reason alone" (Ibid., p. 159).

71 Ibid., pp. 207, 206, 159.

72 The complete passage here embodies Kant's version of the Agathon and what is left of its erotic appeal: "To behold virtue in her proper form is but to contemplate morality divested of all admixture of sensible things and of every spurious ornament of reward or self-love. To what extent she then eclipses everything else that charms the inclinations one may readily perceive with the least exertion of his reason, if it be not wholly spoiled for abstraction" (Ibid., p. 175).

73 Ibid., pp. 178, 177.

74 Alasdair MacIntyre, *After Virtue* (Notre Dame, Ind.: Univ. of Notre Dame Press, 1981), p. 103.

75 Condorcet, *Progress of the Human Mind*, p. 97.

76 Becker, *Declaration of Independence*, p. 279.

77 Joseph de Maistre, *Oeuvres*, vol. 1, p. 69, quoted in Becker, *Declaration of Independence*, p. 279.

78 For a recent argument that "Utilitarianism, for all its vaunted precision, cannot tell us what to do," see Don Herzog, *Without Foundations: Justification in Political Theory* (Ithaca, N.Y.: Cornell Univ. Press, 1985), p. 157.

79 John Rawls, *A Theory of Justice* (Cambridge, Mass.: Harvard Univ. Press, 1971), p. 29.

80 Quoted in Elie Halevy, *The Growth of Philosophic Radicalism*, trans. Mary Morris (Boston: Beacon Press, 1960), p. 84.

81 Alexander Hamilton, James Madison and John Jay, *The Federalist Papers*, no. 51 (New York: New American Library, 1961), p. 324.

82 Leslie Stephen, quoted by Gertrude Himmelfarb, *On Liberty and Liberalism: The Case of John Stuart Mill* (New York: Knopf, 1974), p. 300.

83 For a succinct account of this pattern, see James Fishkin, *Beyond Subjective Morality: Ethical Reasoning and Political Philosophy* (New Haven, Conn.: Yale Univ. Press, 1984), pp. 91–94.

84 See, for example, Sandel's critique of Dworkin's case for affirmative action, in *Liberalism and the Limits of Justice*, pp. 135–47.

85 For example, see MacIntyre's observations about the aspects of Aristotelian thought that at a minimum would require revision or rejection before it could be applicable in a contemporary setting, in *After Virtue*, pp. 152–53.

Two. Rationality in Science and Language: From Syntax to Pragmatics

1 John Herschel, *A Preliminary Discourse of the Study of Natural Philosophy* (London: Longman's, 1831), p. 59.

2 This term was originated by Hilary Putnam in 1962 and is used systematically by Frederick Suppe in his excellent introduction to *The Structure of Scientific Theories*, 2d ed. (Urbana: Univ. of Illinois Press, 1977). Suppe's account provides one of the best available overviews of developments in the philosophy of science during the past fifty years.

3 See, especially, Stephen Toulmin, *Foresight and Understanding* (London: Hutchinson, 1961), and Norwood R. Hanson, *Patterns of Discovery* (Cambridge: Cambridge Univ. Press, 1958). For good first-person explanations of the pivotal role that Wittgenstein's ideas played in their rejection of the empiricist depiction of science, see their contributions to *The Legacy of Logical Positivism*, ed. Peter Achinstein and Stephen F. Barker (Baltimore, Md.: Johns Hopkins Univ. Press, 1969).

4 Each has published extensively, but the major statements of their views on this issue are Michael Polanyi, *Personal Knowledge: Towards a Post-Critical Philosophy* (London: Routledge and Kegan Paul, 1958), and Thomas Kuhn, *The Structure of Scientific Revolutions*, 2d ed. (1962; Chicago: Univ. of Chicago Press, 1970).

5 See, especially, Paul Feyerabend, *Against Method* (London: New Left Books, 1975), and Imre Lakatos, "Falsification and the Methodology of Scientific Research Programmes," in Imre Lakatos and Alan Musgrave, eds., *Criticism and the Growth of Knowledge* (Cambridge: Cambridge Univ. Press, 1970), pp. 91–196.

6 Norwood Hanson, "The Interpretation of Scientific Theories," in Achinstein and Barker, *Legacy of Logical Positivism*, pp. 75–77 (Hanson's italics).

7 Ibid., pp. 74–75.

8 The breakdown of the received view's theory-observation dichotomy implicit in the revisionist account of science was also forcefully suggested by some critics who looked specifically at the nature of actual theoretical concepts deployed in science. See, for example, Peter Achinstein, *Concepts of Science* (Baltimore, Md.: Johns Hopkins Univ. Press, 1968), and Hilary Putnam, "What Theories Are Not," in Ernest Nagel, Patrick Suppes, and Alfred Tarski, eds, *Logic, Methodology, and the Philosophy of Science* (Stanford, Calif.: Stanford Univ. Press, 1962), pp. 240–51.

9 Polanyi, *Personal Knowledge*, p. 254.

10 Kuhn, *Structure of Scientific Revolutions*, p. 146. If the critics were clear and united in their rejection of conventional verification and falsification, they were less clear and less united about what would take its place and about the appropriate strategy to replace quixotic quests for decisive and unambiguous crucial experiments. (These are problems, indeed, that occupy an important place within contemporary discussions in the philosophy of science.) Polanyi seemed willing to accredit the best judgments of the scientific community as generally reliable, although of course not infallible, putting his faith in the rationality of nature and its capacity to reveal itself to inquiring minds. Kuhn's position was underdeveloped and ambiguous—lacunae that played a big role in the counterattacks against his contentions. Feyerabend delighted in his gadfly iconoclasm, advocating theoretical pluralism and leaving more constructive efforts to others. Toulmin sought to develop the "natural selection" analogy that also appeared in Kuhn's just-cited characterization into a full-scale account of theory choice. And Lakatos, conceding a great deal in substance to Kuhn while attacking what he found unacceptable in the implications he found in Kuhn's general formulations, sought to refine Popper's falsificationism into a rational reconstruction of scientific research programs.

11 This line of argument seems to me implicit in all of the revisionist accounts, but it was pursued most explicitly perhaps by Hanson and Polanyi. Hanson sought to illuminate what he called the patterns of discovery by resurrecting and embellishing C. S. Peirce's account of "retroductive" reasoning. And Polanyi sought in parallel fashion to elucidate what he termed the "logic of tacit inference" and its functioning in scientific practice. Besides the larger works of Hanson and Polanyi cited earlier, see Norwood Hanson, "The Logic of Discovery," *Journal of Philosophy* 55: 1073–89, and Michael Polanyi, "The Logic of Tacit Inference," *Philosophy* 40: 369–86.

12 Richard Bernstein, *Beyond Objectivism and Relativism* (Philadelphia: Univ. of Pennsylvania Press, 1983), pp. 16–22.

13 May Brodbeck, review of *Personal Knowledge*, by Michael Polanyi, *American Sociological Review* 25 (1960): 582–83.

14 Kuhn, *Structure of Scientific Revolutions*, pp. 150, 151.

15 Kuhn, "Postscript to the Second Edition," *Structure of Scientific Revolutions*, pp. 205–6.

16 Dudley Shapere, "The Character of Scientific Change," in Thomas Nickles, ed., *Scientific Discovery, Logic, and Rationality* (Dordrecht, Holland: D. Reidel Publishing, 1980), p. 67.

17 This pragmatic turn and its associated emphasis upon the careful examination of historical cases implicitly accredits Norwood Hanson's wry observation that it "never is an elevating spectacle to see philosophers telling the world how it *must* use discourse precisely to describe what the philosophers are presently interested in" ("The Interpretation of Scientific Theories," p. 74). And it is what informs Dudley Shapere's claim that a conception of scientific rationality that does "justice to the variety of patterns of thought and method in the history of science while at the same time allowing for the possibility, and occasional actuality, of true knowledge-acquisition and progress in sciences" would be "perhaps the first truly uncompromising empiricist philosophy ever proposed" ("The Character of Scientific Change," p. 95).

18 Hobbes, *Leviathan*, Part 1, chapter 4.

19 René Descartes to Marin Mersenne, November 20, 1629, in René Descartes, *Philosophical Letters*, trans. and ed. Anthony Kenny (Oxford: Clarendon Press, 1970), p. 6.

20 Bertrand Russell, *The Philosophy of Logical Atomism*, lecture 2, quoted in J. O. Urmson, *Philosophical Analysis* (Oxford: Oxford Univ. Press, 1967), p. 192.

21 Bertrand Russell, writing in *Monist* in 1919, quoted in Urmson, *Philosophical Analysis*, p. 27.

22 "So we may regard the metaphysics of logical atomism . . . as an effort to think out with entire generality, clarity, and consistency the presuppositions and implications of empiricist practice and outlook throughout the ages, with the aid of the new logical tools available" (J. O. Urmson, *Philosophical Analysis*, p. 44).

23 Bertrand Russell, "Introduction," to Ludwig Wittgenstein, *Tractatus Logico-Philosophicus* (1921; London: Routledge and Kegan Paul, 1961), p. x.

24 Wittgenstein, *Tractatus*, 2.02.

25 Ibid., 4.111, 4.003, 4.112, 4.0031.

26 Ibid., 6.54.

27 Russell, "Introduction," to Wittgenstein, *Tractatus*, p. xxi.

28 Ibid.

29 C. L. Stevenson, "Persuasive Definitions," *Mind* 47 (1938): 331–50.

30 John Wisdom, "Metaphysics and Verification," *Mind* 47 (1938): 452–98.

31 John Wisdom, "Philosophical Perplexity," *Proceedings of the Aristotelian Society* 1936–37: 71–88.

32 Ludwig Wittgenstein, *Philosophical Investigations*, trans. G.E.M. Anscombe, and ed. Anscombe and R. Rees (New York: Macmillan, 1953), p. x.

33 Wittgenstein, *Tractatus*, pp. 5, 3.

34 Wittgenstein, *Philosophical Investigations*, p. 13.

35 Ibid., p. 48.

36 Ibid., pp. 11–12.

37 Ibid., p. 14.

38 Ibid., pp. 14–15.

39 Ibid., p. 151.

40 Ibid., pp. 38, 50.
41 Ibid., pp. 47, 48.
42 Ibid., pp. 30–31.
43 Ibid., p. 29.
44 Ibid., pp. 19, 51.
45 John Searle, *Speech Acts* (Cambridge: Cambridge Univ. Press, 1969), pp. 16, 18.

Three. Post-Positivist Praxis: The Constitution
of Rational Enterprises

1   Robert Merton, "Science and the Social Order" and "Science and Democratic Social Structure," in *Social Theory and Social Structure*, 2d ed. (Glencoe, Ill.: The Free Press, 1957), pp. 537–61; Michael Polanyi, *Science, Faith, and Society* (Chicago: Univ. of Chicago Press, 1964), and "The Republic of Science," a lecture delivered at Roosevelt University in 1962 and published as a pamphlet.
2   Merton, "Science and Democratic Social Structure," pp. 558, 556–57.
3   Polanyi, *Science, Faith, and Society*, p. 64.
4   Ibid., p. 54.
5   Merton, "Science and Democratic Social Structure," pp. 558–59 (emphasis added).
6   Ibid., pp. 553, 554–55.
7   Polanyi, *Science, Faith, and Society*, pp. 16, 48.
8   Ibid., p. 16.
9   Ibid., p. 48.
10 Merton, "Science and Democratic Social Structure," p. 553.
11 Polanyi, "The Republic of Science," p. 12.
12 Mill, *On Liberty*, p. 64.
13 Polanyi, *Science, Faith, and Society*, p. 68.
14 Ibid., p. 68.
15 Merton, "Science and Democratic Social Structure," p. 559.
16 Condorcet, *Progress of the Human Mind*, p. 100.
17 Polanyi, *Science, Faith, and Society*, p. 54.
18 Ibid., p. 57.
19 Peter Winch, *The Idea of a Social Science and Its Relation to Philosophy* (London: Routledge and Kegan Paul, 1958).
20 See, for example, the account based upon this misconception in Theodore Abel, "The Operation called 'Verstehen'," in Herbert Feigl and May Brodbeck, eds., *Readings in the Philosophy of Science* (New York: Appleton-Century-Crofts, 1953), pp. 677–88.
21 Other suggestions Winch makes, however, such as those concerning what he terms "limiting conditions" of human life, suggest avenues to a somewhat different outcome. See, for example, the concluding section to "Understanding a Primitive Society," *American Philosophical Quarterly* 1, no. 4 (October 1964): 307–24, and "Nature and Convention," *Proceedings of the Aristotelian Society*, 1959–60: 231–52.
22 Winch, *The Idea of a Social Science*, p. 102.
23 Ibid., pp. 103, 3, 100.

24 Winch, "Understanding a Primitive Society," p. 313.
25 Jürgen Habermas, "What is Universal Pragmatics?" in *Communication and the Evolution of Society*, trans. Thomas McCarthy (Boston: Beacon Press, 1979), pp. 26–27.
26 Jürgen Habermas, "Wahrheitstheorien," in *Wirklichkeit und Reflexion* (Pfullingen, 1973), p. 259.
27 Habermas, "A Reply to my Critics," in *Habermas: Critical Debates*, ed. John B. Thompson and David Held (Cambridge, Mass.: MIT Press, 1982), pp. 254, 227.
28 Karl-Otto Apel, "The Communication Community and the Social Sciences," in *Towards a Transformation of Philosophy*, trans. Glyn Adey and David Frisby (London: Routledge and Kegan Paul, 1980), esp. pp. 158–59.
29 Ibid., p. 159.
30 J. L. Austin, *How To Do Things With Words* (Cambridge, Mass.: Harvard Univ. Press, 1962).
31 Habermas, "What Is Universal Pragmatics?" p. 3.
32 Ibid., pp. 2–3.

Four. Politics as a Rational Enterprise

1 John Locke, "Second letter to Stillingfleet," cited in James Gibson, *Locke's Theory of Knowledge and Its Historical Relations* (Cambridge: Cambridge Univ. Press, 1960), p. 5.
2 Hobbes, *Leviathan*, 1, 14.
3 Hobbes, *English Works*, vol. 4, p. 32.
4 Edmond Cahn, *The Sense of Injustice* (New York: New York Univ. Press, 1949).
5 The phrase "experiments of living" is found in chapter 3 of Mill, *On Liberty*, and the "competent judges" passage is in chapter 2 of Mill, *Utilitarianism*.
6 Robert Nozick, *Anarchy, State, and Utopia* (New York: Basic Books, 1974), p. 310.
7 Shapere, "The Character of Scientific Change," p. 85.
8 John Rawls, "Kantian Constructivism in Moral Theory," *Journal of Philosophy* 77, no. 9 (September 1980): 542, 536.
9 Ibid., pp. 540, 543.
10 Aristotle, *Nicomachean Ethics* 9, 6; 8, 3.
11 Ibid., 9, 9. It is worth noting that Mill appropriates this imagery to make the same point in *Considerations on Representative Government*.
12 Edmund Burke, *Reflections on the Revolution in France* (New York: Liberal Arts Press, 1955), p. 110.
13 Aristotle, *Nicomachean Ethics* 9, 9.
14 Hannah Arendt, *Men in Dark Times* (Harmondsworth, England: Penguin Books, 1968), pp. 31–32.
15 Miller, *Of Thee, Nevertheless, I Sing*, p. 10.
16 Adolf Hitler, *Mein Kampf* (Boston: Houghton Mifflin, 1971), pp. 103, 183, 408, 107.
17 Ibid., p. 582.
18 Jean-Pierre Vernant, *The Origins of Greek Thought* (Ithaca, N.Y.: Cornell Univ. Press, 1982), p. 68.
19 See, for example, Jürgen Habermas, *Knowledge and Human Interests*, trans. Jeremy Shapiro (Boston: Beacon Press, 1971), chap. 3.

20 Condorcet, *Progress of the Human Mind*, p. 97.
21 Charles Taylor, "Neutrality in Political Science," in Peter Laslett and W. G. Runciman, eds., *Philosophy, Politics, and Society*, 3d ser. (New York: Barnes and Noble, 1967), p. 48.
22 Jean-Jacques Rousseau, *"The Social Contract,"* in *The Social Contract and Discourses*, trans. G.D.H. Cole (New York: E. P. Dutton, 1950), bk. 1, chap. 8.
23 David Hume, *An Enquiry concerning the Principles of Morals*, sec. 5, pt. 2.
24 Kurt Baier, *The Moral Point of View* (Ithaca, N.Y.: Cornell Univ. Press, 1958), p. 189.
25 Rawls, *A Theory of Justice*, pp. 130–36.
26 Sissela Bok, *Lying: Moral Choice in Public and Private Life* (New York: Random House, 1978).
27 John Stuart Mill, *A System of Logic* (London: Longman's, 1959), pp. 604–5.
28 Rawls, *A Theory of Justice*, p. 27.
29 Rousseau, "Social Contract," bk. 4, chap. 2; bk. 2, chap. 4; bk. 1, chap. 6.
30 Immanuel Kant, "Metaphysical Foundations of Morals," trans. Carl Friedrich, in Carl Friedrich, ed., *The Philosophy of Kant* (New York: Random House, 1949), p. 182.
31 Ibid., p. 149.
32 Walzer, *Spheres of Justice*, pp. 26–28 and 312–16.
33 Sandel, *Liberalism and the Limits of Justice*, p. 183.

Five. Citizenship in the Republic of Reason

1 Rousseau, *Social Contract*, bk. 3, chap. 15.
2 John Stuart Mill, *Considerations on Representative Government* (Chicago: Henry Regnery, 1962), pp. 58, 55, 50, 72.
3 See, for example, Bernard Berelson, Paul Lazarsfeld, and William McPhee, *Voting* (Chicago: Univ. of Chicago Press, 1954), pp. 306–23; and Lester Milbrath, *Political Participation* (Chicago: Rand McNally, 1965), pp. 142–54.
4 Auguste Comte, "Cours de Philosophie Positive," in Gertrud Lenzer, ed., *Auguste Comte and Positivism* (New York: Harper and Row, 1975), pp. 204, 269.
5 Jürgen Habermas, *Theory and Practice*, trans. John Viertel (Boston: Beacon Press, 1973), p. 40.
6 Karl Mannheim, *Ideology and Utopia*, trans. Louis Wirth and Edward Shils (New York: Harcourt, Brace, and World, 1936), p. 151.
7 Ibid., p. 149.
8 Habermas, "What Is Universal Pragmatics?" p. 66.
9 Mill, *On Liberty*, p. 71.
10 Ibid., p. 68.
11 Ibid., p. 14.
12 Ibid., p. 14.
13 Robert Dahl, *A Preface to Democratic Theory* (Chicago: Univ. of Chicago Press, 1956), p. 45.
14 Nozick, *Anarchy, State, and Utopia*, p. ix.
15 Alan Gewirth, *Reason and Morality* (Chicago: Univ. of Chicago Press, 1978).
16 Kant, "Metaphysical Foundations of Morals," p. 160.

17　Aristotle, *Nicomachean Ethics* 3, 3.

18　Rousseau, "Discourse on the Origin of Inequality," p. 208.

19　Kant, "Metaphysical Foundations of Morals," p. 161.

20　John Locke, *A Letter concerning Toleration* (Indianapolis: Bobbs-Merrill, 1950), pp. 24, 34, 25.

21　Hobbes, *Leviathan*, 1, 6.

22　Locke, *Letter concerning Toleration*, p. 30.

23　Hobbes, *Leviathan*, 2, 18.

24　John Locke, *Essay concerning Human Understanding*, introduction, sec. 5.

25　For an analysis of these difficulties, see my book *The Irony of Liberal Reason*, pp. 203–13.

26　Locke, *Essay concerning Human Understanding*, pt. 4, 3, 18.

27　Bernstein, *Beyond Objectivism and Relativism*.

28　The implicit linkage between rational dialogue and moral equality is, for example, the reason that conversations between parents and children are a fertile source of comic material. Children both are and are not rational beings. They both are and are not the moral equals of adults. Partly and potentially, they are; fully and actually, they are not. Hence parents both do and do not—often in the context of the same discussion—engage their offspring in rational dialogue. And this incongruity possesses a humorous dimension.

29　Bruce Ackerman, *Social Justice in the Liberal State* (New Haven, Conn.: Yale Univ. Press, 1980), pp. 75, 80.

30　Vernant, *The Origins of Greek Thought*, pp. 46, 51.

31　David Hume, *Enquiry concerning the Principles of Morals*, sec. 9, pt. 1.

32　Ronald Dworkin, *Taking Rights Seriously* (Cambridge, Mass.: Harvard Univ. Press, 1977), p. 227.

33　Rousseau, "Social Contract," bk. 2, chap. 11.

34　This account, including the language, follows Michael Polanyi's account of the interplay of freedom and authority in scientific practice; see, *inter alia, Personal Knowledge*.

35　Walter Lippmann, *The Public Philosophy* (New York: Mentor Books, 1955), p. 40.

36　John Locke, *Second Treatise of Civil Government*, chap. 11.

37　Hans-Georg Gadamer, *Truth and Method* (New York: Seabury Press, 1975), p. 248.

38　Condorcet, *Progress of the Human Mind*, p. 100.

39　MacIntyre, *After Virtue*, p. 177.

40　Locke, *Second Treatise of Civil Government*, chap. 11.

41　Ibid.

42　Ackerman, *Social Justice in the Liberal State*, p. 75.

43　Lippmann, *The Public Philosophy*, p. 102.

44　Mill, *Considerations on Representative Government*, p. 31.

45　Compare, for example, the strictures against excessive individualism in *Habits of the Heart* with the concerns expressed in Don Herzog, "Some Questions for Republicans," *Political Theory* (14, no. 3) (Summer 1986), pp. 473–94.

46　Christopher Lasch, "The Communitarian Critique of Liberalism," *Soundings* (69 nos. 1–2, Spring/Summer 1986), p. 75.

Six. Understanding Liberal Democracy

1   MacIntyre, *After Virtue*, pp. 38, 49.
2   Ibid., p. 52.
3   Charles Frankel, *The Faith of Reason* (New York: King's Crown Press, 1948), pp. 2–3.
4   Ibid., pp. 3, 156.
5   Ibid., p. 158.
6   George Sabine, "The Two Democratic Traditions," *The Philosophical Review* 61 (October 1952): 466.
7   MacIntyre, *After Virtue*, pp. 175, 211.
8   Sandel, *Liberalism and the Limits of Justice*, p. 183.
9   Amy Gutmann, "Communitarian Critics of Liberalism," *Philosophy and Public Affairs* 14 (1985): 314.
10 Stephen Holmes, "The Polis State," *The New Republic* (June 6, 1988): 39.
11 Don Herzog, "Some Questions for Republicans," *Political Theory* 14 (August 1986): 481–82, 486.
12 Gutmann, "Communitarian Critics of Liberalism," p. 320.
13 The literature concerning neutrality and the human good in the liberal state is becoming rather extensive. Some of the most incisive accounts, however, can be found in Rawls's Dewey lectures and his "Justice as Fairness"; Ronald Dworkin's essay on "Liberalism," in *Public and Private Morality*, ed. Stuart Hampshire (Cambridge: Cambridge Univ. Press, 1978), pp. 113–43; Bruce Ackerman's *Social Justice in the Liberal State*; William Galston's "Defending Liberalism," *American Political Science Review* 76 (September 1982): 621–29; Sandel's *Liberalism and the Limits of Justice*; and Patrick Neal's "Liberalism and Neutrality," *Polity* 17 (Summer 1985): 664–84 and "A Liberal Theory of the Good?" *Canadian Journal of Philosophy* 17 (September 1987): 567–82.
14 Sandel, *Liberalism and the Limits of Justice*, p. 183.
15 See the account in Herzog, "Some Questions for Republicans," pp. 482–86.
16 MacIntyre, *After Virtue*, pp. 152–53.
17 Leo Strauss, *Natural Right and History* (Chicago: Univ. of Chicago Press, 1953), esp. pp. 202–5.
18 Patrick Riley, *Will and Political Legitimacy* (Cambridge, Mass.: Harvard Univ. Press, 1982), p. 61.
19 This is Rawls's term (see *A Theory of Justice*, pp. 520–29).
20 Rawls, "Justice as Fairness," p. 229.
21 William Galston, "Defending Liberalism," *American Political Science Review* 76, no. 3 (September 1982): 621–29.
22 James Fishkin, "Justifying Liberty: The Self-Reflective Argument," presented at the Legal Theory Workshop, Columbia Law School, November 19, 1984, pp. 12, 13.
23 Barber, *Strong Democracy*, pp. 173, 168 and 178, 175.
24 Charles Anderson, "The Place of Principles in Policy Analysis," *American Political Science Review* 73, no. 3 (September 1979): 711–23.
25 Lowi, *The End of Liberalism*.
26 Ibid., p. 297.

27 Daniel Bell, *The Cultural Contradictions of Capitalism* (New York: W. W. Norton, 1979).
28 Mansbridge, *Beyond Adversary Democracy*, p. 300.
29 Bell, *Cultural Contradictions of Capitalism*, pp. 278, 245.
30 Mansbridge, *Beyond Adversary Democracy*, p. 18.
31 Ibid., pp. 297, 296.

Seven. Approximating a Rational Society

1 A significant literature attends many of the policy issues I discuss in this chapter. I shall footnote only specific references, however, rather than trying to provide bibliographies for further exploration. As a political theorist, I doubt my capacity to make such bibliographic listings sufficiently comprehensive or balanced. Moreover, I would not want to imply that the policy prescriptions in this chapter are more than heuristic suggestions made principally for the purpose of fleshing out a theoretical conception.
2 Barber, *Strong Democracy*, pp. 278–79.
3 For a good discussion, see ibid., pp. 298–303.
4 Milbrath, *Political Participation*, p. 153.
5 Barber, *Strong Democracy*, pp. 287–88.
6 See ibid., pp. 267–73.
7 Alexis de Tocqueville, *Democracy in America*, trans. George Lawrence and ed. J. P. Mayer (Garden City, N.Y.: Doubleday, 1969), p. 238.
8 Rights-based liberals would likely object that this formulation leaves rights in a precarious position. This appearance is deceptive, however, because the moral weight and the prudential worth of adhering to the norms of rationality are so great that the force of "must" in the sentence is exceptionally strong. Or to put it another way, rights may be hypothetical rather than categorical imperatives, but the ends to which the imperatives are connected are so compelling that the logical difference in status has no great practical significance.
9 *Heart of Atlanta Motel vs. U.S.* 379 U.S. 241 (1964).
10 Burke, *Reflections on the Revolution in France*, p. 110.
11 Nozick's tale of a slave carries its libertarian sting only because he conceives of the democratic power over his entrapped individual as a simple majority tyranny. If the choice is one between having multiple masters free to exert their arbitrary will and Nozick's libertarian utopia, then his argument carries the day. But if a democratic society must respect the necessary conditions of citizen autonomy, must subject potential enactments to the discipline of reason, and must embody all dictates in the open and general form required by the rule of law, then Nozick's rhetorical dichotomy loses its persuasiveness (see Nozick, *Anarchy, State, and Utopia*, pp. 290–92).
12 Dahl, *A Preface to Democratic Theory*, p. 137.
13 Michael Walzer, "Liberalism and the Art of Separation," *Political Theory* 12, no. 3 (August 1984): 315–30. This is also a theme of his earlier *Spheres of Justice*.
14 Aristotle, *Politics*, trans. Ernest Baker (New York: Oxford Univ. Press, 1958), p. 182.
15 Ibid., p. 181.

16   Locke, *Second Treatise of Civil Government*, chap. 11.

17   Rousseau, "Social Contract," bk. 2, chap. 6.

18   Alasdair MacIntyre, *Whose Justice? Which Rationality?* (Notre Dame, Ind.: Univ. of Notre Dame Press, 1988), p. 73.

19   Mill, *Considerations on Representative Government*, pp. 30–31.

20   As the supposedly Hobbesian James Madison admitted in the supposedly politically mechanistic *Federalist*, "republican government presupposes the existence of these [virtuous] qualities in a higher degree than any other form" (*The Federalist*, no. 55).

21   Amy Gutmann, *Democratic Education* (Princeton, New Jersey: Princeton University Press, 1987).

22   Sidney B. Simon, "Values Clarification vs. Indoctrination," cited in Gutmann, *Democratic Education*, p. 55.

23   Gutmann, *Democratic Education*, p. 53.

24   See Rawls, *A Theory of Justice*, p. 104; and Nozick's apt observations on p. 214 of *Anarchy, State, and Utopia*.

Conclusion

1   One recent volume containing some suggestive analyses of the general sort I have in mind is *Political Innovation and Conceptual Change*, ed. Terence Ball, James Farr, and Russell Hanson (Cambridge: Cambridge Univ. Press, 1989). See also chapter 5, "Conceptual Revision and Political Reform" in William Connolly, *The Terms of Political Discourse*, 2d ed. (Princeton, N.J.: Princeton Univ. Press, 1983).

2   See, for example, Martin Hollis and Steven Lukes, eds., *Rationality and Relativism* (Cambridge, Mass.: MIT Press, 1982).

3   For a good account, see Thomas McCarthy, "Rationality and Relativism: Habermas's 'Overcoming of Hermeneutics,'" in John B. Thompson and David Held, eds. *Habermas: Critical Debates* (Cambridge, Mass: MIT Press, 1982).

4   Winch, *The Idea Of A Social Science*, frontispiece.

5   Ludwig Wittgenstein, "Remarks on Frazer's *Golden Bough*," ed. Rush Rhees, trans. A. C. Miles (Highlands, N.J.: Humanities Press, 1979), pp. 5,8.

For a provocative and iconoclastic account of Wittgenstein's own spiritual orientation, see Russell Nieli, *Wittgenstein: From Mysticism to Ordinary Language* (Albany, N.Y.: SUNY Press, 1987).

6   Raymond Geuss, *The Idea of a Critical Theory* (New York: Cambridge Univ. Press, 1981), p. 66.

7   MacIntyre, *After Virtue*, p. 177.

8   See, *inter alia*, Michel Foucault, *The Archaeology of Knowledge* (New York: Harper and Row, 1972), and *Discipline and Punish* (New York: Pantheon Books, 1977); Jacques Derrida, *Writing and Difference*, trans. Alan Bass (London: Routledge and Kegan Paul, 1978), and *Positions*, trans. Alan Bass (London: Athlone Press, 1981).

9   Connolly, *Terms of Political Discourse*, p. 231.

10   MacIntyre, *Whose Justice? Which Rationality?* p. 9.

11   Ibid., p. 359.

12   "In this kind of situation the rationality of tradition requires an acknowledgement

by those who have hitherto inhabited and given their allegiance to the tradition in crisis that the alien tradition is superior in rationality and in respect of its claims to truth to their own" (Ibid., p. 365).

13 Ibid., p. 395.

14 It is worth remembering in this context that Kant and Hobbes, who are logically linked with the middle and third layers of liberal democratic association, both allowed themselves to be excessively optimistic about the power of political institutions in the absence of bonds of political friendship. Kant averred that even a society of devils could be well governed if it had the right constitution; and Hobbes thought his sovereign could maintain civil peace and a commodious life for a society of almost pathological egoists. Our claim that the "Aristotelian" layer is necessary, though not sufficient, for a liberal democracy to prosper is based on doubts about this form of optimism.

15 Kant, "Metaphysical Foundation of Morals," p. 199.

16 Condorcet, *Progress of the Human Mind*, pp. 179, 194.

17 Voltaire, cited in Ernest Cassirer, *The Philosophy of the Enlightenment*, trans. Fritz Koelln and James Pettegrove (Boston: Beacon Press, 1955), p. 169.

Index

About the author. Thomas A. Spragens, Jr. is
Professor of Political Science at Duke University. His many publications include *The Politics
of Motion: The World of Thomas Hobbes, Understanding Political Theory*, and *The Irony of Liberal
Reason*.

Library of Congress Cataloging-in-Publication
Data
Spragens, Thomas A.
Reason and democracy / Thomas A.
Spragens, Jr.
ISBN 0-8223-1050-3.—ISBN 0-8223-1068-6 (pbk.)
1. Democracy. 2. Reason. I. Title.
JC423.S75   1990
321.8—dc20   89-71474 CIP

1580